Jim Smallman is a writer and award-winning stand-up comedian. Performing comedy around the world since 2005, he has established a loyal following amongst those who enjoy hearing his brand of silly storytelling and improvised idiocy.

He has been published in *The Guardian, The Mirror, FSM, The Leicester Mercury, Skin Deep* and *The Huffington Post.*

He is the co-owner of PROGRESS Wrestling in London, now one of the most successful independent wrestling promotions in the world.

'1'M SORRY, I LOVE YOU'

A HISTORY OF PROFESSIONAL WRESTLING

★ JIM SMALLMAN ★

HEADLINE

First published in 2018 by
HEADLINE PUBLISHING GROUP

First published in paperback in 2019 by
HEADLINE PUBLISHING GROUP
1

Cataloguing in Publication Data is available from the British Library

ISBN 978 1 4722 5423 8

Typeset in Sabon MT by Palimpsest Book Production Ltd, Falkirk, Stirlingshire

Printed and bound in Great Britain by Clays Ltd, Elcograf S.p.A

Headline's policy is to use papers that are natural, renewable and
recyclable products and made from wood grown in sustainable forests.
The logging and manufacturing processes are expected to conform to the
environmental regulations of the country of origin.

HEADLINE PUBLISHING GROUP
An Hachette UK Company
Carmelite House
50 Victoria Embankment
London
EC4Y 0DZ

www.headline.co.uk
www.hachette.co.uk

For my wonderful wife and children.

Thank you for understanding that I adore professional wrestling; the only thing I love more than it is you three wonderful humans. You guys are my world.

Contents

Acknowledgments

I would like to thank a lot of people for their help, knowledge and general awesomeness. I may well have forgotten somebody; if I have then I apologise profusely.

Huge thanks to my business partners Jon Briley and Glen Joseph, not just for the past six and a bit years of working together and doing something cool with PROGRESS, but also for being so understanding when I was working towards deadlines for this book and covering for me; also thanks to them both for reading the initial drafts and, in Glen's case, making a case for Vince Russo to be number one on every top ten list.

I wouldn't even be around wrestling if it wasn't for my dear friend Chris Brooker, who I met through comedy. Without him encouraging my love of wrestling I wouldn't be anywhere near as involved in it as I am now, and I certainly wouldn't have written this book.

Huge thanks to fellow friends Matthew Richards and Craig Michael Hall for doing their bit reading through my initial drafts, just like Chris did as well.

Thank you to William Regal and Mick Foley, two of my absolute heroes who have been inspirational to me for decades and who now I'm lucky to count as friends. Without these two fine gentlemen again, this book may not exist. I've enjoyed supporting them both in their stand-up pursuits and never tire of hearing their stories and insight.

I'm super grateful to Scroobius Pip for having my podcast – Tuesday Night Jaw – on his Distraction Pieces Network. That's enabled me to connect with thousands of wrestling fans across the globe and forms the basis for many of the lists in this book.

Special thanks to Andrew O'Neill for writing the fabulous A History of Heavy Metal. If I hadn't have tweeted about that, I may not have met my publisher Richard Roper through Twitter. Of course, my eternal gratitude to Richard and everyone at Headline for letting me write this book, and their brilliant support throughout the process.

Enormous thanks to every single wrestler, manager, referee, commentator, booker and writer who has been involved in professional wrestling during the course of my lifetime. From the heights of WWE to the very smallest independent company, I have enjoyed tens of thousands of hours of this wonderful art form, and without the amazing people that make it possible across the globe then my life would have been very different and nowhere near as fun.

To every wrestler that has worked for PROGRESS, thank you.

You've made my dreams come true. To every fan who has supported our shows and, indeed, purchased this book, thank you for coming on a journey with me and my friends.

Finally, thank you to my family. From my wife and toddler son for tolerating me as I wrote this book; to my teenage daughter for trying her best to understand why her dad loves wrestling so much; to my father and late mother for bringing me ECW tapes and nWo t-shirts back from Florida in the late 1990s; all the way back to my Grandmother for making me watch World of Sport as a child. I'm a very lucky man to have the family that I do.

Preface

I'm Sorry, I Love You: a Note on the Title

I know the subtitle to this book is *A History of Professional Wrestling*. That's what it's about, honest. But I feel the need to explain the main title before we get started, just in case you've been expecting a Mills & Boon novel rather than a man from the Midlands detailing over a century's worth of grappling.

Before I get to that, I'd like to give you a mission statement of sorts as well. I'm fully aware that if I go into extreme detail about everything that has ever happened ever in the entire history of wrestling then this book will run to about five hundred volumes. I know I'll skip over a few things and that a lot of the focus will probably be from 1984 onwards, for reasons that will become apparent as you read on.

I'm not a historian or a scholar. I'm a huge wrestling fan who has been watching for decades, and I've managed to start making my living working within the world of wrestling (as well as my original field of expertise, stand-up comedy). If you want a scientific dissection of any year since wrestling began, then trawl through the archives of Dave Meltzer's *Wrestling Observer Newsletter*. I'm here to have a laugh, walk you through some of the defining moments in wrestling history and try to nail down why I – and so many other people – adore this quasi-sport so much.

So here's my statement:

There's far too much history in professional wrestling to go through the full history of professional wrestling in this history of professional wrestling. Let's keep it fun, shall we?

Anyway, the title . . .

The Citrus Bowl in Orlando (now renamed as the much less iconic Camping World Stadium), 30 March 2008. WrestleMania XXIV. Following immediately after a match that lasted all of 11 seconds (Kane winning the ECW (Eastern Championship Wrestling) title from Chavo Guerrero), two legends took to the ring. Ric Flair, the bleached blond veteran who somehow survived a plane crash at the start of his career in the 1970s to go on to be considered the greatest of all time by millions. His opponent, Shawn Michaels, nicknamed 'Mr WrestleMania' because of his knack for having the best matches at the annual showcase, another man who is considered by many to be one of the very best to lace up a pair of boots.

Under a cloudy central Florida sky, the two legends went at it. The storyline mainly concerned Flair, who had been wrestling for most of 2008 with a cloud over his head. The next time he lost a match, he would have to retire. After being told he would be entering the WWE (World Wrestling Entertainment) Hall of Fame in February, he challenged Shawn Michaels to a match with both men knowing the emotional stakes at hand. You don't retire from wrestling like you do from working in a building society branch in Yorkshire, as far as I'm aware.

The match lasted a shade over 20 minutes. With his career on the line, Flair kept kicking out of pinfall attempts and escaping submission holds, matching the younger Michaels hold for hold, counter for counter. Flair had already kicked out of Michaels' signature move – 'Sweet Chin Music', a superkick to the jaw – once when Michaels caught him with it again. As Flair got to his feet, groggy, Michaels wore a look of concern, but did what needed to be done. A 35-year career was about to end.

Flair circled around the ring, on unsteady legs, ready to be beaten. His eyes locked with Michaels, who seemed to be welling up. Time stood still, the near 75,000 crowd lowered their voices and Michaels said to his foe:

'I'm sorry, I love you.'

With that, a third superkick connected with Flair and he was pinned in the centre of the ring, ending his career on the grandest possible stage with a moment that fans like me still speak of now. I've seen it parodied countless times, and other wrestlers try to better it. For me, it's one of the finest and most emotional moments in wrestling history and it's just a few words at the end of a match. But wrestling isn't just oiled-up guys in spandex having a scrap, it can take you on the same rollercoaster that any good film, book or album can. When done well – like this match – it can make you cry your eyes out.

Of course, this is professional wrestling. You'll learn from this book that it frequently skips from the sublime to the ridiculous quite quickly, and a few minutes after this landmark moment in the sport the crowd was watching a Playboy Bunnymania Lumberjill match. I was too busy crying to know what that was, and I still don't. You'll also learn that nobody ever retires. Ric Flair was wrestling again a couple of years later, slightly taking the gloss off what I consider to be the greatest retirement of all time by, you know, not actually retiring.

This book takes its title from that one moment because it encapsulates one of many reasons why I love wrestling. Anyone as nerdy as me already knows what it refers to, but probably got a little twinge reading through the events again.

There's a double meaning though. My dad has no idea why I love wrestling. When I worked in an office, pre-stand-up, I never told any of my colleagues that I had a whole room full of video tapes that I'd sent off to the USA and Japan for, so I could absorb as much wrestling as possible. Until I became a comedian, I always hid it. Now I'm genuinely not sorry that I love it so much, but I think that some people may need to know the full scale of the wonder of wrestling to understand why I and millions of others adore it so.

So that's the title explained. If you accidentally bought this book for your sister Maureen to read after her hip operation, then I'm truly sorry. But she's about to learn a heck of a lot about wrestling. Lucky Maureen, I say.

A Glossary of Useful Wrestling Terms

I won't lie, dear reader. I am probably going to slip into using a few specific wrestling terms here and there, and while I'll always try to explain them and give them context, if you're new to wrestling then you may wonder what on earth I'm talking about. So, I present this absolutely non-exhaustive list of terms for you to dip into before you dive in to the main event.

Please don't use them in real life though. Everyone involved in wrestling cringes when we accidentally do that from time to time.

Agent: a backstage person, usually an ex-wrestler, who helps the wrestlers put their matches together, come up with their *spots* and *finish* and so on, acting in accordance to what the *booker* wants out of the match.

Angle: a wrestling storyline that can span the course of a show or two, all the way up to several years. Also surname of Kurt, Olympic gold medallist, Atlanta 1996.

Blading: cutting oneself (or allowing a trusted opponent to do it for you), usually on the forehead or in the hairline, in order to bleed to further the drama of a match or *angle*.

Booker: a person within a wrestling promotion who is responsible for setting *angles* and making matches between wrestlers. It's part-writer, part-director. I'm one of the three people that *books* PROGRESS, the wrestling promotion I founded in 2011. Also, forename of T, many-time world champion.

Botch: a move that goes wrong inside the ring, recently expanded to include anything within wrestling that goes wrong thanks to the YouTube video series *Botchamania*, which I have been in.

Bump: the art of a wrestler taking a fall to the mat or ground in order to *sell* the move of an opponent. Most *bumps* are taken either flat-back or on the stomach. More dangerous bumps include head drops, where a wrestler is taking much more of a risk by landing on their upper back and neck to *sell* that they've been dropped on their head.

Bury: relegating a wrestler further down the *card* in order to lower their worth, sometimes deliberately as punishment for their actions, sometimes out of spite. Methods of *burying* someone include long losing streaks, taking away promo time or giving someone a silly *gimmick*.

Card: a set of matches at a particular event. The *main event* would be at the top of the *card*, everything beneath that is technically the *undercard*.

Carry: an experienced wrestler will often *carry* a newer, *green* opponent. Ric Flair was notable for being able to *carry* anybody to a good match, with it often said that he could wrestle a broom to illustrate this point.

Catch-as-catch-can: sometimes just shortened to *catch wrestling*; a style of grappling that originated in regions of the UK like Lancashire and was popularised by travelling carnivals in the late 19th century. Mainly submission-based, it remains a big part of mixed martial arts.

Championship: a wrestling title, usually in belt form. Most often awarded to a wrestler who is a good *draw*, so you would expect one of your most beloved *faces* or most despised *heels* to hold the company's *championship*.

Curtain jerker: a derogatory term for wrestlers who have to go out first at the start of a show, often in a *dark match*. It symbolises that they're not *main event* level yet.

Dark match: a contest that takes place before the cameras are live for a TV recording or pay-per-view event. In the past, many wrestlers earned their contracts in companies after first performing in *dark matches*. These days, WWE often has *dark matches* after the cameras have finished rolling at shows like *Smackdown* in order to send the fans home happy with a quick, unfilmed win from a popular *face*.

Deathmatch: not a literal fight to the death. Used to describe more extreme *hardcore* matches, often including the use of terrifying objects like glass, barbed wire or, in some circumstances in Japan, crocodiles.

Double cross: something that happens within a match that leads to a change in result without one party being aware of it previously. For example, the famed *Montreal Screwjob* that we'll discuss at length in these pages is an example of a double cross, where one man (Bret Hart) definitely didn't think that he was going to be beaten by Shawn Michaels, but ended up losing.

Draw: anyone within wrestling who makes the company he works for money. A *draw* is somebody who sells tickets and fans want to see win (if a *face*) or lose (if a *heel*). Veteran wrestlers will often complain about newer talent by insisting that they 'never drew a dime in this business'.

Dusty Finish: a term popularised by veteran NWA (National Wrestling Alliance) wrestler and *booker* Dusty Rhodes, used often in the 1980s. A *face* looks like he/she has won a big match, only for the decision to be reversed, either there and then or the next night, on a technicality and awarded to the *heel*.

Face: a good guy; also known as a *babyface* or, in the UK, a *blue-eye*. In the past, usually heroic and brave; since Steve Austin changed wrestling in the 1990s, it's now more down to if the fans cheer for you rather than your actual behaviour.

Fall: the end of a match, be it obtained by pin or submission. Some matches are two-out-of-three *falls*. Wrestling fans like to shout 'one fall' when announcers say it to introduce contests; I refuse to say it for that reason.

Finish: the planned series of events that lead to the *fall* at the end of a match.

Foreign object: any weapon or hidden item that a *heel* wrestler (usually) uses in order to gain an illegal advantage in a match. Can range from a baseball bat or a chair, to a pencil, roll of quarters, knuckleduster or brick conveniently hidden in a handbag.

Gimmick: broadly speaking, the character that a wrestler portrays. Can also be used in reference to any particular character traits, their costume and so on. A wonderfully overused word by some older wrestlers, who will often say the word 'gimmick' 17 times in one sentence.

Gorilla position: named after Gorilla Monsoon, WWE legend; the area behind the curtain right before the wrestlers enter the arena. In WWE, it's where the producers and *agents* watch the matches on TV screens. In smaller companies, it's probably just a dark place behind a curtain.

Green: term used to describe a new, inexperienced wrestler.

Hardcore: a match that involves weapons like chairs and tables, and a lack of rules such as disqualifications or count outs. Matches like 'street fights' or those conducted under 'extreme rules' are *hardcore* matches. Anything even more violent and bloody could be considered a *deathmatch*.

Hardway: blood that arrives, usually from a broken nose or a busted eyebrow, from an actual physical blow (be it accidental or otherwise) rather than *blading*.

Heat: both used to describe the negative reaction from a crowd that a *heel* receives, and also to sum up ill-feeling between wrestlers and/or management backstage. 'I can't believe that I'm getting *heat* because I went out there and got good *heat*'.

Heel: a bad guy, also known as a villain or in Mexico, a *rudo*. Traditionally someone who was underhand and devious, but those traditional, easily defined boundaries are long gone these days.

Hooker: a *legitimate* tough guy who can be relied upon to injure someone for real if need be. Not as in demand as they were in the 1950s, when they were very handy to have around.

Hot Tag: what most *face* v *heel* tag team matches are built around. A *face* takes a long, sustained beating (Ricky Morton of the Rock 'n' Roll Express was the best at this) but eventually swings the match in his team's favour by making the *hot tag* to his partner, and crowd (hopefully) goes wild.

House: the money that a show makes. A good *house* would mean you sold out or thereabouts, everyone got paid and you made a profit. A bad *house* means you may well lose your *actual* house.

House show: not something that your partner drags you around to look at new interior design trends. An untelevised show. WWE puts on several of these a week, often having the same matches each night for that week. They're often a lot of fun.

Independent promotion: a wrestling company that doesn't have a television deal and doesn't tie wrestlers down to exclusive contracts. PROGRESS, PWG (Pro Wrestling Guerilla) and Evolve are independent promotions. WWE and NJPW (New Japan Pro Wrestling) are not.

Jobber: a wrestler whose main job is to lose to more established wrestlers to make them look credible. Some wrestlers become career *jobbers* like Barry Horowitz or the Brooklyn Brawler. If you're slightly higher up the *card* but still lose, just to bigger names, then you could be called a *jobber to the stars*.

Kayfabe: the pig Latin term used for trying to maintain that wrestling is a real sport and protect the secrets of how it is run from the fans. Until the advent of the internet, *kayfabe* was a much more important thing. Now many more fans are aware of how wrestling works, but good companies still keep a level of *kayfabe*, even if it isn't as strict as it used to be.

Legitimate: a wrestler who has a real background of being a tough competitor in real life. Kurt Angle, Brock Lesnar, Matt Riddle and Minoru Suzuki are all *legitimate* competitors as well as professional wrestlers.

Lucha libre: meaning 'free fight' in Spanish, is the main way of describing Mexican wrestling which is recognisable by its use of masked competitors, a sometimes more choreographed style and a fair bit of high flying.

Main event: the final match on a *card*, and often the contest that most of the fans have come to see. A wrestler who regularly appears in these matches and is a good *draw* would be called a *main eventer*.

Manager: someone who accompanies a wrestler to the ring, often acting as a mouthpiece for a talent who perhaps isn't the best talker. Bobby Heenan would be a great example. Traditionally, it is more common for a *heel* to have a manager, but some *face* wrestlers do too.

Mark: a fan who absolutely, 100 per cent believes everything that happens inside the ring is real or is often over-enthusiastic for one wrestler or brand. The term comes from old carnival speak. Nearly always used in an insulting way, usually by people on Twitter.

Mid-carder: a wrestler who is not a *jobber* or *curtain jerker* but has not yet found his or her way to the *main event*.

Monster: an often massive and/or terrifying wrestler who gets *pushed* as being unstoppable. It's more common to have a *monster heel* than face.

Muta Scale: the level of blood generated after a *bladejob*, named after the gory crimson mask donned by The Great Muta in 1992 in a match against Hiroshi Hase in Japan. 1.0 on the Muta Scale would be incredibly gory, like that match or Eddie Guerrero v JBL in WWE in 2004, whereas, say, 0.2 is just a trickle of blood.

Near-fall: a very, very close two-count that the fans believe could well have ended the contest.

No-sell/No sold: when a wrestler chooses to not react to any moves or strikes from their opponent. Sometimes done to be unprofessional, *no-selling* was also part of some wrestlers' *gimmicks*: from The Undertaker sitting up to *no-sell* because he was a zombie, to Hawk from the Road Warriors *no-selling* piledrivers because he was Hawk from the Road Warriors.

No-show: a wrestler not bothering to turn up for work. Usually blamed on hard living in the 1980s, and on Southern Rail in modern-day Britain.

Over: how much a wrestler is achieving the reaction that they or their *booker* want from the fans. For a *face*, being *over* means loud cheers, lots of merchandise sales and people naming their kids after you. For a *heel*, being over means that thousands of people are ready to riot every time you win a match by nefarious means. In Puerto Rico, they may actually go through with that threat.

Open challenge: in the carnival days, this would be what the resident *hooker* would do: take on all comers for a wager. Nowadays it is used by a wrestler to issue a challenge, usually to 'anyone in the back' who fancies having a grapple. Often used to introduce a new or returning star, or to cover for a *no-show*.

Parts unknown: where nearly all *heels* with a vaguely mysterious *gimmick* would claim to be from. Also, where I claimed to be from on Twitter for years, thinking I was the only wrestling fan to do so – I most certainly was not.

Pop: a loud, positive reaction from the crowd. A huge *pop* can accompany the entrance of a popular *face*, or a surprise return. A *Road Warrior Pop* signifies a particularly loud reaction, named after the response that the legendary tag team used to get in the Eighties, especially in Chicago.

Psychology: the actual thinking behind wrestling. Why would a wrestler choose to use one move over another? How would they react after taking a blow? Wrestlers who demonstrate great *psychology* can bring all of this together inside the ring and tell a story without needing to speak.

Puroresu: the Japanese word for professional wrestling.

Push: using all the elements of professional wrestling to elevate a performer up the card. If someone goes from *curtain jerking* to the *main event* in a very short space of time, then you could say that they have been *pushed to the moon*.

Ref bump: a moment in a match where the referee is accidentally taken out of commission, often leading to other shenanigans. While most wrestlers can be back on their feet a few seconds after a hefty blow, referees are known to lie unconscious for several minutes sometimes after taking the lightest of strikes.

Run-in: one wrestler interfering in another's match to further their feud or *angle*.

School: where wrestlers train. They used to be secretive places, now there's one in most large cities. The most famous currently is the WWE Performance Centre in Orlando, and they stretch all the way down the food chain to weekly classes in a church hall. In Japan, wrestlers will often physically live in their school, or dojo.

Screwjob: the *worked* finish of a match being turned into a *shoot* or something similar in order to change the outcome of a match without telling one of the wrestlers. The most famous example of this was in Montreal in 1997 between Bret Hart (screwee) and Shawn Michaels, Vince McMahon, referee Earl Hebner and the then-WWF (World Wrestling Federation) (screwers).

Sell: how you make your opponents offence look good, therefore establishing them as a threat. It is possible to *no-sell* and also to *over-sell*, notably Shawn Michaels v Hulk Hogan at *Summerslam 2005* where Michaels *sold* every blow from Hogan like he'd been shot by a sniper with explosive bullets.

Shoot: if a wrestler chooses to go off script, either during an interview or worse still, during a match, that's a *shoot*, basically meaning 'real'. Wrestlers are known to end long stories with the phrase 'and that's a shoot, brother' to give it extra authenticity. Akira Maeda and Bruiser Brody were well known for occasionally choosing to shoot on their opponents in the ring.

Smark: a contraction of the words 'smart' and 'mark'. Didn't used to be an insult, basically referred to the growing number of fans who enjoyed wrestling but had a good knowledge of how things worked behind the scenes, while never actually being involved themselves. Is now mainly used to sum up any fan who is a tedious know-it-all. I was definitely a *smark* before becoming a promoter made me see the error of my ways.

Sports entertainment: how WWE have referred to themselves since the 1990s, instead of calling their product 'wrestling'. It does sum up what wrestling is about though: about half is about athletic ability, the other half is about drama or comedy or performance skills.

Spot: a planned move during a match. A *highspot* would be something a bit riskier, possibly leading to a *near-fall* or the *finish* of a match.

Squared circle: a fun nickname for the wrestling ring. Because a ring is a circle, but a *wrestling* ring is a square. Geddit? Also, it's super-fun to say and pretend to be American.

Squash: seen less these days, a match where an established star or up-and-coming *monster* rapidly beats a *jobber* in order to look impressive.

Stable: a team of three or more wrestlers, joined together with a common goal. Some great *stables* include the Four Horsemen, the New World Order (nWo), D-Generation X and Bullet Club.

Stiff: using a bit more force in your moves and strikes than might be necessary. Some wrestlers are just *stiff*, some choose to be so when annoyed. Wrestling in some nations is also, broadly speaking, *stiffer* than others. The style in Japan is very physical; in Mexico a lot less so.

Swerve: a change in plans to what the fans are expecting. They could be expecting to see one wrestler and be given another, or a title and company direction could change hands because of a sudden *turn* from one wrestler. Vince Russo built his career on swerves.

Turn: a wrestler moving from being a *face* to be a *heel*, and vice versa. A *double turn* is one of the hardest things to do, where two wrestlers turn to their opposite alignment during their match or angle. The most well-known of these is Bret Hart and Steve Austin turning heel and face respectively at *WrestleMania 13*.

Tweener: somebody who is neither *face* nor *heel*. It could be a wrestler who acts like a *heel* and yet still gets cheered like Pete Dunne; a wrestler who acts like a *face* and still gets booed like Roman Reigns; or someone who splits the crowd exactly 50/50.

Valet: usually a woman who accompanies a wrestler to the ring. An archaic term; nowadays female managers are as strong characters as male ones.

Visual pinfall: often occurring during a *ref bump*, a moment where one wrestler pins the other, clearly for a count of three, but there is no official there to count. Can often give a *face* an excuse for a rematch if they're then screwed out of a victory.

Work: what wrestling is. Wrestling is a *work*; it's pre-planned with the knowledge of everybody involved.

Worked Shoot: something else that Vince Russo enjoyed. Usually a promo where a wrestler sounds like they're *shooting* on their co-workers or bosses by using insider terms, but it's actually just as much of a *work* as everything else.

Workrate: a performer with a high *workrate* puts absolutely everything into their matches, works hard, goes all out to please the crowd and make their opponent look good. Low *workrate* is the exact opposite.

The Rules of Wrestling

The rules vary a little from country to country, but this is a rough guide if you've somehow never seen a wrestling match ever before.

To win a match, you must do one of the following:

1. Pin your opponent's shoulders to the mat for a count of three, administered by the referee.
2. Make your opponent submit to a hold, either by them saying they give up or, more commonly since the rise of UFC (Ultimate Fighting Championship), by them tapping out.
3. See your opponent disqualified because of any form of cheating, such as using a weapon, not breaking when instructed to, interference from another wrestler and so on.

4. Have your opponent not meet a ten count from the referee (20 in some companies and countries) when they are outside the ring and you have returned to the ring before the count has concluded.

A pinfall or submission can be broken by grabbing one of the ring ropes or putting a limb underneath the bottom rope.

The referee can administer a five count if a wrestler does not break a hold when instructed to at their discretion. If they get to five, then that wrestler is disqualified.

In tag team matches, upon tagging their partner in a team they will have five seconds where they are allowed in the ring together. After that the referee must eject the non-legal man.

Usually, championships cannot change hands by disqualification or count out, a method often used to keep a title belt around the waist of a heel character.

Of course, if you're promoting wrestling then you can make these rules work for you in whatever way you choose, thanks to literally hundreds of different match stipulations being available to help tell stories.

Introduction

> 'We have all felt every emotion today. Remember today, the
> next time a family member or workmate tells you that
> wrestling is stupid. We've laughed, we've cried, we've
> screamed our lungs out. Professional wrestling is the greatest
> thing in the entire world.'

I said that. Sat cross-legged in the middle of a wrestling ring,
with 700 fans on their feet applauding the sentiment. My name
is Jim, and I love professional wrestling.

To give you a little bit of context, I'm the co-owner, ring
announcer and executive producer of a little independent wrestling company called PROGRESS, based in London. We had just

put on one heck of a show at the Electric Ballroom in Camden, a show where good guys had turned bad, despised villains had carved a path of destruction against valiant heroes and then we sprung a huge surprise on everyone at the end of the show. Two wrestlers returned to our company and the resultant explosion of crowd noise for their comeback is among the loudest I had ever heard in my 30-plus years of being a fan. It all worked very well. If I smoked I would have reclined backstage at the end of a show with a well-earned Benson & Hedges.

Wrestling genuinely makes me emotional. I care enormously about the product that we present to our fans, and I really want everyone to have the most amazing time. I want people to think that we're one of the best companies in the world. It's not that I have a massive ego – 13 years as a stand-up comedian have flattened out that nicely – but purely because I am a massive, huge wrestling fan. I don't watch comedy on TV because that's my day job. I still watch hours and hours of wrestling every week because for me, it is the absolute pinnacle of entertainment and I've loved it since I was a kid. Wrestling now helps pay the bills, but it remains tremendous fun.

I can pinpoint the exact moment when I became a wrestling fan. As a kid, I would sometimes spend Saturday afternoons at my grandmother's in Leicester. She lived in a flat above a row of shops and would watch British grappling on *World of Sport* on ITV before the football scores rolled in and her husband would check his pools coupon. Usually, she'd watch and I'd play outside with her dog in the tiny concrete back yard, not interested in grapplers like Big Daddy and Giant Haystacks. I knew at a young age that they weren't for me, immobile behemoths who would win their matches by sitting on their smaller opponents.

One Saturday, when I was probably four years old, it was raining, and I couldn't play outside. Gran had the wrestling on, and I paid no attention to the screen, expecting the usual parade of big lads fending off old ladies – armed with handbags and hatpins – in the front row. I busied myself with my toy cars until I saw the man who would change everything for me. I glanced up at the television screen and was transfixed by a competitor who was part-wrestler, part-escapologist: Johnny Saint.

Mr Saint would have been over 40 years old at the time, and he was a magician in the ring. Despite only being small of stature, everything he did looked believable. He managed to look like he could kill you with crisp strikes and submission holds worthy of UFC, but he also made you laugh by tying his opponent in knots. I had never seen anything like him. From that exact moment onwards, I would sit with my gran every time I visited her on a Saturday to watch the wrestling, becoming a fan of the ground-breaking lightweight British wrestlers who blazed a trail just like Johnny Saint: Rollerball Rocco, Marty Jones, Fit Finlay and more. Mr Saint lives near me in North Wales now, I've been lucky enough to thank him for making me a wrestling fan. Aged 77, you would have no idea that this mild-mannered pensioner is one of the toughest and most influential people to ever step into a wrestling ring.

When wrestling on ITV ended in 1988, the glamorous, American World Wrestling Federation (WWF), as it was called then, came to the forefront and I was lucky enough to have a friend at school whose parents had got divorced. This meant that his dad, in lieu of actual attention, bought him every single WWF video tape that came out. We got Sky TV at home in 1990 in time for me to be able to record *WrestleMania VI*, as I borrowed every one of my mate's tapes to watch all the big shows prior to that. I was obsessed. I bought every magazine that I could, from the official WWF and WCW (World Championship Wrestling) offerings that kept to storylines, to the unofficial ones that came in from the USA that – shock horror – listed the wrestler's real names.

Then as I entered my teens, I changed. My toy wrestling figures were put in a box in the attic as video games took over. I started going to watch football every weekend with my dad. Girls were suddenly vaguely interesting to me. I vividly remember the moment that turned me off wrestling for a fair few years.

Idly watching WWF in the early Nineties, The Undertaker was beating up an adversary. His opponent briefly rallied and fired back with a couple of punches that The Undertaker no-sold. This was the first incarnation of the legendary Undertaker, a man who was almost a zombie; pale-faced and dark-eyed. I was at *WrestleMania* in 2017 when The Undertaker retired as a beloved character and performer, having cycled through variations on his gimmick and having had some of the best matches in the history of the business. I shed a tear when he retired. My opinion of him as a teen in my first throes of puberty was very different.

Vince McMahon, who unbeknown to most fans at the time owned the WWF (now known as WWE – World Wrestling Entertainment), was on commentary. As The Undertaker refused to even blink from the punches of his opponent, he uttered a line of commentary that he didn't realise would affect a pimply teenager in the East Midlands. He said: 'Look at that . . . we're not entirely sure if The Undertaker is alive or dead'.

Click.

I turned the television off and dismissed wrestling for the next few years as childish nonsense. It was a silly cartoon and I had cider to drink in a park and girls to repulse. It wasn't for me anymore. I threw myself into all my other hobbies and presumed that I had left it behind forever.

Fast-forward to the end of June 1998. Aged 20, I had just finished my first year at university and was on the sofa in my parents' front room, idly flicking through Sky Sports, starved of football during the close season, when I chanced upon some wrestling – *King of the Ring* – just as Mick Foley was thrown by The Undertaker (yep, he's a bookmark in my life) from the roof of the Hell in a Cell cage structure to the floor, smashing through the ringside Spanish announce table. I put the channel on literally one second before Mick took flight and watched the rest of the match (because, yes, *the match carried on after this*) with my mouth open. I was blown away. This wasn't a cartoon, it was *very* adult violence.

I now have a Mick Foley tattoo on my arm to show the significance of this accidental epiphany. Having supported Mick on various tours of the UK, he finds this hilarious.

I spent the next few weeks learning everything that I could about wrestling: the current scene, what I'd missed, all of the gossip. Because the internet was now a firm part of wrestling fandom, it was easy to find out *everything* about wrestling. Not just the storylines that I had missed out on, but also the behind-the-scenes information that I'd had no concept of when I was first a fan. I started buying videos of every big WWE show from that era, then everything that I had missed, then went online to buy tapes from overseas of other shows and matches that I had heard about. I would then trade these tapes with other fans. I even started doing something called E-Wrestling, where I invented various characters and wrote promos for them. I guess it's a natural progression for me to be doing what I do now, even if I blush a little bit knowing that I used to do that.

Certain tapes were in high demand. I waited for weeks for deliveries from the USA of long-play, NTSC VHS tapes that had grainy, sometimes hand-held footage of non-televised shows on them. This is how I fell in love with a little company called ECW, known for their bloodshed and violence on one hand, and for truly excellent matches on the other. I ordered one tape because it had the notorious 'Mass Transit Incident' on it – where an untrained wrestler was bloodied in the ring to the point of hospitalisation – but also on that tape was a stellar match between Eddie Guerrero and Dean Malenko that made me appreciate technical wrestling and how a crowd can display unbridled emotion for two competitors. That became my thing. I love good promos and storylines and plot development, but I *really* love hard-hitting technical wrestling.

The tapes I ordered introduced me to Japanese wrestling as well, in particular the work of a company called All Japan Pro Wrestling (AJPW). I had a six-hour-long tape that I watched again and again, eventually wearing out the tape as I became obsessed with the 'Four Pillars of Heaven', four talented wrestlers who would often wrestle each other, every time finding a way to make their bouts more entertaining and different. Mitsuharu Misawa, Toshiaki Kawada, Akira Taue and Kenta Kobashi showed me exactly what wrestling could be. They genuinely approached perfection with everything that they did.

As video on the internet kicked on in the mid 2000s and smaller promotions put out DVDs, I started amassing a collection of independent shows from the USA. All my favourite talents from that time ended up in the WWE at a high level – stars such as CM Punk, Samoa Joe, Daniel Bryan and more. The more I understood wrestling, the more I realised that the days of territorial companies had gone, and independent companies were a production line for the big companies. I would eagerly watch smaller shows, trying to predict who would go on to be the next big thing, enjoying the storytelling that comes from every wrestling show, no matter what the size.

I started stand-up in 2005, aged 27. At that point, I worked in an office and kept my love of wrestling secret. It would have been less embarrassing for me to list my sexual fetishes to my colleagues than it would be to explain that I was often tired on a Monday because I had stayed up till 4 a.m. to watch a WWE pay per view. But once I entered the comedy world, it was much more acceptable to chat about my hobby. Loads of comedians were into it. One, Chris Brooker, took me to a live show in Coventry in 2008. Our friendship grew from there, and its thanks to Chris having me support Mick Foley and William Regal on stand-up tours that I started working within wrestling rather than just being a fan.

I get asked a lot about how we started PROGRESS. We've grown massively in the past six-and-a-bit years, but to me it's still just three mates messing about. Jon used to be my comedy agent, and during the Edinburgh Fringe in 2011 I showed him a Pro Wrestling Guerrilla DVD. PWG are a tremendous independent promotion who host all their shows in a scout hut in Reseda, California. Jon watched it for a while and said, 'We should have a go at this', specifically in London where it was always said it was too difficult to run wrestling shows. By the second show Glen was on board, and over six years later we're now spoken of in the same breath as PWG. Life is weird.

So now, at 40 years of age, I'm as much of a wrestling fan as ever. Thanks to technological advances I'm watching an old WWE show from 1997 via the internet as I'm writing this. Tomorrow morning I'll get up early to watch New Japan Pro Wrestling live through their on-demand service, and this year I'm going to the USA, Australia and Germany to host our shows.

I spend a lot of my time reading about wrestling, and that's where the idea for this book came from. There are dozens of excellent autobiographies of superstars out there, and they're certainly worth hunting down. But in terms of historical documents, most wrestling books are concerned with what went wrong in a certain period; how a company failed, why the in-ring product sucked and so on. I don't buy into that. Wrestling as an industry will always have its ups and downs, but in the main it has kept me entertained for about 30 years. I want to tell the complete story of the history of professional wrestling in my own way, hopefully with humour that's appreciated but always with as positive a spin as I can manage on things. Because I really do love it. Because the complete history of wrestling should be told, and now is the time to do it. I want everyone to appreciate what isn't just entertainment, but in the eyes of many, an art form.

Professional wrestling is the greatest thing in the entire world.

Chapter One:
In the Beginning

From 'real' to 'fake':
the pioneers to the Gold Dust Trio

Any wrestling fan will tell you about the constant struggle that they have with acquaintances who *don't* enjoy the grappling arts. At the age of 40, I've suffered through countless friends and relatives who feel the need to ask me the same question every time my hobby comes up:

'You know its fake, right?'

Well, yes. Of course I do. But I also know that Luke Skywalker isn't a real person (nor has he, or anyone else, ever piloted an X-Wing to destroy the Death Star in real life) and I still love *Star Wars*. My mother was comfortable knowing that everyone in *Coronation Street* was an actor, but that didn't stop her crying whenever someone died on a street with the highest mortality rate in Northern England. My nephew enjoys first-person shooter video games, but nobody is giving him grief because he's not out in a war zone firing a missile into someone's face.

Wrestling is escapism and has been for me since the age of four. I don't think I've ever thought it was real, and I'm completely fine with that. The first wrestler I ever saw on television was Big Daddy and even as a little kid I knew everything that he did looked hokey. The A-Team was more realistic, and nobody on that ever got as much as grazed by any of the thousand bullets fired in any given episode. But it was bright and loud and fun, and that's what I fell in love with then and what I still enjoy now, even if some of my sensibilities have changed with age.

Don't get me wrong, I enjoy legitimate combat sports like MMA (Mixed Martial Arts) and boxing, but you never know what you're going to get. You could get a brutal, athletic, fast-paced slugfest; or you could get two grown men hugging each other for an entire fight. With wrestling, at least you're getting two (or more) competitors who are going out there to entertain you, not fight for survival.

I'd equate it to this principle: if you watch a fight scene in a film it's invariably exciting and well-paced. Ever seen a real fight? It's often some hugging and some badly thrown punches and a woman shouting, 'Leave it, Gary, he's had enough'. Thing is, wrestling wasn't always this way. It may be considered 'sports entertainment' now, but in its very beginnings it was a legitimate sport that evolved and changed as attention spans grew shorter and audiences became more demanding for thrills and spills.

As a wrestling promoter, I will sometimes hear people throw around a word that is only really an insult within our strange little world. That word is *carny*. A promoter promises a card that he doesn't deliver, then he's a bit of a carny. A wrestler conducts himself in an old-school manner which is a bit obstructive, then he's a bit of a carny. It means 'of the carnival' and is seen these days as a negative but if you know your history then you'll know that without carnies, we wouldn't have wrestling. Or hook-a-duck.

It's pretty easy to forget these days with the huge choices of entertainment that we have, but even in my youth a travelling fair was a genuine treat. Legendary wrestlers such as William Regal learned their chops taking on all comers at Blackpool Pleasure Beach, but the word carny wasn't an insult back then. Go back even further to the 1800s and travelling carnivals and fairs were the biggest of big deals, from across Europe to post Civil War America; and you didn't just go along to see the bearded lady or try to win a prize. Very often, the central attraction of these shows was wrestling.

It's not like wrestling is in any way a new thing. The amateur wrestling they have at the Olympics isn't called Greco-Roman for nostalgia reasons, there has been some form of wrestling in just about every corner of the world since time began. Men have always loved to wrestle, and let's be honest, having a bit of a grapple and a roll around to settle your differences or determine sporting superiority is more fun than getting punched in the face.

I must make this part clear right now; in these early days wrestling was *fairly* legit. Granted, some of the take-on-the-punters challenges may have involved a ringer or two to ensure the respectability of the wrestlers remained intact, but when a big bout was put on between two barrel-chested warriors, they *usually* went at it for real. Wrestling was one of the most popular sports in the world at the turn of the century, with a few real warriors standing out from the herd. Even Abraham Lincoln was known for his wrestling prowess in his youth, with his toughness being brought up repeatedly during his rise to power. Such a shame that he went down the less popular career path of becoming president of the United States (in recent years Donald Trump has been inside the squared circle a few times before millions of American voters gave him the power to destroy us all).

Whenever wrestling has true popularity, it must have some legitimate star power. In the early days, there are three names that stick out as being superstars: Martin 'Farmer' Burns, 'The Russian Lion' George Hackenschmidt and Frank Gotch.

Martin Burns' story sounds a bit like a stereotypical turn-of-the-century American tale: born in a log cabin in deepest Iowa, young Martin developed a love of wrestling during the Civil War when it was a major activity among troops at their makeshift camps. With his father passing away when he was 11 and being from a large family, he worked on local farms to earn money to support his mother and siblings. This is both where he gained his freakish strength and his nickname. Old job titles definitely worked better on that front: 'farmer' is much more interesting and ambiguous than 'agricultural assistant'.

Competing mainly against older men, Burns honed his formidable technique before turning professional at just 19 years old, his first match being far removed from the bouts we see today: a draw lasting two hours and 19 minutes. Burns didn't just earn money from wrestling though, he put his notoriously massive neck to good use at fairs and carnivals by being dropped six feet with his head in a hangman's noose and surviving. (I'm not entirely sure how he worked out he could do that in the first place. Probably best to not ask.)

Burns' big break (not his neck) came in 1889, winning the princely sum of $25 by challenging and beating touring professional Jack Carleek, before becoming Catch as Catch Can Champion by defeating Evan 'Strangler' Lewis. He then defended his title across the USA at fairs, often suckering in easy marks because despite his impressive physique, he only weighed 165lbs at his peak. Instead of just throwing opponents off their feet to win falls, Burns popularised the pinfall victory, as well as utilising countless wear-down and submission holds. In 1895, he won the American title (the unified Catch and Greco-Roman prize) from his old foe Lewis before losing his winning streak (and the title) in 1897. His legacy didn't just come from within the ring though, he trained countless others (more on that in a while) and also put out a famous mail order training course in 1914 called *The Lessons in Wrestling and Physical Culture*. It was very much the P90X of its day, apparently. Would have been massive if they had 3 a.m. infomercials to push that out.

Burns was good and certainly popular, but he was nothing compared to the bona fide superstar that was George Hackenschmidt. Born in what is now Tartu, Estonia, in 1877, Hackenschmidt was an absolute Adonis, with archive photographs showing that he resembled a modern-day Mr Universe competitor. His strength was legendary – the story goes that when he was a schoolboy, he once lifted a horse off the ground. Again, best not to ask . . .

Incredibly proficient at most sports in his youth, Hackenschmidt gave Greco-Roman wrestling a try in 1896 when he challenged Georg Lurich, losing the match but gaining both respect for the sport and the drive to better himself. By 1900 he was winning tournaments across Russia after completing his military service, and by 1903 he was touring the UK, taking on all comers in the catch as catch can style. He would end up spending much of his life in Britain where his talent and good looks – along with the flamboyant management of theatre impresario CB Cochrane – created a massive boom for wrestling in the music halls around the country. He would often grapple multiple foes in one evening, beating everyone easily while gaining recognition from high society for his intellect, nature and philosophy. Ironically, nowadays he'd be regarded as a massive villain by wrestling fans because he was so good at everything.

By 1904 Hackenschmidt was the darling of high society, and London was brought to a standstill twice in 1904 for massive bouts with Ahmed Madrali at the Olympia, followed by Tom Jenkins at the Royal Albert Hall. But news of 'The Russian Lion's popularity and undefeated streak travelled across the Atlantic, creating a rivalry that was the Hogan v Andre or Austin v Rock of its time.

Frank Gotch was a 22-year-old Iowa native when he challenged Farmer Burns to a match in 1899. He lost in 11 minutes, but impressed Burns enough to have him take him under his wing. He wrestled throughout Iowa and the Yukon for a while, often under the pseudonym Frank Kennedy, for reasons that aren't entirely clear. Gotch wouldn't be the last wrestler to use a different name in his career (equally, he wasn't the first). After winning the American Heavyweight Championship in 1904, he turned his attention to Hackenschmidt. What followed remain two of the most famous wrestling matches in history, even if these days we can only rely on their legend being retold and passed on.

Their first clash was in Chicago at Dexter Park Pavilion on 3 April 1908 (incidentally, WrestleMania is usually around that time of the year – probably just a coincidence, but a pretty cool one nonetheless). Hackenschmidt didn't take his challenger too seriously and wasn't in his usual peak condition. Gotch, trained hard for the bout by Burns and his entourage, was both ready and willing to win the fight by any means necessary. He employed headbutts, sneaky blows and was covered from head to toe in oil. That doesn't seem that unusual now if you watch modern-day wrestlers covering themselves in baby lotion and fake tan to bring out their abs, but this was very much a different time. They had a heel and face dynamic before that was really a thing.

After two hours of targeting the leg of Hackenschmidt, Gotch managed to make him submit with his patented toe hold . . . for the *first* fall (matches would usually be best of three falls). The Russian Lion refused to leave his dressing room for the second fall, so gave up his title to Gotch and was gentlemanly in defeat . . . well, for a while at least. When talk of a rematch came about, he started to protest the tactics of the American, stimulating more interest in the bout – this was probably the starting point for the promos that we see today.

While Hackenschmidt was embraced by polite society in the UK and Europe, Gotch became a megastar in the USA where he was regarded as a man of the people. He took a starring role and toured around the country in a play called *All About a Bout* written about him, and became the biggest mainstream hero that the sport had produced, on a par with the biggest stars of boxing or baseball. His first encounter with Hackenschmidt had been major news around the world, and as victor there he knew he had to protect and cement his legacy to continue to enjoy his stardom. Three years after that first bout, the two men met again in Chicago – despite Hackenschmidt wanting the bout to be in Europe – in front of 30,000 fans. On 4 September 1911, Gotch cemented his legacy as the best wrestler of his generation as he beat Hackenschmidt in two straight falls in just under 30 minutes. I'm sure that some fans were disappointed at the relatively short bout, but you imagine many posteriors were relieved.

But the bout was full of controversy. It was claimed that Hackenschmidt was injured in training by a sparring partner who was paid off by the Gotch camp, and the champion continued to use his dirtier tactics to his advantage, targeting the injury and taking any shortcuts that he could. Fans were still discussing the contest decades later. Heck, some British comedian is writing about it more than a century on (and you're reading about it right this second).

Gotch retired in 1913, having only wrestled 160 matches in his career (winning 154). A wrestler's career back then was much closer to a boxer or MMA fighter now, training for big bouts and not being physically able to perform at peak competitive level every single day of the week. Gotch's retirement left a massive void in the wrestling world (tragically, four years of hard living later, he passed away at the age of 40, with the ghastly sounding uremic poisoning given as his cause of death). Fans drifted away, annoyed at the lack of star power and tired of how long matches could often go on for. I've watched 20-minute-long time limit draws at shows and heard fans chant 'Bullshit' at the lack of a conclusive result. Imagine watching a match for three hours, where two burly men lock up and then don't move for pretty much that entire time, then it's a draw? That happened, repeatedly.

Let's be honest, there was another similarity to boxing and MMA back then as well. Audiences were starting to question the legitimacy of the sport more and more. It was often rumoured that stars like Gotch would have officials in their back pockets, and at some point between Gotch and three gentlemen known as the Gold Dust Trio (more on them soon . . .), wrestling went from a *mainly* legitimate contest at the turn of the century to being 100 per cent fixed by 1925 (with the occasional exception). Maybe that's where boxing will be in 30 years' time. The blurring of lines between competing in sports halls and stadiums but then taking on all comers at carnivals didn't help the feeling that wrestling wasn't always on the level even at the very turn of the century, so as the 1920s began popularity was at an all-time low.

Someone had to shake things up a bit. Three men did so much in the space of a few years to revolutionise wrestling and turn it into something much closer to the product that we enjoy now. Incidentally, the Gold Dust Trio didn't get that nickname until after their heyday; but they are at least partially responsible for the naming of one of my favourite characters from the 1990s – Goldust – through their legendary status.

Like Gotch, Joseph 'Toots' Mondt was another Iowan. Born in 1894, he learned to wrestle through the Farmer Burns correspondence course that I mentioned a little earlier. He got so good that he eventually toured the USA with Burns and became known as a legendary hooker (no, not like *that*, get your mind out of the gutter). As those of you who bothered to read the Glossary will know, a hooker or shooter was someone who had all the legitimate skills to really hurt an opponent if he needed to. As Mondt became well known for his toughness, he was asked to join the entourage of Ed 'Strangler' Lewis and his manager Billy Sandow, who could also shoot if need be. These three men, all similar ages, absolutely changed the wrestling world during the 1920s.

Sandow would do most of the promoting, Lewis was usually in the main event and Mondt was the genius working behind the scenes, coming up with finishes to the matches to keep things entertaining for crowds and using ideas like drawn matches and no contests to be able to draw more money when the show rolled back into town a few months down the line; as well as being able to keep Lewis as champion if it suited the group. The 'Strangler' was a tough guy who was pretty legit, but he knew that losing from time to time to a challenger only kept audiences engaged and away from boredom.

Crowds were utterly bored of mat-based grappling. As other sports and forms of entertainment became popular, audiences required a little bit more razzmatazz for their hard-earned money. The Trio devised a new form of wrestling that wasn't limited to either catch as catch can or Greco-Roman styles but used the best parts of both and utilised elements of boxing, gymnastics and showboating. While still nowhere near the product we see today, it was called 'Slam Bang Western Style Wrestling' and it did exactly what it said on the marquee. This was the first promotion where you would see suplexes, body slams and hip tosses all in the same match, moves where it actually requires two men working together for them to work. Wrestling was no longer a sport, it was entertainment. Looking back, it is hard to imagine that such basic moves were massive high spots back then when you're used to what wrestling offers these days. An audience in 1920 would lose its mind if it saw Will Ospreay v Ricochet.

With audiences once again on the up in the early 1920s, Sandow started signing wrestlers to exclusive contracts with the Trio, meaning that they controlled touring wrestling shows and for a while at least, killed off much of their competition. The group became the first notable wrestling promotion, repeating storylines in different cities and offering wrestlers many chances to work. Up until 1925 everything was a roaring success. Then somebody threw a spanner in the works by bringing the real fight to a pretend fight.

The Trio could all certainly handle themselves, but their wrestlers always did what they were told not because of fear, but because of money. Everyone was making loads of it, so why rock the boat? Stanislaus Zbyszko was one man making good money from the Trio, winning Lewis' title in 1921 but losing it back under a year later as his title reign didn't do the box office that was expected. In 1922, just after the title switch, Joe Stecher left the Trio to start his own promotion. Another well-known hooker, Stecher had been a long-time rival of Lewis and believed he could run a promotion to rival the Trio.

By 1925, the Trio had a different champion in Wayne Munn. A giant of a man, Munn was a former football player and unusual in wrestling in that he wasn't a shooter or a hooker, just a tough guy who was massive and had a ton of charisma. He was a pet project of the Trio, who saw him and immediately saw dollar signs. To make Munn look more credible, he had tough challengers lined up, including Zbyszko. The role of Zbyszko was to make Munn look good and lose to him, but instead he turned the worked match into a shoot, repeatedly pinning the big man until the referee (who was clued in to knowing who was meant to be winning) had no choice but to award the match and title to Zbyszko, mainly to avoid the contest becoming even more of a farce.

Zbyszko wasn't done though. He rapidly dropped the title to Stecher in his promotion, causing huge embarrassment to the Trio. They countered by claiming the Munn v Zbyszko match was null and void and reinstated Munn as champion to ensure that they had control over their own title. Lewis obviously won it from Munn rapidly, with the big lad's career in ruins as his lack of legitimate toughness was exposed. This double-cross can't be underestimated, as it's arguably the last time a major wrestling championship has changed hands legitimately rather than being scripted (well, until a little something that happened in 1997, as we'll see later . . .). With Lewis and Stecher now seen as champions of the same stature, the Trio's reputation was irreparably harmed.

Lewis, Mondt and Sandow worked together until the 1930s, but never saw that same amount of power and glory as a group again. Lewis remained a legitimate champion and tough guy; indeed, the Munn debacle meant that it would be a long time before non-shooters were trusted to hold titles again. For the longest time, a champion would be someone with the right mix of pedigree, charisma and a very real ability to be able to shove an opponent's head up their own backside if things started getting a bit suspect. Lewis was a long-running champion, and one of the biggest parts of his legacy was training Lou Thesz who would certainly follow in his coach's footsteps.

Sandow managed other champions and promoted other shows, but it was Mondt who arguably had the longest-lasting legacy. He was key in the training and rise of dozens of major stars from the 1930s onwards, but more crucially invested his hard-earned money in 1952 into a little start-up company called the Capitol Wrestling Corporation with his friend Jess McMahon, a boxing promoter. That company would morph into the World Wide Wrestling Federation in the 1960s. It's safe to say he did okay for himself.

Once the Trio's dominance subsided, wrestling became fragmented. More promotions sprang up, more wrestlers held titles, and nobody really kept any order. Wrestling was ready to surge forwards again after the Second World War, but it needed tidying up. It required some kind of wrestling alliance.

Hang on. That's a heck of a name.

Chapter Two:
Acronyms and Television

**The NWA is born, then splintered;
and the first true wrestling TV star**

After the Second World War, the wrestling scene in the USA consisted of dozens of regional territories, all with their own rotating rosters and with their own champions, nearly always called 'world champions' despite never defending their titles outside of the couple of states that their territories operated in. With television in its infancy and the internet the stuff of science fiction at this stage, that was fine. You often didn't know what was going on beyond your local area. It's probably why baseball's biggest game is called the World Series and the furthest a team has ever come from for that is Canada. I demand a British representative in that tournament to disappoint us all and somehow lose on penalties to Germany. Or something. I don't know how baseball works.

Sometimes – and you'll find this is a running theme in this book – it takes one guy to come up with an idea that in retrospect seems so simple, but at the time was astonishingly ground-breaking. That man was Paul 'Pinkie' George, but as you'll shortly learn, this trailblazer has rather become the wrestling equivalent of Joseph Swan to Sam Muchnick's Thomas Edison; it's just a different kind of lightbulb moment.

George came up with the 'crazy' concept of trying to unify as many disparate wrestling promotions as possible, in order for them all to draw more money. His idea was to attempt to have one world champion who could travel to all the different promotions defending the belt, giving status to the title and enabling different territories to loan talent to one another to keep 'approved' companies on top and squash competition. It seems all kinds of shady now, but this idea gave rise to the NWA – not Ice Cube and Easy E; the National Wrestling Alliance. (To make things more complicated, there was already a National Wrestling Association.) This force would be one of the most dominant in wrestling until the early 1990s. It's still a thing today, weirdly owned outright by Smashing Pumpkins lead singer Billy Corgan. This is but one of many utterly ridiculous turns in the history of wrestling and the NWA in particular.

George was installed as the first president of the NWA with a unanimous vote, making him the first person in history nicknamed Pinkie to hold a position of power.

Promoting his territory out of Des Moines, Iowa, George invited five other prominent Midwest promoters to a show of his on 18 July 1948. Backstage, they had the first NWA conference, agreeing to work together and voting to crown the first NWA World Heavyweight Champion, who happened to be

George's champion at the time and one of the other promoters (covering Iowa, Kansas and Missouri), Orville Brown. A 19-year veteran, he fitted the image of being a believable tough guy that the NWA could count on. He'd set out to then unify his title with other championships across the land, firstly with American Wrestling Association and Maryland World Champion Frank Sexton in March 1949. Because he was part of the organisation, he could certainly be relied upon to carry the NWA forwards; that's if fate didn't intervene. (Spoiler: It did.)

Sam Muchnick is the name that most people think of if they talk about the early days of the NWA. Massively important to the NWA over a 25-year period, he was one of the initial founders at that first-ever meeting, and based on what we now know, was possibly sat in a comfortable chair, plotting like a Bond villain.

Muchnick ran the St Louis Wrestling Club in Missouri (to be fair, I'm surprised they let him take that white cat in) and before the formation of the NWA he was struggling to promote in his region, having to use veteran wrestlers that had been cast aside by his rivals. He did the best that he could with limited resources, drawing good crowds and gaining respect until his closest rival group was taken over by Lou Thesz. A few months after this happened, Muchnick struck up a friendship with Thesz that meant a lot more than just keeping things harmonious in the Gateway to the West.

First off, Thesz and Muchnick merged their promotions, then Thesz became champion and the main draw. During that first NWA conference, it was arguably between Thesz and Brown to become the first NWA champion; politics ensured that Brown got the nod. But in 1950, things changed. Yet again, fate intervened.

Brown and Thesz were due to have a unifying title match in November 1949, when Pinkie George was in his second term as NWA President. However, Brown was seriously injured in a car accident just 24 days before the contest, badly enough to immediately end his career. Nowadays a promoter would scramble around to at least make a token contest to crown a new champion, but in 1949 wrestling still had an air of sporting legitimacy. Therefore, Thesz (as next appointed challenger) was awarded the NWA World Heavyweight Championship, unifying it with his other titles and giving the organisation more power. Muchnick was his biggest supporter and closest ally, and he became president of the NWA in 1950, easily winning the votes as he commanded so much trust among the other promoters in the now rapidly expanding group.

That was just about it for Pinkie George. He fell out with the NWA and drifted away, trying to sue the group for $200,000 in 1963 as he struggled to promote shows of his own without access to the top talent and best arenas that NWA controlled. I'd suspect that he probably regretted starting the monster that eventually consumed him, but you have to take your hat off to the man for being a visionary.

Incidentally, I cannot confirm or deny the rumours that he was the inspiration for the character Pinky (of *Pinky and the Brain* fame) in the cult cartoon *Animaniacs* though, or that he ended that first NWA conference by declaring: 'We're going to take over the world'.

Muchnick took the NWA from strength to strength. He was president from 1950 until 1960, only stepping down because of illness and so the group could take on new ideas. He returned to the helm in 1963 and remained in charge until 1975. He oversaw the rapid expansion of the NWA, including deals that took them overseas and grew the brand massively. He was also behind revolutionary ideas for wrestling on television and his peers regarded him as a visionary. With Thesz as champion for most of the 1950s, the NWA became pretty unstoppable.

In total, Thesz spent 3,749 days as NWA World Heavyweight champion over the course of his numerous reigns. A legit shooter, learning from his experience training under Strangler Lewis, he could be relied upon to draw good crowds, have great matches and be tough enough to never get double-crossed. He did, as we'll learn, end up being involved in more than his fair share of controversial matches that ended up shaping wrestling as much as the Zbyszko double-cross did, but in the main he ploughed on through his career making a lot of money and helping the NWA's growth in its first full decade.

In 1952, he beat Los Angeles World Champion Baron Michele Leone in a unification match, becoming the closest thing to a 'true' unified World Champion since the 1930s. He took some time off for injury in 1957 after losing his title to Whipper Billy Watson, but seven months later the belt was back around his waist. It's hard to imagine such a dominant champion now, speaking from my personal experience of running a wrestling company. I've seen fans vociferously complain when someone holds a title for six months after defending it a couple of times a month; Thesz was all over the country, every day of the week defending the belt and trying to tighten the stranglehold of the NWA.

Everything spread from the Midwest to every corner of the states, like votes for the Republican party. The NWA had allegiances from Hollywood to Florida, and Ontario to New Mexico, as well as in Japan and Mexico. By the 1960s, some groups would drop away, but the NWA would continue to make gains.

Thesz was the driving force for much of this expansion. The deal with JWA (Japan Pro Wrestling Alliance) in Tokyo was inked based off a couple of drawn matches with their biggest star (and promoter) Rikidōzan, for example. But he wasn't everyone's cup of tea. With his close ties to Muchnick, when an NWA-affiliated promoter had an axe to grind then his status as champion could be a bone of contention and it did lead to the first cracks in the NWA organisation, with some pretty industry-changing results.

Édouard Carpentier (born Édouard Weiczorkiewicz) was a French-born son of Polish and Russian parents who emigrated to Canada in the 1950s after decorated combat as part of the French Resistance during the Second World War. With excellent gymnastic ability, he was one of the first talents to bring this side of performance and athletics to wrestling, gaining a stellar reputation for exciting bouts (well, for the time. If someone in 1950 had seen the likes of 1996 Psicosis or Rey Mysterio Jr, they would have absolutely lost their minds).

On 14 June 1957, Carpentier had an NWA title match with Thesz; with the action tied at one fall each (title matches were nearly always best of three falls; for the sake of drama, it was very rare that anyone ever won a title match 2–0), Thesz was forced to retire due to a legitimate injury (the same one that forced him to lose his title to Watson as mentioned earlier). This meant that Carpentier won the title, but it wasn't recognised by the NWA as it was the result of an injury. Some territories did acknowledge Carpentier as the new champion, though, leading to questions over the absolute authority of the NWA.

Carpentier would lose his version of the NWA title in fairly short order to Minnesota promoter and former NFL star Verne Gagne. The kind of tediously talented man who could turn his hand to any sport and excel at it, Gagne had a couple of years in the NFL before deciding to start his wrestling career in 1949 because – and this is hard to believe these days – it paid better. The NFL really wasn't big business until the 1980s, so it was common for football players to take on wrestling jobs during their close season until the 1970s. At least an NFL player would be of a certain size and level of fitness. Gagne didn't do any sneaky wrestling himself while employed by the Chicago Bears, mainly because they were aware that one of their biggest stars in the 1930s, Bronco Nagurski, was the first guy to do it. You can only wonder if the management there reminding Gagne of the money and notoriety that Nagurski gained was enough to make him eventually take the plunge.

Making his debut in Texas, Gagne started picking up titles in the early 1950s then started getting involved in promoting. In Omaha in 1958, he won Carpentier's version of the NWA title and it set his brain in motion. The NWA affiliate in Nebraska recognised him as champion now, not Lou Thesz. Maybe he could use the friction to his advantage? At the time, he held the title for three months before dropping it to Wilbur Snyder; he then took a break from wrestling every night as he was an independently wealthy man. But in 1960, he got back into the game in the biggest way he could manage: he started his own promotion. Not a territory; he'd done that and had been told what to do by the NWA overlords. He wanted to be king.

We can only speculate as to how Gagne came up with the name for his rival to the National Wrestling Alliance, but I imagine he was thumbing through a thesaurus while listening to the Star-Spangled Banner. His American Wrestling Association (AWA) was born in 1960, and the reigning NWA champion Pat O'Connor was named as its first champion.

O'Connor held the NWA World Heavyweight Championship between 1959 and 1961, winning it from Dick Hutton before becoming a bit of a political pawn in a long-standing rivalry between Sam Muchnick and Chicago-based promoter Fred Kohler, who was particularly vocal in not wanting O'Connor as NWA champ. He was even cheeky enough to ask that O'Connor pay *him* to wrestle on his shows before he would pay him his fee, which would be less than he paid previous champions. Maybe Kohler had a severe aversion to anybody from Down Under because it was undeniable that, as television became more important in the 1950s, New Zealand born O'Connor was a star. After initially refusing, at the height of his title reign and of his popularity O'Connor would go on to work for Kohler.

O'Connor drew over 30,000 fans to Chicago's Comiskey Park for a bout with Yukon Eric in 1960, and I sincerely hope that he really did utter the phrase 'I told you I was good at this' to Kohler in the back when he was counting up the ticket receipts.

Back to Gagne's AWA (although we're not finished with O'Connor by a long stretch). Gagne was around a lot of key people in the early 1960s, and as a result is very much the Kevin Bacon of wrestling in that time, by which I mean that he was only ever a few degrees of separation from something absolutely massive occurring, rather than him introducing the love of dancing to a straight-laced Midwest town.

Gagne needed a champion at the top of his AWA, so he named O'Connor as his first ace. Now holding both the NWA and AWA

World Titles, O'Connor was given 90 days by Gagne to defend his AWA title or be stripped of it. As he never asked for it in the first place and was probably wise to the alpha-male power move by Gagne, he never did. In a move that was a surprise to nobody, after 90 days Gagne was named AWA Champion. He would go on to hold the AWA title ten times during the remainder of his career, at one point keeping it for over seven years (1968-75). In fact, if you remove Gagne's hand-picked successor (and multiple time AWA champion) Nick Bockwinkel from the equation, in the history of the AWA, 1960-1991, Gagne held the world title there for longer than every other champion *combined* – Gagne had 4,677 days as champ, Bockwinkel had 2,990, everyone else combined had 3,492.

I suppose you can always trust yourself to carry the company more than anybody else. After all, you're not likely to leave for another promotion.

When Gagne retired in 1981 from in-ring competition, he didn't even observe the time-honoured tradition of putting someone over on his way out. He retired as an active wrestler while AWA Champion, and again the title was just passed on to someone – the admittedly excellent Bockwinkel, as Gagne always preferred amateur-style tough guys – when he chose to finish up. It's not to say that Gagne didn't get what wrestling was about. The AWA was successful for a long time, and Gagne would go on to be involved in the training of a who's who of professional wrestlers: Ric Flair, Bob Backlund, Ricky Steamboat, The Iron Shiek and Curt Hennig among others. He would train anyone who wanted to be a wrestler and had the necessary athletic skills on his farm, in often brutal conditions. Flair quit the first time he signed up for training because he couldn't take it, returning the next year to stick it out.

The breakaway of the AWA wasn't the only loss that the NWA felt in the 1960s though. Another company took its leave, and although it stayed on pretty level footing with the NWA and AWA for the next couple of decades, by the early 1980s it would grow into a company of titanic proportions.[1]

Remember NWA affiliate promoter Fred Kohler? He was the bloke that didn't like Pat O'Connor being champion. In 1961 he had a run at being NWA President for a year, during Sam Muchnick's three-year hiatus from the job. A challenger to the champion had to be voted for. The board voted for someone Kohler knew very well, a man with bleached-blond hair who had been selling out venues in Chicago throughout the 1950s: Buddy Rogers. Rogers didn't use the mat-based style that so many of his contemporaries did, instead using flashy moves like piledrivers and neckbreakers and utilising a style that was more high-octane (and some would say unrealistic, especially compared to what wrestling had been up to this point).

The O'Connor v Rogers clash happened on 30 June 1961 at Comiskey Park in Chicago, with a crowd of over 38,000 setting a gate receipts record for professional wrestling that would last for the next 20 years. The match was choreographed so that Rogers capitalised on a missed O'Connor dropkick to win the match by two falls to one.

Make no mistake about it, Rogers was an absolute superstar, but very much the antithesis of what the NWA had been built on. He was brash and bold and the first wrestler to use the 'Nature Boy' nickname (which in turn was an evolution of his

---

[1] I'm aware that is a really good joke that you won't actually get for the next few chapters if you're not a nerd. But trust me, the pay-off is wonderful. Store it in your memory now. You'll thank me.

original 'Natural Guy' nickname that didn't exactly have the same ring to it). He invented the figure four leglock and was one of the most innovative villains in all of wrestling. By being loud and flashy, he was very different to the calm, athletic champions of the past like Thesz. Not that he wasn't tough himself, but he would often raise the ire of the shooters in locker rooms with his attitude. Upon winning the title, he took the microphone and uttered his catchphrase: 'To a nicer guy, it couldn't happen', becoming arguably the first wrestler to have a signature catch-phrase. Ever since then, grapplers have been desperate to find one that sticks.

It was always said that Rogers favoured certain promotions, especially around the North East of the USA. When he became NWA champion, this greatly annoyed some of the plainer, tougher guys that he had to spend his time around. Legend has it that he sustained several real injuries during his two-year reign as champion, including a broken hand from Karl Gotch and Bill Miller, both gentlemen considered two of the most dangerous legitimate fighters of the day. After a few instances of injury lay-offs during his reign, in 1963 the NWA voted to put Lou Thesz back in place as champion. At the time, Thesz had a genuine, deep dislike for Rogers, the two men very much chalk and cheese.

The title switch took place in Toronto on 24 January 1963. Rogers, knowing that things might get a little bit dodgy, was reticent about losing his belt to Thesz, so Sam Muchnick, back in the role of NWA president, managed to put a few safeguards in place to ensure that nothing untoward happened: the match would only be one fall to a finish, not the usual two-out-of-three-fall encounter. Thesz was in the match, and if he had to, he would just shoot on Rogers and take the belt. Finally – and this was most likely the deciding factor – Muchnick threatened to donate Roger's $25,000 champion bond to charity. Each NWA champion would have to put up $25,000 upon winning the title as a deposit on the belt and to ensure no shenanigans. (The same issue would arise again in the 1990s, just a different Nature Boy that time.)

As far as the NWA was concerned, everything went smoothly. Rogers dropped the title as requested. Business could carry on as usual, right?

No. For all that Thesz and Muchnick may have not been fans of Rogers, he did have his supporters. Two that were particularly prominent were Toots Mondt and Vincent J McMahon (who we shall refer to as Vince Sr from now on), promoters of the Capitol Wrestling Corporation in the North East. Because of the population density of their geographical region, they controlled much of the NWA's business in the 1950s. In 1963 they didn't want Thesz as the NWA champion, so decided to make a break for it and start up their own stand-alone company: The World Wide Wrestling Federation. And yes, you're right. There were too many Ws back then.

Even these days, the company that has gone from being WWWF to WWF to WWE is still called 'New York' by some people, a throwback to those territorial times.

In the beginning, nobody could predict just how massive the WWWF would become, but Toots and Vince Sr had their plans ready to set in motion. Rogers was named their initial champion; they didn't recognise the title change to Thesz as it took place over one fall. Rogers would eventually be awarded the WWWF title in April 1963, with his reign beginning with a tournament win in Rio. Of course, that tournament was entirely fictional, but this was 1963: you had to make it sound legit and nobody in New York knew anybody in Rio who could prove it didn't happen. It sounded perfectly reasonable.

Rogers would end up being champion for just a month, and would never hold a WWWF title again after that. He had a mild heart attack just three weeks after being awarded the belt, but he had always been likely to be replaced by a champion chosen by Mondt and McMahon anyway. He was merely the reason for them to break away, and in May 1963 he was beaten in 48 seconds by an Italian-American superhero, Bruno Sammartino. Legend has it that Mondt – who we know was a shooter in his day – dragged Rogers from his sick bed to the arena so he could switch the title. He doesn't seem like the sort of chap who would accept a note from your mum.

All this wrangling in the early 1960s over power and money in wrestling was a direct side-effect of the huge growth that the business had seen in the Fifties. Some of that was down to the NWA, undoubtedly. But the main reason that it caught fire so quickly after the Second World War? The same reason that anything big in entertainment did: television.

Wrestling was ideal for television: it was happening across the country already, it was exciting, and the pre-determined nature of it meant that you could plan television episodes around it fairly easily. The DuMont Network was one of the first to be set up in the USA and because it didn't have the massive budget of its rivals CBS and NBC, it needed cheap programming to fill its schedule. Wrestling was one of its biggest successes, routinely the most-watched show on the station with around 20 per cent of the homes that had televisions tuning in. Imagine those kinds of figures now. If one in five homes are watching *Celebrity Big Brother* or some other nonsense, then I'm very disappointed in humanity.

In the early 1950s as TV ownership grew rapidly, wrestling was on network television and a seriously big deal. *Wrestling from Marigold* was one of DuMont's biggest success stories, lasting for six years between 1949 and 1955 and showcasing NWA-affiliated action – produced by Fred Kohler – from the Marigold Arena in Chicago. The show remained on non-network television until 1957; after that, it would be three decades until professional wrestling was once again seen as mainstream enough to be shown on every television in the USA.

That's not to say that wrestling's relationship with TV didn't lead to some massive advances, both technically and artistically. *Wrestling at the Chase* began in May 1959, the brainchild of Sam Muchnick and Harold Coplar, the owner of the Chase Park Hotel in St Louis and, as luck would have it, the KPLR TV station that happened to be next door. Although only shown in the local area, it was wildly successful and ran until 1983. It's certainly one of the reasons that Sam Muchnick remained as powerful as he did in the NWA hierarchy, with his St Louis territory always seeming hot. Technically, Muchnick was smart too; they would eventually start to tape three weeks' worth of episodes in one day, charging nothing for entry but reaping rewards in live ticket sales for other shows and advertising.

Wrestling at the Chase is now looked back upon fondly (you can view some archived episodes of it online) as a show that put many of the biggest stars in wrestling in front of a camera for the first time. It was also the show that featured something incredibly ground-breaking in an episode taped on 27 December

1983: the WWF debut of some bloke called Hulk Hogan (daft name; whatever happened to him?). That was the end of one era on television and the beginning of something very different indeed.

With TV, it wasn't just enough to be strong and tough anymore, or to have a stellar amateur background. What really caught on with a channel-hopping television audience was the characters. A legion of five-feet-10-inch white guys in black trunks didn't exactly scream excitement to the neutral.

We haven't mentioned Gorgeous George up until this point as he never held the NWA World title and was sadly dead by 1963. But the man born in Nebraska as George Wagner was as important to wrestling in the 1940s and 50s as Hulk Hogan was in the 1980s and Steve Austin was in the 1990s. His attitude and style in the ring led him to draw a ton of money and influence hundreds of imitators: most notably, Muhammed Ali who cited George's arrogance and poise as something he admired. Go back and watch old Ali interviews: he was doing wrestling promos.

George's first TV appearance was in 1947 and the golden age of wrestling on TV thrust him into the spotlight. Nicknamed 'The Human Orchid', he was a massive crossover celebrity – on a similar level to Dwayne 'The Rock' Johnson these days – and spent the 1950s earning over $100,000 per year, a ludicrous sum of money at the time, swelled by insisting on a large percentage of gate receipts for any show he was on. Promoters would readily agree to pay him; George being on your show meant you would sell out.

With a character like George being such a draw, it led to a rise in gimmick matches, where the stakes were raised even more, promoters playing with the conventions of wrestling to deliver something new for their audience. In Toronto in 1959, 20,000 fans watched with glee as Whipper Billy Watson won a hair v hair match and shaved a horrified George bald post-match. On other occasions, fans would be ready to riot as George took to the ring, carefully inspecting himself in the mirror and spraying perfume into the crowd to ensure the watching public smelled better. Nowadays, this seems like a tired act; the preening prima donna character has been somewhat overdone. But it's been hammered into the ground purely because George was so unbelievably successful.

George actually had a decent amateur background, but it took him bleaching his hair, using female valets, acting distinctly more effeminate than he actually was and taking the name 'Gorgeous' from a heckle to really catch on the way he did. I could steal a heckle aimed at me for a nickname, but I can't find one that I can write here without blushing or weeping.

George was forced to retire on medical advice in 1962 as decades of heavy drinking led to liver problems. He died on Boxing Day 1963, penniless following his recent divorce and unsuccessful investments. People remember him fondly though, even if fans at the time would boo him until their throats were sore. He was the first wrestler to make such a ceremony out of his entrance, spending an age getting to the ring as *Pomp and Circumstance* would play over the venue PA, pulling golden bobby pins out of his long hair and handing them to the audience. He also ramped up the idea of being a heel to the next level, always cheating and acting cowardly. His catchphrase was 'Win if you can, lose if you must, but always cheat'. Very much how I play Monopoly.

JIM'S TOP TEN: WRESTLING MOVES

If we didn't have wrestling moves to punctuate matches, then we'd be watching a whole lot of hugging. Here's my favourite moves; I've tried to describe them as well as I can, but it might also be worth typing them in to YouTube so you can see them for yourself. And before you tweet me about it; I know there's no Canadian Destroyer in here. I've seen it destroyed by overuse, no pun intended.

10. Penalty Kick – Zack Sabre Jr/Katsuyori Shibata

Your opponent sits up in front of you and you kick them hard in the chest, as if you were booting a football into a goal. When done well this is a brilliant spot and a believable finish to a match. Sabre Jr was the first person I saw do it in person; it's up for debate if it's him or Shibata who had the best version.

9. Tour of the Islands – Jeff Cobb

A reverse-spin powerslam with about a million, dizzying rotations in it, this move is a great showcase for the athletic ability of Cobb, a former Olympic athlete who is destined for big things in the world of wrestling.

8. La Mistica – Mistico

Easily the biggest draw in Mexico in the mid 2000s, Mistico would finish matches with an incredibly elaborate submission: a tilt-a-whirl headscissors into a single arm DDT, which he then transitioned into a fujiwara armbar. Mistico was expected to be the new Rey Mysterio when he signed with WWE and became Sin Cara, but it didn't quite work out that way and he's now back in Mexico as Caristico.

7. Total Elimination – The Eliminators

Seeing tag team Perry Saturn and John Kronus looking like they'd killed an opponent with their roundhouse kick/leg sweep combo, coupled with ECW commentator Joey Styles screaming 'TOTAL ELIMINATION!' is one of my favourite moments from rediscovering wrestling in the late Nineties.

6. Package Piledriver – Aja Kong/Kevin Steen

Invented, like so many wrestling moves were, in the world of Japanese women's wrestling in the 1990s, Aja Kong was the first to wield this super-deadly version of the piledriver, itself a move that was always treated as unbeatable for years. With the opponent squashed into a package, they're dropped on their head. Steen's use of it in RoH (Ring of Honor) and PWG brought it to my attention. He can't use it in WWE, but every time he teases it the internet goes insane.

5. Poison Mist – The Great Muta

Muta wasn't the first to use this tactic of spraying coloured mist into his opponent's faces, but he's the reason I was initially aware of it (Great Kabuki used it before him; Tajiri, among others, afterwards). Any wrestler performing this spot would have a condom full of food colouring in their mouth and would bite down on it when required in order to break it. Different colours have different mysterious powers: green just blinds for a while, black blinds for a long time, yellow paralyses, red burns and blue sends the opponent to sleep. I desperately want to work as a manager just once and spray mist as my gimmick.

4. Psycho Driver – Super Dragon

Super Dragon is one of the founders of PWG and although semi-retired now, a great wrestler in his own right. Another piledriver variant, the Psycho Driver starts from an Argentine backbreaker position before the opponent is flipped into a piledriver. Super Dragon has variations on this move, plus another move called the Barry White Driver which is nearly as deadly.

3. The Cop Killer – Homicide

Another of my favourite RoH wrestlers, Homicide would destroy opponents with this move, also known as a Vertebreaker (and used by Shane Helms). It was actually invented in Japan by Megumi Kudo, and when she used it referred to it as the Kudo Driver. It's a double underhook back-to-back piledriver and is incredibly dangerous. Homicide gave it the coolest name though (and renamed it 'The Gringo Killer' when he was more PG-rated at TNA (Total Nonstop Action Wrestling).

2. Rainmaker/Acid Rainmaker – Kazuchika Okada/Jimmy Havoc

I love a lariat; it's different to a clothesline as the attacker swings his arm rather than leaving it straight. Stan Hansen had arguably the best in the business. The Rainmaker is a wrist lock into a short-arm lariat. I've listed both Okada and Havoc here; Havoc's has a cooler name, but Okada's is accompanied by theatrics and his own dramatic camera shot.

1. Burning Hammer – Kenta Kobashi

Sometimes, people in wrestling will talk about 'protecting' a move; having nobody kick out of it and use it sparingly to make it special. Kobashi's burning hammer is exactly that, an inverted Death Valley driver that he only used seven times between 1998 and 2006 and for good reason: it flat-out killed dudes. I have seen it used in independent matches many times since, and it has never finished a match. I prefer the original.

Chapter Three:
Foreign Menaces and Immigrant Heroes

The rise of WWWF and
'The Italian Superman' Bruno Sammartino

In less cynical times, making good guys in wrestling was pretty easy; certainly, much easier than today. You'd take a guy who had a decent athletic background and was in good condition, have him prove he was a good fighter and decent human being and that was pretty much it. But for every babyface you needed a decent villain, and the likes of Gorgeous George and Buddy Rogers couldn't be in 17 different places at once. In post-war America, with television fanning the flames, promoters came up with a way to create new super villains: the foreign menace.

Wrestling pre-war was much more concerned with legitimate fighters performing in a pre-determined sport. As television audiences required more – forgive me using the term so soon – *sports entertainment* to give the casual fans a reason to tune in, the easiest narrative was taking an American hero and putting him up against a terror from overseas. (It wasn't exclusively post-war; in the 1930s Turkish wrestler Arteen Ekizian was briefly National Wrestling Association champion as the villainous Ali Baba.)

While this may sound simplistic, it still works now, although the levels of jingoism and xenophobia have been dialled down a lot over the past couple of decades. That said, as long as Donald Trump is president it might shortly make a massive comeback. We've not had a North Korean villain yet, although in Trump's eyes maybe a Mexican heel is more viable.

Goose-stepping Nazis would push the buttons of the post-war crowd fantastically, with characters such as Hans Schmidt and Fritz Von Erich. The former was actually a Canadian named Guy Larose; the latter, Texan promoter Jack Adkisson. Adkisson would remain named as Von Erich for the rest of his life, eventually dropping the overtones of his heel character to become the beloved patriarch of one of the most important families in wrestling history. Would have made his life easier to maybe go back to his real name, but I guess he reasoned that a gimmick is for life, not just for *Weihnachten*.

Smart promoters wouldn't just tar all foreigners (real or portrayed) with the same brush though. If you really wanted to make money, you needed to appeal to as many potential audience members as possible. In larger cities, it made sense to try and attract an immigrant fanbase who wanted to support someone of a similar background – one of the reasons that Pat O'Connor caught on as well as he did was his Irish surname (despite being from New Zealand). The New York territory, both pre- and post-WWWF, was very smart in using talent that appealed to the Italian and Hispanic fans, as well as enabling the same talent to cross over into mainstream adulation from fans who didn't have that background.

Antonino Rocca was one of the first of these stars. Born in Italy but moving to Argentina before the Second World War, he had seven years of headlining shows at Madison Square Garden (MSG) during the 1950s. Rocca would draw numbers to New York shows that rivalled even those of 'The Golden Greek' Jim Londos in the 1930s and was seen – through his exclusive contract with Capitol – to be the main reason that wrestling returned to MSG after a lengthy absence (he would also be central to wrangling over the MSG contract in 1959–60).

Combining film-star good looks and athleticism with a repertoire of moves that revealed his experience playing soccer and rugby, Rocca utilised acrobatics in a way that really hadn't been seen before. Fun fact: he was the losing finalist in the 1963 tournament to crown the first WWWF Champion, won by Buddy Rogers. Yep, the tournament that never happened. Rocca also had the distinction of appearing on the front cover of a *Superman* comic in 1962, wrestling the man of steel in a rare face v face contest. I think it went to a double count out.

A tag team partner of Rocca in the early 1960s was another Italian-born star, Bruno Sammartino. Moving to the USA in 1950 at the age of 15, he decided to combat being bullied at school by throwing himself into bodybuilding and weightlifting. By 1959, he was broad-shouldered enough to carry a log under each arm and was setting bench press world records, before moving into professional wrestling in his adopted home of Pittsburgh. The local wrestling TV show – *Studio Wrestling* – was a huge part of Sammartino's star rising; as well as his natural strength, he exuded charisma and was pretty close to being a genuine superhero. That's the great thing about wrestling; you can get up close to actual, real-life superheroes. I'm never likely to meet Batman . . . well, not unless I join Fathers for Justice.

Sammartino is known for his two massive WWWF World Title reigns, from 1963 to 1971 and then 1973 to 1977. But they nearly didn't happen. In 1961 he jumped from Capitol to a rival New York promoter over money, only to find he ended up earning even less. From there he tried to move to San Francisco to wrestle, only to find that he was suspended indefinitely by the Athletic Commission for missing a show in Baltimore (when he was actually double-booked). Unable to wrestle in the USA, he briefly returned to Pittsburgh to work as a labourer before heading to Toronto to work for promoter Frank Tunney. There he successfully resumed his career, getting to wrestle for various promotions all over Canada and having NWA title matches with Lou Thesz (a draw and a loss, designed by Sam Muchnick to make his then-rivals in New York look weak as Sammartino's name was still associated with them) and prior to that, Buddy Rogers, who he actually beat in 1962 as a result of an errant head to the groin (I'm aware that sentence is strange; Rogers mistimed a leapfrog). When Rogers couldn't continue (and presumably as he wasn't meant to win the title), Sammartino remained the total babyface by refusing to accept the belt. I would have taken it and ran.

He did of course beat Rogers in 1963 once he returned to the WWWF, Mondt and Vince Sr paying the fine to ensure that Sammartino's suspension in the USA was lifted. From there the entire company was built around him for the next couple of decades, with Bruno the blue-collar hero to the masses in the North East of the USA. He of course needed decent opponents to be fed to him though, and a number of his feuds in the 1960s are remembered fondly.

One such feud was with Killer Kowalski (real name Edward Spulnik), a giant Canadian who stood six feet seven inches tall (genuinely massive for a wrestler in that era) and who earned his nickname by his actions in the ring. In reality a softly spoken vegetarian who refused to smoke or drink, he's known chiefly now by fans for being the man who trained Triple H. His massive size enabled him to work as an effective, vicious heel, and he was soon known for a fantastic feud with Sammartino that lasted for much of the 1960s, as well as being in a tag team with fellow legend Gorilla Monsoon, also a giant man.

Kowalski is also credited with being the first man to beat Andre the Giant in North America in 1972, but he's known more widely for a much-discussed incident in 1952: He hit another wrestler so hard that his ear fell off. That's one way to cement your nickname of 'Killer'.

Yukon Eric was the unfortunate opponent of Kowalski in Montreal. Eric was prone on the mat when Kowalski performed a knee drop, tearing off his foe's ear with the impact. In reality, this was just an accident. Many old-time wrestlers had cauliflower ears from years of grappling for real, and Eric's were incredibly calcified. That would have been enough in the eyes of the fans to cement him as a villain, but the story wasn't over. Kowalski went to visit Eric in hospital – they were actually friends – and upon seeing his head swathed in bandages, started giggling. Eric joined in. The next day, a newspaper reported on the meeting but only mentioned that Kowalski was the one wetting himself with laughter. This only made him more notorious and made both men richer as they continued their feud over the next couple of years.

The USA in the 1950s and 1960s was constantly evolving. You've probably noted that so far wrestling has been mainly about white men; like every part of American life, diversity did start to slowly spread throughout the wrestling industry. Baby steps for now, but some steps nonetheless.

Nowadays, women's wrestling is huge. We've been through over a decade of 'Divas': women hired more for their looks than their in-ring talent and matches designed to titillate and come out the other side, no doubt influenced by female stars of UFC like Ronda Rousey (who is now signed to a WWE contract). But before we had that in the late 1990s, aside from GLOW (yes, the Netflix show is based on a genuine company), female wrestlers could really tear it up and while less in number, those who achieved success did gain respect.

Mildred Burke was the first trailblazer, even though her career ended in retirement in 1955. But her legacy was great; she was known as being incredibly tough and the first big star in women's wrestling, someone who many women wanted to emulate. One of these women was Lillian Ellison, better known by her ring name: the Fabulous Moolah.

Starting out as Moolah the Slave Girl, she managed another wrestler, Elephant Boy, who was originally from Mexico. At a show in Oklahoma City, she did what she did every other night and kissed her charge on the cheek as he was making his entrance. A racist in the crowd, under the impression that Moolah and Elephant Boy were in a mixed-race relationship proceeded to try and stab her despite the fact that Elephant Boy was definitely white; he merely had a particularly deep tan.

Moolah became Fabulous in 1956, given the name by Vince Sr after she won a variation of the NWA Women's World

Championship. She would hold this title – and gain others to add to it and make undisputed – for the best part of 30 years. Moolah became an often controversial, divisive but very well-known figure, and was the first woman to wrestle in Madison Square Garden after they lifted the ban on female wrestlers in 1972. She remained around wrestling for the next four decades, although her legacy has been somewhat tarnished by some quite serious accusations about her conduct outside of the ring.

We've briefly touched on race with Moolah's story. In the 1950s seating at many wrestling shows in the South was still segregated between blacks and whites, but it would take only the most stubborn Confederate to ignore that times were indeed a-changing. Black audiences loved wrestling as much as white audiences, and they had their own stars. A few of these stars crossed over to become beloved or despised by everyone in the crowd as the 1960s rolled around and racial barriers were gradually eroded.

The first African-American to make a challenge to the NWA World Heavyweight title was Luther Lindsay, a tall, rangy submission specialist who impressed then-champ Lou Thesz when he made three attempts to win the belt between 1953 and 1956. He spent time in Japan, the Pacific Northwest, Canada and Hawaii before meeting an early demise. In 1972, at the age of 47, he climbed to the top rope during a match in Charlotte to deliver his big splash to his fallen foe. He landed it but immediately died of a heart attack, winning the match but losing his life.

Other black stars earned names for themselves, like Sailor Art Thomas and Bearcat Wright, the latter refusing to wrestle in front of segregated crowds and helping remove that barrier. Arguably the biggest African-American star of the era was Bobo Brazil, who can be considered the first African-American to have won the NWA World Heavyweight title – although like all things in wrestling, it's not that simple. Taking on Buddy Rogers for the belt in October 1962, Brazil was victorious but initially refused the title as Rogers was claiming an injury. After a doctor checked on Rogers the next day and found him to be in a clean bill of health, the title was awarded to Brazil; the title change isn't recognised by the NWA, however. It would be 30 years before the first 'proper' world title reign for an African-American, Ron Simmons.

Change was a slow process. By 1970 cities like Atlanta were only just having their first mixed race wrestling matches, but the star power of Brazil no doubt sped up that slow process. Brazil, Wright, Thomas and Lindsay are all now members of the WWE Hall of Fame – as are Burke and Moolah – as recognition for their hard work changing an industry in rapidly evolving times.

By 1971, Bruno Sammartino had been WWWF champion for over seven years. That's an incredibly long time to stay in one territory, let alone as the champion and main hero. It was decided to switch the title on to a new star, and WWWF booking always preferred a babyface champion.

The WWWF formula was pretty much this: establish a strong, charismatic, popular star as your champion; Sammartino was obviously the blueprint. Build up a strong heel enemy to him, probably with a manager like Lou Albano or the Grand Wizard. Have them do battle around the territory, with shenanigans including drawn matches and disqualifications or count outs (a title cannot change hands under those means) to maintain interest. Have a huge blow-off match at a show in Madison Square Garden or Shea Stadium in New York. Find a new foe and repeat.

This was working out pretty well and Bruno was still doing good business, but seven years at the top will make anyone grow weary. The schedule was pretty brutal, and the pressure of having to main event every show meant he wanted a break. He asked if he could drop the title, so his successor had to be found. They wanted the same kind of champion: full of fire, a draw to the ethnic community in the New York area, a talented, believable wrestler and, most importantly, a babyface.

Trouble is, Sammartino couldn't lose to another babyface character because it would hurt the new champion. Face v face matches were incredibly rare in those days, so what was needed was a transitional champion, someone to shock the world, take the title from Bruno, and be beaten by the new chosen one in order to shotgun some of Bruno's massive popularity on to them. Oreal Perras was that man. Perras had been raised on a dairy farm in Canada, and previously wrestled as an Irish character, Red McNulty, but since 1967, thanks to his sinister look and manicured black beard, he had taken the name 'The Russian Bear' Ivan Koloff.

Talk among the 22,000 fans at Madison Square Garden on 18 January 1971 was that Bruno was nursing an injury, broken ribs suffered at the hands of green-tongued Wildman George 'The Animal' Steele. (Steele, who would later star in the Johnny Depp film *Ed Wood*, playing wrestler Tor Johnson, also worked as a high school gym teacher for most of his wrestling career). The crowd was nervous, but still didn't expect the Italian Superman to be anything other than victorious against the villainous, hated 'Russian'. The boos for Koloff were deafening, as were the cheers for Sammartino.

The match went as most during Bruno's reign did at that

time: the champion getting on top with his tests of strength and virtuous grappling skills while Koloff would draw heat with underhanded tactics. As it looked like Sammartino was heading to the final stretch before another victory, Koloff caught him with a knee to the midsection, seemingly knocking the air from his lungs. Sammartino's selling caused a gasp from the crowd as they recalled his rib injury (which was of course, a work, a way to give Sammartino a believable excuse for losing – a virtuous babyface in that era was never properly bested by a villain in a straight fight). Koloff climbed the ropes, standing tall over the fallen Bruno and delivered a knee drop to his foe, making the cover and winning the title. The Garden was absolutely stunned.

Crowd riots would sometimes happen back then, so, mindful of this, the handling of everything after the match had to be well staged. A wrestling crowd nowadays is too smart; they'll watch a babyface lose and boo a bit, but then head home and wonder what'll happen next as we now consume wrestling in a very different way. In 1971, 22,000 New Yorkers had just seen their idol, an actual superhero, lose his title that he'd held for seven years to a hated Russian, and a lot of people in that crowd would have believed that what they witnessed was 100 per cent real. Wrestling may have been fully pre-determined since the 1920s, but the culture of protecting it behind the scenes and presenting it as real was still in full force. The stunned silence gave way to anger. Koloff paced the ring, having his arm raised in victory but crucially not being handed the title belt. Sammartino got to his feet, looking out at the crowd and took their sympathetic applause so Koloff could leave the ring and be presented the title for photographs backstage. It was genuinely felt that if he had been handed the belt in the ring that the place would have been burned to the ground.

Sammartino left the WWWF and headed to California for what he hoped would be another successful chapter in his career. Koloff – who continued wrestling into the 1990s – would hold the title for just three weeks. Bruno's successor had been chosen: Puerto Rican immigrant Pedro Morales, who had moved to New York as a teenager and fallen in love with wrestling. A keen sportsman in his youth, he had amateur wrestling experience and the potential to play baseball professionally, before becoming the plucky, stocky hero to wrestling fans and a real Hispanic superstar to WWWF fans. He was, despite a difference in nationality to Bruno, part of that same blueprint of working-class, immigrant hero to the masses.

By the end of the Seventies, it would be a different breed of talent that resided at the top of the card in the WWWF. A giant and a bodybuilder changed wrestling as we knew it. And a mere ring announcer, the son of the owner, would change the business forever.

Chapter Four:
Larger than Life

Morales, Andre, Graham, Backlund and Vince Jr

Pedro Morales wasn't exactly a newcomer to wrestling, as he had spent his time working around the USA honing his act. By the time he got to the WWWF, Vince Sr recognised that the Hispanic crowd attending shows adored him, and the non-Hispanic crowd appreciated his fiery Latin temperament and in-ring skill. He wasn't quite Bruno in terms of getting reactions, but he was pretty close. On 8 February 1971 he began a 1,027-day reign as WWWF Champion, beating Koloff at MSG. Sammartino's last move before packing off for the west coast was handing the title to Morales, passing the torch and ensuring that the new champ got a little bit of the love that he'd commanded for the past seven years.

Trouble is that as soon as Bruno left for California crowds in

New York took a bit of a hit. WWWF wasn't exactly on the brink, but not every show was selling out and Vince Sr, appreciating the safety of the cartel, quietly rejoined the NWA. He had another plan to help business: he called Bruno and asked him to come back, albeit with a much-reduced schedule.

The WWWF repeated the formula of building up a heel challenger to Pedro and running that feud round the horn before moving on to the next villain, like the weirdest job-centre queue you'd ever seen, but with Morales and the returned Sammartino both the best-drawing babyfaces in the WWWF, it made sense to try and put them together. You couldn't turn either of them villain though; they were both too beloved. WWWF had to get creative to position both men against each other.

The set-up for their encounter came in July 1972, with Morales and Sammartino teaming up against the evil Professor Toru Tanaka and Mr Fuji. It seemed to everyone that night that the current and former champions would be taking the hated villains down, but it didn't pan out that way. Fuji threw salt into the face of Sammartino, who attacked Morales by mistake while blinded. With Morales down, Tanaka tossed salt into his eyes and the match ended with the two most popular wrestlers in the company attacking each other by mistake as fans desperately squealed in horror and tried to warn them what they were doing.

That set the stage for what many people called 'The Match of the Century', which I appreciate is a bit overused. But if you lived in New York and loved your wrestling, it probably felt like that at the time: two working-class superheroes going at it to prove who was the best. Both had proven themselves to be pretty much unstoppable. One of them had to be halted. But who? The answer was . . . neither.

22,000 fans attended Shea Stadium on 30 September 1972. That's a good attendance, but not quite the crazy numbers that WWE hits in stadiums these days. It was a cold and rainy night, and Pedro v Bruno was quite rightfully the main event, starting late in the evening as the crowd huddled together for warmth. Morales was, surprisingly, the crowd favourite. He'd worked hard to appear everywhere and defend the title like a true champion; some New Yorkers were mildly annoyed that Sammartino was working a more relaxed schedule and wasn't making every single show.

Both men tried their best to put on a technical spectacle worthy of their names, exchanging near-falls and keeping the fans on the edge of their seats (although a few of them may have shifted into that position because of the shivering). George 'The Animal' Steele tried to get involved. More near-falls were exchanged. The two superheroes continued to go toe to toe, nose to nose, in a battle that I guarantee was definitely better than the *Batman v Superman* movie showdown.

At the 75-minute mark, the bell was rung, and the match was declared a draw thanks to the New York curfew laws for any events. While the match would be seen as slow-paced today, back then both men (and Vince Sr) would have decided to have the match as a draw to protect both of their careers. Usually matches would go an hour to be declared a tie, or *broadway*. 75 minutes was a step above, and they must have just decided to wrestle and tell a story within the ring until the stadium switched the lights off. To keep an audience in rapt attention for so long is truly amazing, an art form of 'calling the match on the fly' and improvising everything, reacting to crowd peaks and troughs; that is somewhat of a lost skill these days as the advanced, more complicated choreographing of matches has become more widespread.

Not sure I would have fancied being the bloke who had to flick the light switch though.

Of course, this was New York. Some fans were absolutely incensed at the lack of conclusive result, and despite Sammartino and Morales embracing in the ring and renewing their friendship, a few jumped into the dugouts to remonstrate with the wrestlers, shaking their fists with rage, barely thinking of the value for money that they got from their admission price. At least the rage might have warmed them up a bit. In hindsight, the match is seen as a classic of WWWF at the time, but the anger at the lack of resolution shows you exactly why wrestling went down the pre-determined route in the 1920s, and why innovative heels like Buddy Rogers showed the way in terms of making matches infinitely more exciting. The time of Thesz had long since passed.

Morales would hold the WWWF title until 1 December 1973, when the decision was made to put the belt back around Sammartino's waist, although he'd keep his agreed slower schedule. In order to do this, WWWF needed another transitional champion, and this chap wouldn't even get three weeks on top like Koloff did. His name was Stan 'The Man' Stasiak, and he got nine days. Stasiak was the first man to win the WWWF title outside of New York – in Philadelphia – but that was just to ensure that Bruno won it back just over a week later in the Big Apple. Stasiak didn't even know he was getting the title until the backstage agent told him that night.

Morales didn't do bad business, he kept things ticking over. Sammartino's second reign pretty much did the same, maintained the status quo but didn't draw in too many new fans. WWWF needed a new attraction. Something massive. The Eighth Wonder of the World: Andre the Giant.

It didn't hit me just how cool Andre was when I was a kid. Sure, I'd seen him wrestle in the twilight of his career and of course, he was just a massive, humungous dude. It was in my twenties, when I became fascinated with graffiti and street art that I started to read up on – and really appreciate – the man born Andre Rousimoff. In 1989, artist Shepard Fairey started a stickering campaign in the USA that spread from his home in Rhode Island all across the nation and beyond, mainly carried by the enthusiasm of the skating community. Fairey would go on to create the OBEY clothing brand borne out of the notoriety of this one campaign, a simple sticker featuring an image of Andre's face, the slogan 'Andre the Giant has a Posse', plus his height and weight. It made very little sense, but it really caught on and became a cult sticker (I used to have lots of them) by the mid 1990s. The OBEY logo these days is a close up of the middle of Andre's face.

Andre was, for much of the 1970s, the highest-paid wrestler in the world. It was reported at one point that he was pulling in as much as $400,000 per year, a colossal amount for a wrestler at that point in time. Born near Grenoble, France in 1946, Andre's nickname wasn't just for effect. He was a true giant, afflicted with gigantism that would become acromegaly in his adult life and be responsible for his slightly out-of-proportion head and other features. It was this unusual look that would convince anyone that he was exactly as tall as billed – seven feet four inches – when in reality he was probably around six feet 11 inches. Photos would surface of him stood next to basketball player Wilt Chamberlain in the 1980s, with Chamberlain (a genuine seven feet one inch tall) appearing to be slightly taller.

Despite all that contentious stuff, Andre was a genuinely huge boy as a result of his gigantism and by the age of 12 he had been over six feet tall and weighed over 200 pounds. Oddly, he was befriended as a child by Samuel Beckett who lived nearby, the Irish playwright helping Andre get to school in the back of his pick-up truck as he wouldn't fit on the school bus. Andre would work on his father's farm once he left school, being a real asset as his strength meant that he could do the work of several others. He was never happy there though, and sought more in life, wanting to use his freakish size to his own advantage. This ambition took him to Paris at the age of 17, where he trained to be a wrestler in the evening and worked as a removal man during the daytime, presumably shifting pianos on his own and taking up two seats in the van. He was initially billed as Géant Ferre, based on a French folk hero to capitalise on his unique presence and look. Local promoters quickly realised that a wrestler of his size and strength – even if he was new – would easily be able to make them a lot of money.

By 1966, Andre had met Canadian promoter Frank Valois, who managed to take him overseas as a very special attraction. He saw the UK, Germany, Africa, New Zealand and Australia before visiting Japan for the first time in 1970, being billed there as 'Monster Rousimoff'. It was in Japan that he was first told of his acromegaly, and it's thought that being told the disease would affect the quality of his life made Andre live every day as if it was his last. Tales of how much he could drink – 150 or so bottles of beer in one sitting – have become legendary.

Andre would move to Montreal and initially become a huge draw there, but his pulling power diminished as he conquered every wrestler that challenged him. He couldn't really be bettered by anybody in a believable way, especially while he was still in his twenties and fairly athletic for a man of his size.

Every now and then, Andre would travel to the USA as a special attraction. On one of these visits, Valois was advised on how to maximise the money that Andre could make by Vince Sr. The main thing was to keep moving him around, so his act never got stale. Take on all comers, beat them all, then move on and come back in a few months or a year later and repeat it again. WWWF started acting as Andre's booking agent (he would now be known by the name we know him best for) at this time to help with that.

Vince Sr's other tip has been copied by all big wrestlers since and that was *not* to move around: Andre was to become an immovable object, no longer leaving his feet to deliver dropkicks or running the ropes. This would help him seem even bigger than he was. The way he acted, along with his acromegaly, made him seem believably eight feet tall, at least if you squinted.

On 26 March 1973 Andre made his WWWF debut at Madison Square Garden. As a smiling fan favourite he beat Buddy Wolfe in short order. A sign of his popularity to come was that on his MSG debut he was already in the semi-main event. This would start a long-standing undefeated streak that would last the best part of 14 years; well, as long as you only count WWWF matches. But compared to most wrestlers, he was the *most* undefeated man on the planet, a couple of well-hidden losses and a couple of draws with big stars the only stains on his record. But seriously, who could ever beat him? Surely nobody could conquer the beloved giant? Either it was coincidence or just amazing forward thinking, but we'll see later on just how important that win-loss record was in a sport where none of that stuff usually matters.

A giant wasn't the only striking visual change to the WWWF

roster. The biggest surprise with Andre is that he was never called upon to be champion in the 1970s, whether that's down to Vince Sr feeling he was better as a special attraction, being worried about his broken English or just concerned that if he was booked as champion, who on earth would beat him? Sammartino remained champion until 1977, when one man changed what would be expected of wrestlers aesthetically for the next couple of decades. His name was Billy Graham. No, not *that* Billy Graham.

Without *this* Billy Graham (younger, somewhat less vocal about his devout Christian beliefs, infinitely more hench) we wouldn't have had Hulk Hogan, Rick Rude, The Ultimate Warrior and countless other wrestling luminaries from the 1980s. Born Eldridge Wayne Coleman in Phoenix in 1943, Graham took the nickname 'Superstar' during a run in AWA in the early Seventies, he had the flamboyance and talking skills of a Gorgeous George or a Buddy Rogers, was trained in Calgary by the legendary Stu Hart in his dungeon, and most importantly of all, was the first massive name to marry bodybuilding to wrestling. Graham was even a friend of Arnold Schwarzenegger in the late 1960s, before one man went into acting and the other chose wrestling.

It's important to give this some context: Graham had 22-inch biceps, was tanned and ripped. Most other wrestlers, even if they were legitimately tough and had useful, workable strength, were not in the same league in terms of their look. Graham stood out, an Adonis in a sea of men who looked like (and often were) barroom brawlers rather than Mr Universe competitors. During his wrestling career, Graham would only get more muscular. Some of that was down to hard work and training. Some of it was down to just a *little* bit of help.

Graham had developed a niche gimmick during his early days in California, challenging other wrestlers to gimmicked arm-wrestling contests in front of the live audience so he could prove his strength. As he was a villain, he'd often use these opportunities to sneak attack his opponent just as they were about to beat him, leading to a wrestling feud that they could take around the loop. That shtick and his extreme (for the time, anyway) look led to him being in demand across the globe, enjoying tours to Japan before settling in the WWWF at the beginning of 1977.

In Baltimore on 30 April, it was time for Graham to ascend to the top of the business, in the North East territory at least. Playing off the bodybuilding history of both men, they repeatedly tested each other's strength in a match that today feels slow-paced, but still had blood involved, Graham's head striking the ring post and crimson-staining his bleached-blond hair. While the challenger was certainly hated by the crowd, it's doubtful that anyone would have seen the switch coming, until Graham pinned Sammartino with his feet on the ropes for leverage after nearly 14 minutes. Graham was new champ, the crowd was stunned, and that was the end of Sammartino's time as WWWF champion. His second reign had lasted nearly three-and-a-half years, but Graham felt like the future. And for once, the heel champion of the WWWF was going to get to hold the title for a bit more than a week.

Graham realised his worth to WWWF but also wanted to use the heat he was getting to springboard himself into a babyface position as nobody in WWWF at that time had his charisma, speaking ability or unique look. Problem is, this wasn't the mid Nineties. Someone on the fringes of being good or evil wasn't going to get cheered by the crowd. It would be too hard to turn someone who was so good at being bad into a good guy. Also, Vince Sr had promised the WWWF title to a man who was the exact opposite of Graham when he'd agreed to join the territory: Virtuous. A technician. Quiet. A lot more pale.

That's not to say that Graham wasn't a huge success as WWWF Champion; he absolutely was. He sold out 19 out of 20 MSG shows while he was on top, but after dropping the title his career faltered a little, including a very messy break-up with the WWF in the Eighties, occasionally acting like its best friend, sometimes like a jilted lover. We also can't overlook the fact that Graham was the reason that two of the less-loved practices in wrestling became hugely popular.

Firstly, steroids. Graham is an admitted steroid user, and his unique look was thanks as much to what he was jamming into his veins as it was the weights he was lifting and the protein he was eating. There is no question that guys like Hogan, Warrior and many, many more looked to him for inspiration, and certainly followed in his footsteps by becoming as knowledgeable about pharmaceuticals as they were about wrestling holds. Graham denounced his steroid use years later and has gone to great lengths to advise up-and-coming wrestlers against taking them, especially as his body has repeatedly failed him in recent years.

Secondly – and arguably even worse than mainlining horse testosterone – is a habit that I heard on my TV all through the 1980s, and now in my professional life I hear in locker rooms every week. Graham would refer to everyone as 'brother', perhaps a side effect of attending evangelical revivals as a teenager where he would combine sermons with feats of strength. Hulk Hogan would take that idea on board (and to extremes) as well. If only

Graham had been raised an atheist, his sins would ironically have been halved.

If it had been a real fight, then the night when Graham lost the title would have been a no contest. For all of his bulk and swagger, he wasn't anywhere near the legitimate fighter that his opponent was. Bob Backlund may have been smaller and less flashy, with pale skin and plain trunks, but the Minnesota native was hard as nails and had a legitimate, stellar college amateur wrestling background. For the first time in WWWF history, it felt like they might have found their version of Lou Thesz.

Backlund had made his debut in 1973 and had then wrestled everywhere before making it to WWWF in 1977. Vince Sr had a handshake agreement with Backlund that he would be his new, legitimate, all-American champion and on 20 February 1978 he took the belt from Graham, who desperately didn't want to lose it. Vince Sr was always a man of his word though, and Backlund would reign as champion (aside from a couple of sneaky switches that lasted a few days) for the best part of five years, WWWF having restored the norm with a babyface champion once again.

In 1979 – the year that the 'wide' was dropped from the company name and it became WWF – it was felt that a new title was needed in order to help mid-card guys get over with crowds, especially with the main champs tending to hold their belts for a few years at a time. It was decided that a new title – the WWF Intercontinental Championship – would supersede the WWF North American Heavyweight Championship by unifying that one with a mythical *South* American title. Guess where the tournament was to crown the first champion? That's right, Rio de Janeiro. You already know the answer to whether it *really* happened or not.

The first Intercontinental champion was French–Canadian veteran Pat Patterson, who moved to the USA in 1962 with a limited command of English and whose grasp of the language would become discussed in many wrestlers' autobiographies. Winning (yeah, honest) the IC title in Brazil in September 1979, Patterson was an experienced and fabulous worker who radiated a tough-guy image after years of being in the 'Blond Bombers' tag team with Ray Stevens, mainly in California. They were trailblazers in the ring for their bombastic style, but it was behind the scenes that Patterson was also a trailblazer. A gay man who was proud of his sexuality, those close to him got to know his long-time partner and while not everyone knew about it, those who did never treated him differently.

It was fair game for the IC title to change hands more often than the main belt, so Backlund could continue unbeaten in the main event (or close to it at least) while new challengers could be built up using the secondary title. By 1983 it was around the waist of Don Muraco, a heavy-set Hawaiian veteran who would go on to be involved in the wrestling equivalent of the Sex Pistols at the Free Trade Hall in Manchester; a match that about 100,000 people claim to have been at and which influenced wrestling for decades later.

I'll cheerfully admit that I wasn't aware of this match until I read Mick Foley's first book, hearing how the future hardcore legend hitchhiked his way to New York to watch it. While it was certainly a big deal at the time, knowing that Mick adored this match so much and that it influenced his wrestling career immeasurably means it's only grown in stature as time has passed.

Muraco was involved in a feud with Fijian wildman 'Superfly' Jimmy Snuka, a recently turned babyface who was riding a wave of enormous popularity. The feud had begun in June 1983, gathering in intensity until it could only be settled in a steel cage: a 15-feet-high structure surrounding the ring at Madison Square Garden in October 1983 where victory could only be achieved by pinfall, submission or escaping the cage. Watching the match now, there's a real sense of electricity in the air at MSG, with fans hoping to see a new champion crowned and Snuka getting some justice by beating Muraco down with nobody there to aid him.

What actually happened was sensible wrestling booking. Notoriously as wild outside of the ring as he was inside it, Snuka wasn't necessarily somebody that you would want holding one of your titles, no matter how popular he happened to be. In May 1983, Snuka's girlfriend Nancy Argentino was found injured in their hotel room, eventually dying in hospital from her wounds. Snuka was long considered the only suspect in her suspicious death, although he was only charged 32 years later in 2015. Charges would eventually be dropped due to Snuka's worsening dementia.

So, WWF couldn't really put a title on Snuka, but they knew that he was so wonderfully popular with the fans that he couldn't just get eaten up by Muraco. This is where wrestling can be quite beautiful; structured as well as your favourite television drama. Muraco won the cage match on what looked, to the audience at least, like a sheer fluke: Snuka was getting carried away beating him up and, with both men drenched in blood, Muraco tumbled out through the cage door and thus retained his title.

The match itself was decent, but it was the post-match action that everyone recalls: Snuka brought Muraco back into the ring and beat him until he lay prone in the centre of the canvas, before climbing to the very top of the cage. Snuka had tried to deliver his splash from the top of the cage the previous year, but he was a villain then, attempting it against Backlund and missing. On this occasion he hit it, a huge high spot at the time, replayed for years afterwards and making Snuka's career.

In the audience that night as well as Mick Foley (and countless other people who claim to have been there) were future wrestlers The Sandman, Bubba Ray Dudley and Tommy Dreamer. It was a landmark event that felt extreme and ahead of its time in 1983 and shaped a very different style of wrestling by the 1990s. *Extreme* would become the operative word by the mid 1990s and all four of those men helped change wrestling – stylistically at least.

As the 1980s rolled on, though, the biggest story in the WWF wasn't the wrestlers so much as the ownership of the company. Vince Sr was getting older, and one of his two sons was knocking at his door and wanting to change everything.

Senior's company Capitol had known its place during the Seventies. It had hooked back up with the NWA and ran big shows at MSG and other key arenas monthly rather than weekly, to both keep costs down and increase chances of selling out key cards.

Vince Sr was a magnanimous promoter. He had managed to keep the then-WWWF on television in some form until 1971 and had been the first promoter to split large gates with his wrestlers, ensuring loyalty from them. His territory, thanks to the general affluence and large population, was arguably the most lucrative in the USA so he never had trouble attracting new talent to come in and shake things up when it was needed. He was a little set in his ways though, believing that wrestlers should be wrestlers and not crossover media stars. He also kept himself backstage and out of the spotlight, not needing to pull power plays like whoever was head of the NWA at any one time or have himself as star talent like the AWA's Verne Gagne.

Vince Sr had two sons, Roderick and Vincent Jr. The latter didn't see his father until he was 12 years old, instead growing up with his mother and abusive stepfather in Virginia. Senior took junior to Madison Square Garden at around this time, and even though the younger McMahon desperately wanted to be part of his dad's business, the elder didn't want him to be around it. Vince Jr got a job as a travelling salesman after graduating from university in 1968. It's insane to imagine that he wasn't good at selling stuff when he's made his fortune out of guys selling (just in a different way), but he wasn't.

With his son's career floundering, Vince Sr gave him a chance to work his way up in the family business, working as a ring announcer. By 1971, he was a regular commentator and trusted with some small, limited creative decisions. But once he got to grips with the business, Junior really went for it. His tenacity paid off as WWF managed to hugely improve their television syndication towards the end of the 1970s, generating extra income from that and, as a consequence of greater exposure, through increased ticket sales. And it was Junior that would push for the renaming of the company in 1979, having floated the idea for a few years previously.

Junior had bigger plans though. In 1976, he was behind the ill-fated boxer v wrestler match as Japan's Antonio Inoki, claiming professional wrestling was the greatest form of fighting in the world, took on the one and only Muhammed Ali in Tokyo. Senior managed to sell over 30,000 tickets for a closed-circuit screening of the match at the Shea Stadium in New York. Trouble was that the match itself is remembered for all the wrong reasons, as neither man had agreed to lose, the contest rapidly descended into farce and the fans nearly rioted at the end.

Vince Jr started a new company, Titan Sports, in 1979 with his wife Linda, basing their operation out of a minor league ice hockey stadium. They took out loans, called in debts, did whatever they could to raise money for their next venture. In 1982, with his father in poor health, Vince Jr and Titan Sports took control of Capitol. It would be both Vinces who chose to pull WWF from the NWA in 1983. Bob Backlund's time as champion was soon to come to an end. Vince Jr had a vision. It was the end of the old school in New York. Things were about to explode.

JIM'S TOP TEN: TALKERS

It was always said that the very best promo guys in wrestling could actually talk you into a building. Here's my ten favourite talkers in wrestling history:

10. Zack Gibson

As I write this, Gibson may not be well known to you, but he certainly is to me; he's technically one of my employees. An absolutely unbelievable talker when it comes to getting heat from a crowd, he's a fine wrestler who just happens to become the biggest villain in the country the second he opens his mouth. Watching a crowd of 2,500 pelt him with toilet paper on one occasion is one of my very favourite moments in wrestling.

9. Paul Heyman

In both his role as a manager, of the Dangerous Alliance back in the day and of Brock Lesnar now, every Paul Heyman promo is worthy of you stopping whatever you're doing and listening. Furthermore, the speeches he used to give to fans at ECW shows made everybody want to take a bullet for his little company.

8. Roddy Piper

Sure, he'd sometimes veer off into absolute craziness, but Piper was the best talker in 1980s WWF, which meant to the majority of wrestling fans in the USA that he was the best in the world. It wasn't a surprise when he went into acting, and when he returned to wrestling his body may not have been able to deliver great matches, but his voice could still knock a promo out of the park.

7. Ric Flair

With so many transitions in his career between heel and face, it's the intensity that always marked a great Flair promo for me, such as the one on *Nitro* where he started stripping off his clothes, screaming abuse at Eric Bischoff. Oh, and of course his interviews and segments are the reason that we all scream 'Whooo' at certain things within wrestling.

6. Chris Jericho

Criminally underrated in WCW, despite some brilliant promos like his '1,004 moves' one, Jericho has always reinvented himself but his skill as a talker has never diminished. From the arrogant Y2J debut promo on *Raw* to his more recent 'list of Jericho' stuff and on to his amazing work to promote his NJPW match with Kenny Omega, you feel that Jericho always has another great promo up his sleeve.

5. Steve Austin

When one promo single-handedly turns a company around and sells about a million T-shirts, you know you're doing something right. Check out Austin's promos during his brief stay in ECW – they are hilarious. So entertaining is Austin's voice that I pop for every advert he reads out on his excellent podcast.

4. CM Punk

The 'pipebomb' promo is what most people will remember from *Raw* in June 2011, but Punk has always been a great talker, from his days in RoH and the 'Summer of Punk' to his first work on WWE television on the relaunched ECW show. His no-nonsense way of speaking has led to a legal case between him and WWE, but I hope it gets resolved and we see him in a wrestling ring again someday.

3. Dusty Rhodes

Not only a brilliant talker in his own right, but the man who is responsible for a whole generation of WWE Performance Centre graduates finding their own voices. The 'Hard Times' promo that Dusty cut in the early 1980s remains one of the greatest ever, and for him to overcome a speech impediment and go on to become the finest talker of a generation is genuinely inspiring.

2. The Rock

When he started in WWE, The Rock was Rocky Maivia, all smiles, a forced babyface that the fans turned on. When he turned heel and became The Rock, shooting from the hip about everything that irritated him, he became a megastar. Of course, he was *so* cool that in the end he turned face, but it was his tremendous speaking ability, comic timing and turns of phrase that elevated him (and his catchphrases) to the top of wrestling, and then in turn to the very top of Hollywood.

1. Mick Foley

Under three different personas – four if you count him just being himself – Foley has managed to deliver amazing promos and spellbinding story-telling for nearly three decades. Now a stand-up comedian and occasional wrestling persona, his intensity as Cactus Jack in ECW was brilliant; his insanity as Mankind in WWE was amazing; the silliness of Dude Love shouldn't be forgotten; and the blend of comedy and tragedy within his promos is almost Shakespearean in breadth.

Chapter Five:
Blood, Sweat and Tears

Tragedy to Triumph in the NWA:
Harley Race, Ric Flair and Starrcade

By 1966, Lou Thesz had been NWA Champion since the WWWF split in 1963, but he was getting on in years. He was nearly 50 years old when he dropped the title to Canadian former footballer Gene Kiniski. Spending the following three years as champion took its toll on Kiniski though, and by the 1968 NWA convention he was looking to drop the title to someone suitable. The man chosen was Dory Funk Jr, tough-guy son of Dory Funk Sr, NWA promoter in Amarillo, Texas. While the WWWF was creating unbeatable supermen, the NWA felt grittier, more real. To be the NWA champion meant a lot of blood, sweat and tears. Mainly blood.

'Red makes green'.

That's a common phrase that was thrown around wrestling

back in the day, meaning that if you bled for your art then you had a better chance of making an obscene stack of money. By the start of the Seventies, with the golden days of the 1950s a fading memory, something needed to happen to keep getting the fans through the door. The easiest solution was to ramp up the violence. There had always been blood in wrestling, but as styles changed and as films and television gradually became more violent, the level of bloodletting had to reach a new, more extreme level. It's purely a coincidence that the movie *Carrie* came out in this decade. Blood provokes a deep, instinctive reaction.

If you talk to someone who doesn't like wrestling, they'll often insinuate that any gore seen in a match is 100 per cent fake. I'll let you into a secret right now: 99 per cent of the blood you see in wrestling matches is real. This is one of the reasons that, in a more enlightened and aware society, you don't see anywhere near as much blood in wrestling nowadays. It's a risky tactic. In the 1970s wrestlers would willingly bleed on dirty mats, running the risk of blood-borne diseases and painful staph infections that were seen as much part of the job as sprains and bruises. The whole 'red makes green' stuff didn't really pan out when everyone was willing to bleed and clearly, not everybody was a millionaire.

So then, how do wrestlers bleed? There's two ways. The first was the most traditional as the 1970s began; by the end of the decade, an easier way was more popular as many bigger shows started to have a similar amount of spilled plasma as seen in the new slasher films.

Let's put you in the position of a wrestler . . .

The first method is shockingly simple. The promoter has told you to 'get some colour'. You realise that it's going to hurt but might earn you some more money. You then hope that your opponent is calm, precise and sober. You brace yourself, and he punches you with the point of his knuckles over your eyebrow, hopefully achieving the desired effect and splitting you open, spilling blood everywhere and giving you a headache for the next week. Mick Foley is famous for bringing up this method in his autobiography *Have A Nice Day: A Tale of Blood and Sweatsocks*, when he asked both Harley Race (by then the manager of Vader) and Terry Funk to bust him open; it took quite a bit of effort. This is called bleeding *hardway*, so basically as a result of a very real injury.

The other option is now the norm, and certain wrestlers in the 1970s elevated this way of spilling their own blood to an art form; every photograph of them from the era has them wearing the proverbial 'crimson mask' (a term coined by the legendary commentator Gordon Solie) and their foreheads were so scarred that they'd look like road maps or tree bark. It was said that magazines in the Seventies always sold better if there was blood on the front cover, and nearly every publication followed this principle. Every single month.

So again, you are the wrestler . . .

Before the match, you take a razor blade. You cut a small section from the blade, then wrap it in tape, leaving a small point exposed. You then wrap tape around your wrists or fingers, leaving room to tape your blade under one of the layers. If you're really brave (or foolish, depends on your view) then you'll pop the taped-up blade into your mouth for safekeeping, to be spat out when needed. If you're insane, you'll pop it into your trunks and hope that you don't get a cut-price castration.

At the right point in the match, when your opponent has hit

you in the head, you roll out of the ring and wedge your head under the apron or lie face down on the mat and cover your head with a free arm, depends on your level of sleight-of-hand mastery. Take out your blade. Cut yourself on the forehead, close to the hairline. Puff your cheeks out a bit. Hope that you didn't tap right into a vein. Then get back to your feet, making sure you circle around slowly so that everyone can realise that blood, mixed with sweat, is cascading down your face.

Nobody ever bleeds like this in an MMA fight; that's all bloodied noses and lips and eyes, vicious-looking but sometimes lacking in actual blood. Blading means that your face is covered for a minimum amount of pain, and usually not needing stitches afterwards. If you are less experienced, you'll sometimes let your opponent blade for you.

Blading was around in the 1940s, and was a carny trick even earlier than that, but certainly became more commonplace in the 1970s as wrestlers started to tire of being punched in the face for real. Fair enough – I wouldn't fancy having to do that every night. Most of the big stars from the era wound up in their later years being absolutely covered with blading scars, a badge of honour to them that recent generations of wrestler's lack as the industry has undoubtedly become much safer.

As a side note, when I found out about blading as a university student, I decided to try and do it myself. It's not quite as easy as you'd think. Snipping a razor blade requires a GCSE in metal-work. It does hurt a fair bit, which I managed to be surprised by even though I was essentially stabbing at my own face. If you're not used to doing it, then the skin on your forehead is tough and leathery, even if you think it's beautiful and soft because you moisturise it. I finally managed to puncture my skin after ten minutes of trying and produced a trickle of blood that dried up a couple of minutes later. Now try to imagine doing that in front of a crowd, keeping it secret and doing it in a window of a few seconds. It's not easy. Shawn Michaels once bladed in the time it took him to be thrown over the top rope to the floor, spitting his blade out of his mouth and cutting himself in mid-air in one amazing motion. I'd have choked half to death, tripped over the top rope and have been laying on the floor weeping. Chances are that I would still have been bleeding, albeit accidentally.

Big draws in the 1950s and 60s were often positioned that way because of their legitimate wrestling skill first, and their charisma second. By the Seventies, some wrestlers became stars purely because of their willingness to bleed and bloody their opponents with a level of viciousness that bordered on legitimate assault. Freddie Blassie was a trailblazer for this in the 1960s in the USA and Japan, sharpening his teeth into points so he could bite the foreheads of his opponents. He was followed by two men who wouldn't hold much in terms of major titles in the USA but would sell tickets for the next couple of decades as they guaranteed excessive amounts of chaotic violence.

Abdullah the Butcher was billed as 'The Madman from Sudan', but in reality, was a man with a surprisingly high-pitched voice (that's why he never spoke in character, although the excuse used was that he spoke no English) called Larry Shreve from Windsor, Ontario. A near-400-pound man with a penchant for using weapons, he had bladed so much in his career that by the 1980s he could actually line up casino chips in the massive divots in his forehead. I guess that's one way to keep them safe.

Abdullah – Abby for short, making him seem much more

fluffy and cuddly than he was – became a notorious heel that anyone could bring in to increase business in their territory. Often using a fork, hidden in his tights, he would bloody his opponent before they made a comeback and bloodied him. Abby remained popular and active well into the 21st century, wrestling into his seventies. His feud with Carlos Colon in Puerto Rico rumbled on for much of his career.

Abby owned a restaurant in Atlanta for many years; I cannot confirm or deny that he would attack you with a fork if you ordered your steak cooked in any way other than extremely rare.

Another man who feuded with Abdullah was The Sheik, billed from the Syrian Desert but actually Detroit-based promoter Ed Farhat. Already in his fifties by the mid 1970s, he also wrestled well into his seventies and had a formidable reputation in Japan as well as in his home territory, and in Toronto, where he worked feuds with Lou Thesz, Bruno Sammartino and Tiger Jeet Singh. While Abby favoured the fork as a weapon, The Sheik would use a pencil to gouge at his opponent and would also often throw fireballs, a gimmick that involved using a lighter and magician's flash paper. By the 1990s, The Sheik was passing the torch of insanity to his nephew, Sabu, and he would revolutionise violence in spectacular ways.

These men, and many others, would be the standard-bearers for a new level of violence during the 1970s. And the three major companies all shed their own blood, both literally and figuratively, as the decade wore on.

Meanwhile, in the NWA, Harley Race became the absolute man during the 1970s, even if his first title reign was out of necessity to get the status of the belt to the level the bigwigs wanted it to be. Race was the toughest of the old-school guys in this era, with the tattooed forearm of a docker, a man who overcame polio in his youth and who was expelled from school for attacking the principal while fending off a bully. Trained on the Zbyszko farm in his home state of Missouri, he broke into the business by agreeing to drive around guys like the massive Happy Humphrey (and Humphrey, incidentally, really was a massive unit, weighing on average around 750 pounds, often billed at 802 pounds and at one point reportedly tipping the scales at over 900 pounds!).

Race was never far from tragedy. After breaking into the business as a worker at 18 under the name Jack Long and being seen as having a bright future, he was in a massive car accident that killed his wife and unborn baby. Promoter Gust Karras managed to stop the hospital from amputating Race's leg, but he was told he would never walk again. The stubborn kid that beat polio managed to defeat the odds again, going through a painful and arduous period of recovery and returning to wrestling in 1964 under the name he'd become famous for. He was originally portraying the storyline 'brother' of his tag team partner; his father advised him to go under his real name, so he wasn't making anyone else's name famous. If you call your kid Harley Race from birth, you'd better believe that you're a kick-ass dad and your kid simply has to become a pro wrestler. That's why I believe that my son will succeed: little Johnny Nepotism.

Gaining a name by teaming with Larry Hennig in the AWA, his first NWA title reign was an upset. Dory Funk Jr was recovering from a truck accident in 1973 and needed to drop the NWA title. He didn't want to lose it to Jack Brisco, the NWA panel's choice to take it from him, either because of ego issues or because he didn't want to have a face v face encounter. Harley was used instead and told backstage that he *had* to win. He was picked because he was tough, and it was thought because of that ruggedness that he could take the title by force if he really needed. He won the belt (with Funk's full cooperation) but only held it for a couple of months before dropping it to Brisco. His willingness to do what needed to be done made the NWA board love him, and the way he carried himself during his brief reign as champion raised his stock massively in the eyes of the fans. By the end of the decade, he'd be the biggest star in the organisation.

While Harley had the look and reputation of a gritty street fighter, Jack Brisco was a huge fan of Lou Thesz and embodied the amateur skillset that the NWA loved. Jack was the first native American to win an NCAA (National Collegiate Athletic Association) amateur wrestling championship and was another legitimate tough guy. It was during a good run in Florida between 1969 and 1972 that he really started taking off, both as a singles competitor and as a tag team with his brother Jerry; the Brisco brothers had a long-lasting feud with the Funk brothers that bubbled on for about a decade.

Once Jack had taken the title from Harley in July 1973, he held it for over a year before a one-week switch in December 1974 with Giant Baba in Japan. He then kept it around his waist until 1975, taking on challengers like Stan Stasiak, Abdullah the Butcher, Gene Kiniski, The Sheik and Johnny Valentine. The last name there was a grizzled, respected veteran, always good to challenge for a top title and sell tickets. Everybody loved Valentine backstage (crowds hated him, as was his gimmick), and even though he was 47 years old it was felt that he had a long career still ahead of him. He was the biggest draw in the Mid-Atlantic region and the reigning US champion. On 4 October he would get on a plane with a handful of other wrestlers. He would never wrestle again.

A twin-engine Cessna 310 had been chartered by promoter Jim Crockett to fly the short hop within North Carolina from Charlotte to Wilmington. It was just a 45-minute plane ride rather than a lengthy drive, although Jim wasn't on the plane that night as he had the flu. His brother David was; he worked as an announcer as well as helping with the promoting side of things. Johnny Valentine got a seat on the plane thanks to his seniority and respect. Another big star was on the trip, Tim 'Mr Wrestling' Woods, alongside two relative newcomers: former football player Bob Bruggers (who had been given Jim Crockett's seat), a three-year veteran who had just won (and lost) his first-ever singles title, the Mid-Atlantic TV Championship, and a kid working and learning alongside Valentine. His name was Ric Flair.

A few miles out from Wilmington, the plane ran out of fuel and plummeted to the ground. The impact of the crash would be devastating: pilot Mike Farkas would slip into a coma and pass away a couple of months later; Valentine broke his back and was paralysed from a bone fragment entering his spinal column; Bruggers also broke his back and had reconstructive surgery – he could have wrestled again but chose not to; Crockett and Woods were the least seriously injured.

Woods gave his real name (George Woodin) at the hospital to avoid the embarrassment of exposing the business – he was the only babyface on the plane and sworn enemies were not meant to travel together. When stories came out that he might have been in the crash, he rushed back to the ring far too early, wrestling in immense pain to avoid having the secrets get out. Kayfabe had to be protected at all costs, for the sake of the business as well as his own reputation.

Flair also broke his back, but in hindsight the crash may have been the event that shaped his career the most. At the time, he was working a powerhouse style that fitted his athletic background, and was a new villain performing alongside Valentine in a feud with Woods. Doctors told him that he would never wrestle again, but after eight months he was back in the ring, modifying his style (he would try to avoid taking big flat-back bumps for the rest of his career, usually turning on his side) and riding a wave of popularity from being the man who survived a plane crash and carried on fighting. A couple of years later, he would feud with Buddy Rogers over the name 'Nature Boy' and his transition from understudy to superstar was complete. It's bizarre to consider that his career may not have ever got going if he'd have taken a different seat on that plane.

Two months after the crash, Terry Funk won the NWA title from Jack Brisco in Miami. Brother of Dory Funk Jr, Terry had a similarly athletic background, attending West Texas State University and being a standout in football and wrestling. He would follow into the family business with his father and brother, splitting his time between his own Amarillo territory, All Japan and CWF (Championship Wrestling from Florida) in Florida. The match with Jack Brisco only helped pour fuel on the feud between the two sets of brothers, but after a 14-month reign as champion Terry started meandering following his switch with Harley Race, who was ready for a much longer reign at the top. By 1983, Terry would be giving an impassioned retirement speech in Japan.

At last count, Terry Funk has retired roughly 300 times. By the 1990s, he had transitioned from being the respected NWA champion of old to being middle-aged and crazy, sometimes wearing a stocking on his head and spending some time on fire. Literally.

After winning the NWA title in 1977, Harley Race became the dominant force in the organisation for the next four years, with everyone behind the scenes respecting him as much as the fans in the crowds liked to boo him. Thing is, Harley was smart. He understood that sometimes, the best way to pick up business was to drop the title. He was so respected that he'd always get it back in short order. By 1983 he'd be in his seventh reign as champion having made several switches, often very short-term ones, and one important one to Dusty Rhodes, who we'll look at more later on.

Harley's time at the top came to an end on 24 November 1983 at the first-ever Starrcade event in Greensboro, North Carolina. Subtitled 'A Flair for the Gold', it's a miracle that the crowd was in any way surprised at how the show ended up, but it was a simpler time when wrestling was questioned a heck of a lot less.

After the 1975 plane crash, Ric Flair had become huge box office. He'd had significant feuds with Greg Valentine, Ricky Steamboat and Roddy Piper, and five reigns as United States Champion, the secondary NWA title to Harley's big belt. Flair had won the NWA World title in 1981, starting his reign on the wrong foot by beating Dusty Rhodes in Kansas City, a territory where neither man was particularly over. Had that match taken place in the Carolinas, Georgia or Florida, the roof would have come off. It also didn't help that Rhodes was allegedly not in any way happy about being told he had to drop the title.

With such an inauspicious start to his reign, the NWA weren't all-in on Flair being the man to carry them through the 1980s. The decision was made to put the belt on Harley in June 1983 for a few months to help to really build Flair up. The man had survived a plane crash and carried himself like a champion. This roll of the dice had to work, and the NWA threw everything at it. A huge show. A monumental build. And as was often used to symbolise the pay-off of a blood feud: a steel cage.

With Race as NWA champion once again, Flair was in hot pursuit. Race played an excellent villain, avoiding Flair at every turn and offering a $25,000 bounty for anyone who could take Flair out of wrestling, thus solving his problems. In August 1983, Flair was attacked by Dick Slater and Bob Orton, the heels dropping him on his head with a piledriver. Back then, wrestlers sold the piledriver like it had killed them and Flair was no exception, being carried out on a stretcher and announcing his retirement from the squared circle. Slater and Orton collected their bounty, and Race was a happy man.

On 21 September, Flair returned and brutalised Slater and Orton with a baseball bat, calling out Race and setting up the main event for the first-ever *Starrcade*. This became a showcase event, running every year under the NWA/WCW banner until 2000, and WWE recycled the show name in November 2017. It really was a huge supercard featuring some excellent matches, most of which had the obligatory big-match bloodletting in them. Jay Youngblood and Ricky Steamboat took on The Brisco Brothers to win the tag team titles. Roddy Piper beat Greg Valentine in a dog collar match that was so bloody it was still used in advertisements in the wrestling magazines of my youth. But thanks to the build for the show, everyone was really there to see the main event. Throughout the broadcast of the show, which popularised closed-circuit showings of major events, Flair and Race were interviewed backstage, Flair trying to stay calm, but unable to stop himself breaking into rants; Race, calm and softly spoken yet terrifying, delivering promos like a dad telling his kid that he's not angry, he's just disappointed.

The steel cage match was billed as no disqualification (although, by default all cage matches are as you can only win by pinfall, submission or escaping the steel structure) and had former NWA champion Gene Kiniski as special guest referee. By today's standards, the match isn't a stellar one technically, but it is brutal and the heat from the crowd for every Flair comeback is off the charts. Race went after Flair's neck, causing the crowd to scream when he hit a piledriver, everyone remembering the near-career-ending injury that Flair had experienced just a few months previously. Both men bled buckets, Flair taking on his signature look of crimson streaked into his blond hair, like a teenager having done a bad dye job.

Flair managed to apply his finishing manoeuvre, the figure four leglock, but Race broke the hold and moved into the ascendency once again, dropping a head-butt from the top rope. After nearly 24 minutes, Race put Flair into a headlock, but the challenger pushed him off, causing the champion to clash heads with Kiniski. Flair, seizing his chance, took to the top rope and performed a body press to take the win and the championship. It was a passing of the torch from Race to Flair. The NWA in the 1980s would belong to the Nature Boy.

Chapter Six:
Terrymania Doesn't Have the Same Ring to It

The genesis of Hulk Hogan

The AWA was trundling along through the 1970s, but was a little stuck in its ways, leading to the loss of the star that could have made it huge. Verne Gagne, who we've already heard about, held the AWA World Championship until November 1975. It was then that he finally lost it to his hand-picked replacement, Nick Bockwinkel; a man similar to himself and exactly what he wanted from a wrestler.

The son of a wrestler and already 40 years old at this point, Bockwinkel was a wily veteran who was actually a very good talker, but whose style was more akin to his trainer Lou Thesz's than the flashier personas being adopted by more and more wrestlers in the Seventies. Like Harley Race, Bockwinkel learned the ropes by driving around veteran wrestlers when he was starting out, in particular the now one-eared Yukon Eric. Demonstrating intelligence in his interviews that made him stand out as an aloof, superior heel, Bockwinkel was aided by having the greatest manager of all time by his side: Bobby 'The Brain' Heenan. Heenan was an AWA mainstay for much of the 1970s, being able to take a beating even better than most of the wrestlers and being one of the only managers deemed good enough, earlier in his career, to be booked in Sam Muchnick's St Louis territory, despite the former NWA president being known usually to hate such gimmickry.

Bockwinkel was tremendous at being hated, and this only intensified when he was awarded the AWA title for a second time following Gagne's retirement. Being able to lord it over the other wrestlers and the fans with a belt that he didn't even win was enough to have thousands screaming for whomever the latest challenger was to Bockwinkel's title.

On one occasion, it seemed like Gagne and the AWA brain trust had found the perfect challenger, a man with mainstream fame who could shoot the AWA into the stratosphere. Sure, he wasn't a grizzled veteran or a decorated amateur, but he had that mysterious ingredient X: charisma. Nearly everyone wanted to see this man beat Nick Bockwinkel. His name was Hulk Hogan, and the only man who *didn't* want him to win was Verne Gagne.

In the late 1970s, prior to wrestling, Terry Bollea was a bass-playing rock 'n' roll dropout, a sun-tanned beach bum who was in a band called Ruckus (he would claim to have *nearly* been in Metallica years later, but the dates definitely don't add up). Somewhat of a wrestling fan, he was into bodybuilding in a big way and loved 'Superstar' Billy Graham (and he looked a bit like him). Working out in a gym near Tampa in 1976, he was spotted by the Brisco brothers who immediately saw money in the tall, muscular Bollea. They sent him to be trained by the no-nonsense Hiro Matsuda, who promptly broke Bollea's leg in their first-ever session. It was the norm at the time to see if someone really wanted the job by hurting them for real, which makes no sense as wrestling is a work. When I had a normal job, I don't recall ever going into the office to train for a new position and having my new boss punch me in the face. They usually wait a couple of weeks.

Credit to Bollea, he *really* wanted to be in the business. As soon as he was healed, he went back to Matsuda and carried on training. One day at training the Briscos turned up and gave him some ring gear, telling him it was time to debut. His first notable gimmick was under a mask, being billed as the Super Destroyer, utilising the anonymity and a gimmick that had been handed down through other wrestlers to get him used to being in the ring. He got his friend Ed Leslie – later to become Brutus Beefcake – into the business and they started doing the territories together as Terry and Ed Boulder. While working in Memphis for Jerry Jarrett, he appeared on a local TV talk show, sat next to *Incredible Hulk* star Lou Ferrigno. Everyone noticed how Bollea dwarfed the allegedly massive star, so from that point onwards he became Terry 'The Hulk' Boulder – because wrestling doesn't really care about such trivialities as copyright law.

In 1979, Hulk met Vince Sr for the first time, who was impressed by his size and charisma, even if his in-ring work still needed a lot of polish. Proud of his own Irish roots, McMahon gave Bollea the new surname of Hogan, and as legend has it, asked him to dye his hair red for the role. Hulk remained blond, partially out of tribute to Billy Graham and partially as his already balding pate probably couldn't take the dye.

Working as a heel and given Freddie Blassie as his manager, Hogan had a title match with Backlund then a feud with Andre the Giant that led to them clashing at Shea Stadium in August 1980. He also started doing some cool things in Japan, adopting a style that was a little different to what he utilised stateside, with more technical moves (and a different finisher, the brilliantly named *axe bomber* clothesline), and his massive physique and unique look made him stand out. Then Hollywood came calling with his big break. And no, it wasn't *Mr Nanny*.

In 1981, Hogan played the ridiculously named character 'Thunderlips' in *Rocky III*. This thrust him into the mainstream spotlight, against the wishes of Vince Sr who always preferred his wrestlers to just, you know, wrestle. A mid-card competitor in the WWF, he jumped to Gagne's AWA just as the hype around the film really kicked in. He turned babyface quickly, and the film was a huge success (and to be fair, Hogan was really good in it) so his popularity rose at an exponential rate. Jaded wrestling fans often look at past champions and pick fault or complain about them being over-pushed, but in 1982 Hogan was a class apart, a real babyface box-office draw who thousands clamoured to see beat the hated Bockwinkel for the AWA World title. And it did happen, eventually. Kind of.

On 18 April, in St Paul, Minnesota, Hogan finally bested Bockwinkel in a match that saw both men use a foreign object to gain advantage (Bockwinkel, being the villain, used it first). The explosion of joy when Hogan won was one of the most visceral reactions ever from a wrestling crowd; genuine joy from everyone in attendance.

Hogan left with the title, despite remonstrations from Bobby Heenan (who was wearing trunks and kneepads for his managing duties, which seems weird looking back now). This was a typical bait and switch screwjob finish though; a few days later the AWA commissioner 'reviewed the footage' and reversed the decision. Bockwinkel kept the title and, presumably, a riot had been averted by not making that announcement at the time (if you watch the footage, the referee goes to check the trunks of Hogan at the end, after he's used the foreign object).

Hogan was already unhappy at how he had been positioned within the AWA, and he would go back to chasing the title but always coming up short. But Vince Jr – who from now on we'll just call Vince – was now in control of the WWF and he didn't have his father's qualms about wrestlers crossing over into the mainstream. He saw what Hogan was all about, recognised his burgeoning fame and charisma and saw exactly what Verne Gagne didn't: a hero he could build a company around.

On 27 December 1983, Hulk Hogan made his debut on a special recording of *Wrestling at the Chase* that was filmed for WWF purposes, not NWA. That match would be screened in early 1984 as televised wrestling changed forever. Hogan wouldn't be the first talent that AWA let slip through their fingers. Vince had big plans. Huge plans. Bigger than anyone could have ever known. Nothing would ever be the same again.

Chapter Seven:
Mainstream Success

Rock and Wrestling and the first WrestleMania

As 1984 began, Vince had his hand-picked next-generation super-star in Hulk Hogan, hugely over with crowds, dripping charisma and with a dash of mainstream crossover fame. He wanted to build his new WWF around the Hulkster, but to do that he needed to get the title belt around his waist. That meant getting the championship off Bob Backlund, who being champ between Billy Graham and Hogan made him the safe white meat in a decidedly muscular, suntanned, over-the-top sandwich.

This meant the use of the WWF staple: the transitional cham-pion. The man chosen was a former Olympic athlete, Iranian Khosrow Vaziri, seen by the crowd as a bushy-moustached brute who wore curly-toed boots and waved the Iranian flag, a few years removed from the hostage crisis. In reality, he had lived in the USA since the late 1960s and had helped coach the Olympic wrestling team of his adopted home. It's also worth pointing out that since these halcyon days, Vaziri – who became The Iron Sheik in the late 1970s – has become one of the most entertaining nutcases in wrestling.

At Madison Square Garden on 26 December 1983, Backlund faced The Iron Sheik in a match for his WWF Championship. Two days previously on television, viewers had been stunned as Sheik had attacked Backlund with his Persian clubs after the champion had taken up his weekly challenge. Anyone taking this challenge would have to swing the heavy clubs, and on his third attempt Backlund was successful. But the villainous Sheik attacked him from behind, injuring his neck going into their title match.

During that match, Backlund was on top and tried to pin Sheik by bridging his body, but that put too much pressure on his neck, apparently injuring it again. Sheik took advantage, locking on his Camel Clutch finisher. Backlund, valiant and heroic to the end, refused to submit. With his client seemingly in grave danger, his manager Arnold Skaaland threw in the towel, causing the referee to end the match and award the title to the Iron Sheik, ending a five-year-plus reign (admittedly, with a few little sneaky switches) and absolutely stunning the crowd who had always seen Backlund as unbeatable. The way the match was won did give Backlund a bit of an 'out' though, as he hadn't actually submitted, saving face a little.

Sheik would hold the title for less than a month. On 23 January 1984, Backlund was due a rematch at MSG but remained injured. He needed to choose a replacement, and he chose Hogan.

There was the small issue that the last time a crowd had seen Hogan at MSG, he was a villain managed by Freddie Blassie.

But the good thing about wrestling is that you can easily change the persona of a wrestler if you get other good (or bad) guys to say things about him. Backlund said of Hogan that he'd changed his ways and was assuring him that he wouldn't have Blassie around. The fact that he'd been in *Rocky III* meant that his presence at MSG got him a huge crowd pop, even if it wasn't anywhere near the likes of what he'd get later on in his career.

The match wasn't long, nor was it anything approaching a classic. For me, though, knowing what followed, it is undoubtedly one of the five most important matches in the history of wrestling.

A few minutes in, Sheik – with Blassie in his corner, eyeballing his former charge at every turn – had Hogan caught in his Camel Clutch, the very move that ended Backlund's reign. The crowd was on the edge of their seats as Hogan started to power himself upwards, on to all fours with Sheik on his back, then all the way up to his feet with supreme strength, ramming his foe back-first into the corner to break the hold. Rapidly after this, with Sheik down in the middle of the ring, Hogan dropped his 'atomic legdrop' over the throat of the champion, made the cover and the referee counted to three. MSG was delighted, but at the time they wouldn't have known in full what they'd witnessed. It was an industry-changing moment, with wrestling about to go mainstream, carried on the back of Hogan as easily as he'd carried the Iron Sheik just moments before.

Commentator Gorilla Monsoon uttered the phrase 'Hulkamania is here!' on commentary, and it was. From making his return to WWF barely a month earlier to World Champion, it was clear to everyone how much Vince believed in Hogan. The rest of the decade, in the WWF at least, would belong to him. Every kid would soon know his three rules: train hard, say your prayers, eat your vitamins (how you choose to interpret 'vitamins' is up to you). He may not have been the choice of old-school wrestling guys like Verne Gagne, but with a decent Hollywood credit and the right kind of charisma to get new fans – be they kids, teenagers or adults – into wrestling, an empire was about to be built around his popularity.

It's also worth pointing out that Hogan wasn't as terrible a wrestler as some like to make out. Was he a technical wizard? Of course not. But his work in NJPW was perfectly okay. He gets a bad rap among wrestling fans (I'll include myself in this from before I was a promoter, for sure) because of the formulaic nature of his matches. A big heel would be built up to face him, usually someone massive in size, be it bulging with muscles or weighing more than Hogan's billed 300 pounds. They would squash everyone in their path until the showdown with Hogan. In that match, Hogan would start strong, but the heel would cheat to get an advantage. Then for the next ten minutes or so, they would brutalise Hogan until they made the mistake of lingering too long on offence, striking Hogan who would no sell it, shaking his entire body as he 'hulked up', letting blows bounce off him to no effect, getting to his feet and looking his foe straight in the eye. As they panicked and tried to hit him one more time, he would block it, point right at them and hit back, knocking them down. He'd maybe throw in a body slam, but he'd soon be bounding off the ropes, punting them in the face with a big boot before dropping his leg across them and getting the win.

That was nearly all of his matches for a decade, and people absolutely lapped it up time after time.

It's fair to say that Hogan was a genius acquisition by Vince, both for increasing the stature of his company and for weakening a rival in the AWA. Over the next few years, Hogan wouldn't be the only person to come on board to vastly raise their profile. Also nicked from the AWA was Bobby Heenan, the greatest manager of all time and often the character looking after Hogan's conveyor belt of opponents. From the Mid-South NWA territory came Roddy Piper, a Scotsman who had moved to Canada as a child and had led a nomadic life as a wrestler, never the most technically gifted, but easily one of the most entertaining heels in the business. Piper began his WWF life as a manager because he'd suffered injuries to his ear in his dog collar match with Greg Valentine (also soon to jump to the WWF) at *Starrcade* in late 1983. Because he was such a motormouth, Piper was given his own interview segments where he would ask questions to other wrestlers, often just acting like a complete tool towards them and setting up feuds for when he was able to wrestle again. This was revolutionary; up until that point it would always be an interviewer, clad in a suit and acting as the straight man, asking the questions to talent. This created a new dynamic and was a big reason why Piper was so hugely over as a heel, especially when he attacked Jimmy Snuka with a coconut during one of these segments. Borderline racism was a little bit more tolerated in the 1980s.

With Hogan, Heenan, Piper and many others on board for Vince's revolution, it was easy to convince others to sign on, especially once the company really started hitting its stride. Soon other brilliant names would join, talent like Randy Savage, Ricky Steamboat and Ted DiBiase, young wrestlers who wanted to be as well known in the USA as the WWF and Hogan were. And Vince's company was the best place to be, as he didn't just want a territory; he wanted to be a national phenomenon. All he needed was the airtime to spread the word. What he ended up doing led to a moment in wrestling that won't ever be forgotten: Black Saturday. Nobody knew it at the time, but the ripples from this one event ended up changing wrestling forever.

A little background. In Atlanta, an NWA-affiliated territory called Georgia Championship Wrestling (GCW) was doing some amazing things with television. In 1976, it became the first wrestling company to have a nationwide TV deal thanks to the growth of cable television, and it quickly became one of the highest-rated shows on Ted Turner's WTBS Superstation. Three men were in charge of the company, all active wrestlers: Head booker Ole Anderson and stakeholders Gerry and Jack Brisco.

GCW's TV show is remembered fondly, partly because of the sheer wealth of talent that made their names there, but also because of the softly spoken, intelligent commentator Gordon Solie. The man who coined the term 'crimson mask' and pronounced 'suplex' as 'suplay' made every single move mean something, giving even the hokiest of ideas sporting legitimacy. The *World Championship Wrestling* show was seen as rasslin'; all-action, often bloody, portrayed as legitimate competition and in stark contrast to what the WWF presented. To a GCW fan, that product was too cartoonish.

In 1983, WWF already had a slot on the nationwide USA cable channel. Vince got it by simply offering the channel a fee to show his show – the pre-recorded *All-American Wrestling* (these names don't get any less generic, sorry) – instead of what they had been screening previously, Southwest Championship Wrestling. This meant that the WWF had a decent portfolio of TV slots: *All-American* was on cable while *Championship Wrestling* and *All-Star Wrestling* were on syndicated television. Soon, Vince would add the often-bizarre *Tuesday Night Titans* to cable TV on the USA network, a show that showed precious little wrestling but was presented as a chat show with wrestlers in character. These days, it makes wonderfully camp retro viewing.

By 1984, things were going well but Vince wanted a second nationwide cable outlet. He spied GCW's position on WTBS and went after it. Trying a similar tactic to how he secured the USA network timeslot, he went straight to Ted Turner and offered to buy the slot from GCW. Turner refused, loyal to GCW for giving him good ratings. This was the starting point for a feud between McMahon and Turner that got *really* bitter in the mid 1990s.

Vince wasn't completely dissuaded though. He had heard that GCW wasn't a great place behind the scenes. Once McMahon learned that the Briscos were unhappy, he approached them and fellow shareholder Jim Barnett to make a deal. They sold their shares in the company to Vince, giving him control of GCW and in turn, the timeslot on WTBS. Ole Anderson was apoplectic with rage (and trust me, he still hasn't forgotten it); Barnett got a job as an advisor to the WWF and the Briscos were long rumoured to have been given jobs for life in the company.

And so, to Black Saturday itself – 14 July 1984. Fans around the USA who had grown to love GCW were in for one heck of a shock. The show began with regular co-host Freddie Miller introducing Vince McMahon to the audience. Vince, wearing one of the most 1980s suits you'll ever see, proceeded to tell everyone watching that fans would love this new show just as much as they did the old one. And with that, highlights of WWF's other TV programming were introduced. But unlike the quiet revolution that landed Vince the slot on USA, the viewers of GCW were not going to let this one pass quietly.

The network received thousands of complaints. Yes, it was

still wrestling; but it wasn't *their* form of rasslin'. It was, to some extent, the north-south divide in the USA encapsulated in one form of mass entertainment. It wasn't just the audiences who were angry, either. Somewhere else in Atlanta, Ted Turner was really, really pissed.

Turner did two things to try and right what he saw as wrongs as ratings for the timeslot started to decline. He gave Bill Watts's Mid-South territory, which was well-booked and certainly akin to what GCW offered previously, with great star power at the time, their own slot on WTBS during Saturday afternoons. He also gave Ole Anderson a chance for revenge, giving his new company – the imaginatively named *Championship Wrestling from Georgia* – their own slot on the same station, effectively framing the WWF product with wrestling shows that the WTBS audience seemed to prefer. Both shows would go on to beat the WWF in the ratings.

Losing money on the venture, by 1985 Vince was ready to cut his losses. Luckily for him, two great things happened. Elsewhere on television, he was absolutely on fire, setting records for viewers. And a man called Jim Crockett had money burning a hole in his pocket, desperate to make his own bid for national glory with his territory. Crockett would pay $1 million for the WTBS timeslot, which he probably thought was a great deal at the time. Unfortunately for him, while it may have put NWA wrestling back in that prime-time cable slot, that money helped pay for something that would eventually destroy the NWA, at least in the form it had been up till then. That $1 million helped pay for the first-ever *WrestleMania*. Furthermore, that show was going to go stratospheric because of a little thing called *Rock and Wrestling*.

* * *

Have you ever had a chance meeting that has affected your life in some way? Long-time wrestling manager Captain Lou Albano did in 1983, boarding a plane and sitting next to a young couple who seemed really nice. A chap called David Wolff, who worked in the music industry, and his girlfriend, a punkish young lady with bright hair and crazy dress sense who was a singer. She was called Cyndi Lauper and was just a few months away from being one of the biggest stars on the planet.

The veteran wrestler hit it off with the youngsters, and Wolff – who was a massive wrestling fan – asked him to be in Lauper's next music video, playing her father. The song was called 'Girls Just Wanna Have Fun', and with MTV just taking off it thrust Albano into the spotlight, with wrestling fans recognising him as the song went into heavy rotation on the channel. Vince noted the power in this crossover appeal and knew there was a great way to work everything together. It involved Albano, MTV, Roddy Piper, feminism (of sorts), and eventually Mr T and Hulk Hogan.

Lauper and Albano were involved in a Piper's Pit interview segment together. Lauper's very appearance in WWF instantly led to a new, younger audience for the company, teenagers and twenty-somethings who maybe watched wrestling as kids but had forgotten about it until now. Albano had noted the new-found fame he'd got for the video and, being a good heel, played up to it, insisting he was behind Lauper's success. Lauper would appear on a segment with Piper, her bright hair and clothes muted by the garish tartan wallpaper applied to the lean-to walls behind them as they sat and talked, Piper trying to rile the singer up. Then Albano entered, calling her a 'broad', insisting he wrote all her lyrics and was completely responsible for her fame. Crowd shots during this segment are amazing, with youngsters in attendance screaming support for Lauper. Eventually she has enough of Albano's abuse, hitting him with her purse until various people pull everyone apart and the segment ends in abject chaos. It's brilliant television even now, but back then nobody had ever seen anything like it.

Because this is wrestling, this confrontation had to lead to a match. Lauper wasn't a wrestler and certainly didn't have time to train to become one. But a match could be put on that emphasised everything that Lauper represented to the younger generation; both sides would pick a wrestler to compete in a match. Lauper chose Wendi Richter, a young, exciting upcoming wrestler in the women's division. Albano chose WWF Women's Champion the Fabulous Moolah, a veteran who had held the title for decades. It was a battle of the ages and there was only one place to show such a match – MTV.

Called *The Brawl To End It All*, MTV only showed one match from a mammoth MSG card on 23 July 1984. That match, unusually for the time involving two women, would be the first wrestling match broadcast live on cable television. Thanks to the work WWF did in building the story and Lauper did by just being a massive mainstream success already, this match garnered enormous ratings. Record-breaking numbers tuned in to see Lauper help Richter end the ridiculously long reign of the villainous Moolah by hitting the veteran with a loaded purse (basically, her handbag was implied to have a brick in it, every woman should have one) to a massive reaction from the live crowd.

With that show being such a runaway success, it was decided to do a second MTV special, but this one had an even greater goal: set up *WrestleMania*. Taking place a month before that show, *The War To Settle The Score* once again featured Lauper, but this time as part of a match between two men, Hulk Hogan and Roddy

Piper. That contest had been set up at the end of 1984, when, during an in-ring promo, Lauper had been given an award for her services to women's wrestling. She then wanted to bury the hatchet with Albano, who she presented a gold record to. Piper interrupted this, attacking everyone in the ring like a madman: he broke the record over Albano's head, kicked Lauper as she tried to protect him and slammed her boyfriend/manager Wolff to the mat with a powerslam. Hulk Hogan came to the aid of Lauper, offering to be her protector and the match was set, Piper accompanied to the ring by Bob Orton and Hogan by Lauper, Wolff and Albano.

During the match, Paul Orndorff would interfere on Piper's behalf along with Orton to give Hogan the victory by disqualification. This led to chaos in the ring at the end of the show, with *A-Team* star Mr T sitting ringside and jumping the guardrail to come to the aid of Hogan and Lauper. This, again viewed by incredible numbers nationwide on MTV, set up the main event of *WrestleMania* and gave that show a massive leg-up in terms of public awareness. It was set to be the biggest thing in wrestling ever, the crossover success that Vince had wanted to create.

On 30 March 1985, the night before *WrestleMania*, came a PR masterstroke, with Hulk Hogan and Mr T hosting *Saturday Night Live*. This supershow was going to be more than *Starrcade*'s gritty, blood-soaked first show; it was going to feel like the worlds of wrestling and entertainment had collided, a true pop culture phenomenon, the final result of months of hard work collaborating with mainstream media outlets to sell out MSG and break records with closed-circuit pay-per-view screenings.

The 'Super Bowl of Wrestling' did get off to a strange start. Backstage interviewer 'Mean' Gene Okerlund (poached from the

AWA at roughly the same time as Hogan) sang the *Star-Spangled Banner*, now the traditional start to all *WrestleMania* events. It was meant to have been sung by a mystery celebrity who apparently didn't show up, so Okerlund stepped in. Even stranger still is the fact that two singers (Cyndi Lauper and Liberace) were backstage and could have done it, so you have to presume that whoever it was meant to be left it *really* late to leave everyone in the lurch. If I do anything in my life, I will one day find out who it was meant to have been singing to start that show.

These days, *WrestleMania* shows have an official theme song, often performed during the event. I have been, at the time of writing, to two *WrestleMania* shows: Miami in 2012, and Orlando in 2017. Both times I have been forced to see Flo Rida perform, meaning that I have seen more live performances from him than I have artists I actually like. In 2017 that live performance (also featuring Pitbull) was the only thing the fan in front of me got excited about during the whole show – a show that included The Undertaker retiring. Back in 1985, the opening theme was an instrumental version of *Easy Lover* by Phil Collins, proof that this was as 1980s as 1980s could be.

The show, while not spectacular, had some truly memorable moments. Andre the Giant took part in a body slam challenge against Big John Studd, a man nearly as big as him. At stake was $15,000 for Andre if he could slam Studd, but he would have to retire if Studd slammed him first. The beloved Andre managed to hoist his foe up and throw him to the mat, winning a briefcase full of money. The Giant opened it and started throwing handfuls of notes out to the eager audience who all scrambled over each other to retrieve some. Studd's manager Bobby Heenan snatched the case from Andre and sprinted to the back, stealing the money (in storyline) and saving some profit. (It's not clear whether it was real money or not, but the crowd's reaction says it was).

At the last MTV event, Leilani Kai had captured the WWF Women's title from Wendi Richter, so this was the third stage of the feud between the women on the outside of the match: The Fabulous Moolah (in Kai's corner) and Cyndi Lauper (in Richter's). Early in the contest, Lauper saved Richter from Moolah's inter-ference on the outside, giving the challenger the impetus to regain the title. This was pretty much the end of Lauper's involvement in matches in the WWF, but she'd had a great run and set the pop culture thing going in a big way. Wrestlers would continue to appear in her music videos for a while longer too.

Then we had the main event. Nowadays, it feels weird that the biggest match on the show didn't involve the WWF World title (now renamed so with the company firmly out of the trap-pings of the NWA), even if the champion was in the match. Hogan and Mr T took on Roddy Piper and Paul Orndorff (with Bob Orton in their corner) in a tag team match. Mr T was at the height of his fame, having been in *Rocky III* with Hogan and in *The A-Team*, and the celebrity involvement didn't end there, either: New York Yankees manager Billy Martin was special guest ring announcer; Liberace, coming to the ring high-kicking with The Rockettes, was special guest timekeeper; and, on the outside of the ring only, Muhammad Ali was the special guest referee. Of those three names, I only feel that Ali was really in the right role. Ali would get involved too, punching Piper in the face to keep order at one point, which is a bit like being a fireman and putting flames out with paraffin.

Later, with Hogan trapped in a full nelson by Orndorff, Orton got involved with the referee distracted, jumping off the top rope but Hogan moved, and he clattered into his own stablemate. Hogan capitalised and got the victory to the immense delight of the MSG crowd. Business was done after the bell too, with Piper throwing a tantrum and leaving with Orton, while Orndorff remained in the ring with the celebrating Hogan, Mr T and Jimmy Snuka. This led to a face turn for Orndorff and then a turn back heel that would lead to some fantastic business for the WWF.

WrestleMania was a massive gamble, but a huge success. As well as a sold-out MSG, one million viewers watched the show through closed-circuit broadcasts in various venues around the USA. This made big money for Titan Sports, but also had other knock-on effects. With so many people willing to pay to watch one wrestling show, and with the massive MTV ratings in the run-up to the event, it was time for wrestling to return to network television for the first time since the 1950s. Everybody wanted a piece of the action.

Saturday Night's Main Event would draw massive ratings on NBC as an occasional replacement for the incredibly successful Saturday Night Live, usually putting on around five shows a year between 1985 to 1991. These shows would often be the only place that you would see megastars like Hulk Hogan wrestle outside of pay-per-view events as he wasn't usually featured on regular weekly syndicated shows, where lower card wrestlers were the mainstay. Everything was not just going to plan for Vince, it was shattering what he originally had planned and snowballing into some kind of make-it-up-as-you-go-along super-plan. But despite a few companies falling to the wayside, he was certainly not the only game in town.

JIM'S TOP TEN: TAG TEAMS

I've never been the biggest fan of tag team wrestling, as it can often fall into the trap of becoming a bit formulaic: babyface team gets battered, eventually one makes a hot tag, rinse and repeat. But when done well, tag team wrestling can be sublime. Here are my favourite ever teams:

10. The Miracle Violence Connection — 'Dr Death' Steve Williams and Terry Gordy

After a great stint in the early 1990s in Japan, Williams and Gordy were brought into WCW to feud with the Steiner Brothers, although sadly not under their amazingly overblown Japanese name, The Miracle Violence Connection. Two tough dudes, their brawling style got over huge in Japan.

9. The Eliminators — Perry Saturn and John Kronus

Part of the sheer open-mouthed joy I got from watching ECW for the first time, through tapes I'd purchased on the internet, was seeing Saturn and Kronus hit their 'Total Elimination' finisher which was like nothing I'd ever seen before — one man kicking an opponent high while the other went low. Go find it on YouTube now. It's brutal, and they had a high-flying, stiff-kicking style I always enjoyed.

8. Arn Anderson and Tully Blanchard

Known as 'The Brain Busters' during their very brief WWF stint, but mostly referred to simply as Arn and Tully, these two men were a big part of the Four Horsemen and had an almost telepathic chemistry as a team, knowing exactly how to cut the ring off from their opponents. Modern-day team The Revival remind me of Tully and Arn a lot (and I love those guys too).

7. Rick and Scott Steiner

To see the best of the Steiners, I'd recommend watching them on the WWE Network in 1993, when they were destroying jobbers for fun on early episodes of *Raw* before returning to WCW. Often a bit scrappy but always stiff as heck, Scott would morph into an even more terrifying singles competitor as the 1990s wore on.

6. The British Bulldogs – The Dynamite Kid and Davey Boy Smith

Honing their act in Canada in Stampede Wrestling before making it to the WWF and Japan, real-life cousins Dynamite and Davey were more than just a British gimmick, showing off fast-paced tag team wrestling with a reckless abandon for their own safety, especially Dynamite. Both men would also have notable singles careers; Davey as 'The British Bulldog' was at the top of the card in both WCW and WWE, while the Dynamite Kid's matches with the Original Tiger Mask are the stuff of legend.

5. The Hart Foundation – Bret Hart and Jim 'The Anvil' Neidhart

Before he was a huge singles star, Bret Hart had a great grounding in one of the most exciting tag teams of the 1980s. Edging out The Rockers (Shawn Michaels and Marty Jannetty) from that era for me as the Harts managed to actually hold the WWF tag team titles, one of my favourite tag team matches from this time was at *Summerslam 1990* with the Harts facing Demolition in a two-out-of-three falls match.

4. Kevin Steen and El Generico

Just two best friends from Quebec, Steen and Generico did their very best work in Ring of Honor and Pro Wrestling Guerrilla, often working as a tag team where one man was heel (Steen) and the other was face (Generico). Arguably the greatest example of using a tag team breaking up to kick-start an amazing feud, both men went their separate ways before eventually ending up in WWE. Well, Steen became Kevin Owens and Sami Zayn looks a lot like a man who looks a lot like I imagine Generico under the mask would look.

3. The Road Warriors/The Legion of Doom – Hawk and Animal

Starting off in the AWA as green, muscular monsters, nobody had ever seen anything like the Road Warriors. With face paint and spiked American football shoulder pads, they were bigger than traditional tag team wrestlers and manhandled their way through the AWA, NWA and WWF. They absolutely should have been heels, but they were so impressive that people couldn't wait to cheer them. Their Doomsday Device finisher remains one of the most dangerous around and blew minds in the 1980s.

2. The Kings of Wrestling – Chris Hero and Claudio Castagnoli

Now in NXT and WWE respectively as Kassius Ohno and Cesaro, The Kings were another team that did great things in the indies, especially RoH, holding the tag team titles there twice, including one reign that lasted a day shy of a year. There has never been another team with so many ways to either forearm, uppercut or elbow their opponents faces off.

1. The Dudley Boyz – Bubba Ray and D-Von

The most decorated tag team in the history of wrestling, the Dudleys started out in ECW as a thrown-together pairing to represent the entire Dudley clan; they gradually broke loose, establishing themselves as the best heels in ECW, then being part of the two legendary TLC matches in WWE. If I was to shout 'D-Von' at any wrestling show in the world, someone would immediately reply with 'Get the tables!'.

Chapter Eight:
Meanwhile, Elsewhere

**The growth of wrestling around the world:
Britain, Mexico and Japan**

Wrestling may have been massive in the USA, but huge scenes were also erupting in Britain, Mexico, Japan, Canada and Germany and wrestling was a big attraction as far afield as Africa and India. The style of wrestling in Britain, Japan and Mexico was certainly different to what was on offer in the USA and the stories of how those industries took off is as varied and interesting as those in the States. And modern professional wrestling is a hybrid that reflects the influences of all four major nations, taking the best of all of these styles to create the most exciting product.

Let's start with the UK . . .

In 2012, I was in Miami to watch *WrestleMania*, one week after the first-ever PROGRESS show. I went to see a Japanese company called Dragon Gate (many independent companies, my own included from 2017, put shows on around *WrestleMania*, as so many fans are in town. It's a bit like the Edinburgh Fringe, but nowhere near as much of a rip-off). I sat on my own, watched an amazing show and got chatting to a couple of Japanese fans next to me. One of them was obsessed with the town of Wigan.

For those that don't know Wigan, it's a town in Greater Manchester. I live about 40 miles away. If you're British, you probably know of it because of the football team, Wigan Athletic, or the all-conquering rugby league team of the 1990s, or maybe the Heinz factory or the legendary Northern Soul club at Wigan Casino. This Japanese chap wasn't wearing flares and demonstrating his best dance moves, but he insisted we talk about Wigan. The unassuming northern town was his British touchstone. He kept talking about 'Wigan style', which in Japan, it turns out, is a really big deal. Starting from the legendary Wigan gym known as The Snakepit, one little town in England would end up being the place to be when it came to catch as catch can wrestling.

After chatting to my new Japanese chum, I looked into the whole Wigan thing a bit more. It turned out that legendary shooter Billy Reilly built a gymnasium on Pyke Street in his native town and set out to train wrestlers in his own, very legitimate, submission-based style. Countless students would go on to be big stars in the world of wrestling: Jack Dempsey, Karl Gotch, Bert Assirati and – most importantly to my new friend – Billy Robinson.

Robinson had travelled to Japan in the 1970s and, along with Karl Gotch, trained both professional wrestlers and legitimate fighters in the catch wrestling style, taking part in some pro wrestling matches, but helping legitimise a style of wrestling known as 'shoot style' which certainly seemed a lot more real than pro wrestling. Robinson also spent time in the USA, winning titles and being both a great professional wrestler and a tough guy who could stretch people, forever representing the Snake Pit where he was trained.

For me, being raised in the UK, it was crazy to learn that little Wigan was such a big deal to someone from thousands of miles away. But British wrestling has a global respect for its hard-hitting, technical style that was started by men like Reilly, popularised by Robinson globally and adapted into other styles as the 20th century wore on. Stars like William Regal, Fit Finlay, Zack Sabre Jr, Marty Scurll, Tyler Bate, Jack Gallagher and Pete Dunne have all demonstrated the next logical step to this style, adapting and modernising it as they see fit, ensuring that British wrestling is as respected as ever before. My Japanese friend told me that he would visit Wigan one day. I hope he did.

The roots of British professional wrestling started in the world of variety, a match here and there during a night at the theatre modernising the art form at the turn of the century. Before the First World War wrestling was huge, with the Hackenschmidt bouts that I mentioned earlier bringing London to a standstill. After the war, part-fake, part-real shows billed as 'All-In Wrestling' were popularised by promoters Atholl Oakeley and Henri Irslinger, with the crowds firmly believing that everything they saw was absolutely real. The staged stuff started to outweigh the real though, and by the late 1930s wrestling was banned in London thanks to rowdy crowds and in-ring violence, and the whole scene needed a big reset.

In 1947, a bunch of tweed-wearing wrestling luminaries drew

up a set of rules to govern wrestling. Named after the chair of the panel, they were dubbed the Admiral-Lord Mountevans rules, defining what holds were legal and how falls within matches could be won: by pinfall, submission, knockout, TKO or disqualification. In a similar vein to boxing were weight categories, more defined than in the USA. Seven weight divisions existed, with champions required for each, ranging from lightweight to heavyweight. This meant that more wrestlers had the chance to become stars, rather than shows focusing on the bigger guys. It was these weight classes that indirectly led to me becoming a wrestling fan in the early Eighties, so thanks go to Baron Mountevans and his no-doubt pipe-smoking, brandy-swilling chums.

The Mountevans rules were especially important in 1952, when they were adopted by Joint Promotions, a group based on the success of the NWA in the USA. Several promotions came together for this cartel, rotating talent among them and blocking rival companies. With the legitimacy of the rules behind them, and the monopoly on the best talent, Joint Promotions were soon running up to 400 shows a week, despite not always treating their wrestlers as well as they could have. All of the Mountevans titles were defended primarily on Joint Promotion shows, and in the tough post-war financial climate the cartel thrived while other companies outside of it tended to fall by the wayside.

Joint Promotions managed to secure television coverage as well, starting in 1955. By 1965 *World of Sport* became regular programming on Saturday afternoons on ITV, a rival to the BBC's *Grandstand* show, putting football, horse racing and wrestling in the front rooms of the entire country. By the 1960s, Joint Promotions routinely ran 4,500 shows a year, but television exposure meant that rival companies could start clawing back some ground as well, with wrestling in general being seen as a hot property. It helped if your stars were on TV, but it wasn't the be-all and end-all.

The main star everyone remembers from British wrestling was Big Daddy, Shirley Crabtree. Brother of Max Crabtree, who was in charge of Joint Promotions by 1975, Daddy eventually became a beloved, chubby babyface after stints as a villain and even being run out of the business in the 1960s by the incredibly intense Bert Assirati, a notorious shooter who would turn up to events where Daddy was competing as 'The Blonde Adonis' and challenged him for real from the crowd.

I remember buying comics as a kid and seeing Big Daddy in them constantly. He was a massive mainstream star for years, even if rumour had it that he didn't like children very much. His feud with Giant Haystacks was huge in the 1970s and Eighties, and even if it wasn't a technical classic it certainly caught the imagination of the nation.

Haystacks was even bigger than Daddy, standing at six feet 11 inches and weighing nearly 700 pounds. With a big beard and overalls, he terrified audiences around the country (and briefly, in the latter stages of his career, in the USA) but I can't watch footage of him now without remembering stories William Regal has told me about him refusing to share chocolate brazil nuts with him on long car journeys around the UK.

Some form of Daddy v Haystacks encounter would often be part of FA Cup Final day on *World of Sport*, but in June 1981 they had what most people remember as their biggest clash, in front of a sold-out Wembley Arena that could end by knockout only. After around ten minutes of brawling, Haystacks crashed through a table at ringside – ironically one of the stunts that caused wrestling to be banned from London in the 1930s – and Daddy picked up the win, as if that was ever in serious doubt.

For me as a young wrestling fan, it was other stars that caught my eye as I watched *World of Sport*. Thanks to repeats shown on the Wrestling Channel on Sky around a decade ago and the large amount of footage on YouTube, it's easy to go back and experience some of the wonderfully talented and charismatic individuals that made British wrestling such a ratings success. Some of them felt held back by Joint Promotions, though, and ventured abroad to countries like Canada and Japan where they helped to revolutionise the style of wrestling. Stars like Johnny Saint, Marty Jones, Rollerball Rocco and the Dynamite Kid very much shaped what I enjoy about wrestling these days.

Outside of Daddy and Haystacks, Kendo Nagasaki is often the most recognisable star of the era.[2] A kind of masked samurai, he was actually the alter-ego of a quite odd chap called Peter Thornley from Stoke-on-Trent. He was a massive box-office draw across three decades, even after British wrestling disappeared from television screens in the 1990s.

With different masks for different circumstances, Nagasaki was as mysterious outside of the ring as he was within it, but two televised events mark out his career. The first came in 1977, as he undertook a ceremonial unmasking at a show in Wolverhampton, revealing himself to have a tattoo on top of his head in what was one of the most bizarre and anticipated moments in *World of Sport* history. With his manager 'Gorgeous' George (not that one) providing incredibly polite British commentary, an audience of

---

[2] I'd recommend the excellent *The Wrestling* by Simon Garfield to give you a window into the secretive and often bizarre world of Nagasaki.

kids and enthusiastic old ladies looked on as two acolytes assisted Nagasaki in revealing his face for the first time, complete with coloured contact lenses to make the entire spectacle even more surreal. It was part-wrestling angle, part-ITV explanation of martial arts lore. It's got even weirder with age and is easy to watch online. Nagasaki's mask is finally set ablaze in the ring as he raises a sword to the camera, health and safety be damned.

Nagasaki donned the mask again in 1986 but jumped, after a brief retirement, to the rival All Star promotion. With All Star sharing television time with Joint Promotions in the late 1980s, it meant that we got to see one of the strangest storylines in wrestling history in what would be Nagasaki's final ever ITV appearance in 1988. It also happened to feature two of my friends, the Golden Boys: William (then Steve) Regal and Robbie Brookside. In a tag match against Nagasaki and Blondie Barrett, Brookside would be – and I'm not making this up – hypnotised by Nagasaki mid-match and then go after his own partner.

All Star started to get wind of the unhappiness of certain wrestlers who felt they were being held back by Daddy's and Haystacks' dominance and began to poach talent in the 1980s. You could stay with Joint Promotions and have a shot of being on television, but it was accepted that All Star had the more talented wrestlers.

(All Star was run by Brian Dixon, a man who, incidentally, every British wrestler can do a bang-on impression of – it's uncanny, I've never met a wrestler who can't. I can't, though. Must be a wrestler thing . . .)

In September 1985, things started to change massively. *World of Sport* was taken off air, and even though wrestling still had a TV slot, it was at different times each week and viewers started drifting away. Joint Promotions would soon lose their monopoly, as the schedule was rotated between them, All Star and WWF. All three products were very different, and the cycling programme meant that it was hard to have storylines resonate and catch on with viewers. It was a bit like having a soap opera showing every week, but one week it was *Coronation Street*, the next it was *EastEnders* and the next it was *Hollyoaks*.

You could argue that this was a Machiavellian plan by ITV boss Greg Dyke to find a reason to get wrestling off of his channel. Never a fan of what he saw as a downmarket form of entertainment, the dwindling ratings gave Dyke the reason to pull wrestling from national television in 1988.

Joint Promotions would be bankrupt by 1995. All Star maintained a decent business in the immediate aftermath of the cancellation, keeping their storylines going and utilising what was a more exciting roster than their rivals. By 1993 their business had suffered too, but they survived by keeping the holiday camp circuit, something they still do now and a huge reason why some British wrestlers can be full time. It's sniffed at by some fans, but talents like Daniel Bryan speak highly of their excursions to the UK to do the camps when they were starting out.

I'll wager that if you go into a burrito restaurant anywhere in the world you'll see an image on the wall of a luchador, a masked participant in the world of *lucha libre*, as recognisable a symbol of Mexico these days as the Aztec pyramids.

Lucha libre literally means 'free fight', and while there are similarities between wrestling in Mexico and elsewhere in the world, there are a few distinct differences that really set it apart and mean that in certain cities and arenas, wrestling is much more than just entertainment. Some masked wrestlers – *luchadors* – are full-blown walking, talking, grappling legends and Mexican crowds are among the most intense and supportive in the world.

First off, there's the masks. Wearing a mask isn't just a gimmick in Mexico, it's influenced by Aztec history and the very best wrestlers will go through their entire career without ever being unmasked, wearing their hoods paired with a suit in TV appearances and in some cases, being buried in them. Those who have never lost their mask in a match make a huge effort to conceal their identities and removing an opponent's mask during a match leads to an immediate disqualification. Should you lose in a wager match – known as *luchas de apuestas* – where you bet your mask against an opponent's mask, hair or championship, you are forced to remove it in the ring and tell the crowd your real name and hometown, so you don't just lose your mask but all of the mystery around your career. I think anonymous Twitter trolls with fake names and no profile photo should be forced to face similar consequences when you own them with a good comeback.

Not all wrestlers in Mexico wear masks though. Partly to keep such character's special, but also because it's hard wrestling under a mask. It affects your peripheral vision and hearing, and it gets hot under them. It makes it all the more awe-inspiring to see some masked wrestlers doing such amazing things while having some of their senses dulled.

There are a few rule differences between Mexico and the rest of the world. A piledriver is seen as an immediate disqualification, and a reason for *rudos* (heels) to gain a sneaky advantage on their rival *technicos* (babyfaces). In tag matches, you don't actually need to tag in and out; if your feet touch the floor outside of the ring, your partner is immediately legal. Tag matches, in particular six-man matches, are the norm on most cards, and they tend to be two-out-of-three-fall contests. You get your money's worth on a lucha card, that's for sure.

A fun difference in Mexico is that when fans really love a match, they will throw money into the ring to show their appreciation. It's not a common practice, so wrestlers aren't always heading home with handfuls of cash. When it does happen, the tradition is for the wrestlers to collect the money and keep it, rather than spending it, to remind them of the crowd reaction to that particular match. (Obviously, it's much politer to throw notes rather than coins.)

Another anomaly in Mexico is their use of mini wrestlers, with competitors under the height of five feet four inches often being given starring roles on shows, with some having their own gimmicks and some being mini versions of established wrestlers. A few talented luchadors like Rey Mysterio Jr are on the line of being between cruiserweight and mini competitor. In 1997, the WWF had a brief period of using some supremely talented mini wrestlers from Mexico, the tiny luchadors wowing audiences with their quite ridiculous levels of athleticism and gymnastic ability.

If you watch lucha libre now, I guarantee that you'll be astonished at how different it feels to wrestling elsewhere. The style is a little slower, a tad more choreographed and not always as hard-hitting as what you might be used to; that said, it's genuinely wonderful to watch some of the bigger shows as the enthusiasm of the crowd and the heat that good angles generate is really something else. But like all wrestling, it started out as something legitimate and was gradually mutated into what it has become today, by strong characters and Aztec legend.

Enrique Ugartechea is credited as the man who started lucha libre, using influences from Greco-Roman wrestling to kick-start the sport in 1863, during the Second French Intervention in Mexico. It remained a mainly regional industry until the 1930s when Salvador Lutteroth, a property inspector and former soldier, fell in love with wrestling after watching shows across the border in the USA, primarily in El Paso, Texas. Lutteroth would start Empresa Mexicana de Lucha Libre, or EMLL, in 1933, a company that survives today, making it the longest-running wrestling company in the world.

In 1934, Lutteroth used his first masked wrestler, an American rudo called Maravilla Enmascarada, and the attention that drew led to more masked talents and very good crowds. EMLL even had to build their own arenas that still host wrestling to this day: Arena Coliseo and the 16,500-capacity Arena Mexico, the latter being the largest purpose-built wrestling arena in the world.

The explosion of popularity for EMLL came about thanks to one massive star: El Santo. Starting his career in the 1930s, he became 'The Saint' in the 1950s, initially a rudo but winning the crowds over by being so committed to the mystery of his persona. Never removing his mask or losing a wager match, by 1952 he was starring in comic books, and by 1958 he started appearing in films. Not as a random background figure or stuntman, but the star of a whopping 52 movies that have a wonderfully camp, B-movie charm. Many wrestlers are superheroes; El Santo tended to play a wrestler who was a superhero on the side. He was buried in his mask after his death, having briefly revealed his face just once, in a television appearance a few weeks before his passing.

El Santo's biggest rival was Blue Demon, another luchador who never lost his mask and was buried in it. Often starring in films alongside or against El Santo, they had an in-ring rivalry as well as one in real life, jostling for position and prominence in the movies. Completing the 'big three' of the initial lucha libre explosion is Mil Máscaras, a man so famous in Mexico that he has appeared on postage stamps; well, I suppose his mask has at the very least. It was Máscaras (his name means 'thousand masks') who first took the lucha libre style overseas, mainly because he was a heavyweight competitor so could easily be matched with the leading American and Japanese competitors of his day.

EMLL was hugely successful but it wasn't without its failings. In the 1970s Salvador Lutteroth's son, Chavo, was in charge of the company but not everybody was enamoured with how conservative and restricting the brand could be. Francisco Flores and Ray Mendoza made their break for it, leaving EMLL and setting up UWA (Universal Wrestling Association), becoming a huge rival to EMLL pretty much overnight. With a newer, faster style of wrestling and a younger, exciting roster, UWA made stars of Dos Caras, El Canek, Fishman, Perro Aguayo and the Villanos, and set up partnerships with WWF and NJPW. This was the first, but certainly not the last, instance of Mexican wrestling becoming a bit like the Wild West. EMLL would steady the ship and be back on top by the late 1980s, but then another upstart booker from within the company – Antonio Pena – would tire of restrictions and want to set up on his own. In 1992 he formed AAA (Lucha Libre AAA Worldwide), found newcomers from areas outside Mexico City, like Rey Mysterio Jr and Psicosis from the Tijuana circuit, and experienced insane levels of success. So much so that EMLL (rebranded now as CMLL) took a huge hit on business and UWA went out of business by 1995. AAA and CMLL are still rivals, but every now and then a company will spring up, talent raids and switches are common, and Mexico always seems a more lawless place when it comes to contracts and allegiances.

In Japan, professional wrestling is known as *puroresu*, literally 'pro-wres' after the Japanese pronunciation and abbreviation of the term. It's one of my very favourite words to say out loud, and it's also one of my favourite forms of grappling. Japanese wrestling is traditionally hard-hitting and has much more of an undercurrent of legitimacy, while fringes of it are so weird and wonderful that they could only ever exist on an island so isolated from outside cultures.

Sumo is, of course, an ancient and sacred sport within Japan. It would be a former star of sumo who would be the first man to make puroresu a success, but he wasn't the first man to try to bring it to the shores of Japan. Sorakichi Matsuda moved to the USA in the 1880s, living his life virtually in poverty as he pursued his dream of becoming a professional wrestler. He tried unsuccessfully to popularise the hybrid of wrestling styles that he had seen in the States back in his home nation, but died in penury in New York, aged just 32.

It would only be after the Second World War, and with a combination of post-war anxiety and westernisation of the nation through American occupation, that professional wrestling really took hold in Japan. Television, as elsewhere, also helped the situation.

The 'Father of Puroresu' was born Kim Sin-Rak in Korea but became known as Rikidōzan as he broke into the world of Sumo in the 1940s. Performing in that art form at a decent level – but never attaining grand champion status – he quit in 1950 for what he described as financial reasons, but what also may have been down to racism. As a Korean he was struggling to get the opportunities that the Japanese nationals were getting in the ancient, fiercely tribal world of sumo. His identity during much of his wrestling career would be kept incredibly secret, his Korean background rarely being spoken of as he became a national hero. His 'real' name would be given as Mitsuhiro Momota.

Legend has it that Rikidōzan befriended Harold Sakata, the man who played Oddjob in *Goldfinger* and a long-standing professional wrestler from Hawaii during a barroom brawl. Sakata introduced Rikidōzan to Bobby Bruns, and both men would take a role in training him, mainly during an excursion to Hawaii. Rikidōzan's first-ever match was against Bruns in Tokyo, starting a trend that built his career: the former sumo wrestler standing up to American enemies.

Rikidōzan founded the Japan Pro Wrestling Alliance, or JWA, in 1953. It quickly became a huge success, becoming part of the NWA and making Rikidōzan – who was also the company's biggest star – incredibly wealthy and very famous in short order. The roster initially consisted of legitimate fighters from sumo or judo backgrounds, retrained as professional wrestlers and *gaijin*, or foreigners, usually from the USA who would normally work as heels.

One of the judoka who became a big star was Masahiko Kimura, a spectacularly tough man who had already achieved a high level of fame thanks to his tour of Brazil and in particular, a legitimate fight with Hélio Gracie in Rio. In the early 1950s, Kimura founded his own puroresu company, Kokusai Pro Wrestling Association. While he would also work for the JWA, both teaming and opposing Rikidōzan, Kimura was often aggrieved at not getting the same level of attention despite his storied legitimate background. When the two men squared off for the JWA title for the first time, the match was meant to end in a draw, to enable both men to make more money by having rematches further down the line. What happened was quite different, and the consequences of the match could well have led to Rikidōzan's early death.

During the encounter, Kimura set himself up to receive a chop from Rikidōzan. Offering his chest up for the move, Kimura braced himself but Rikidōzan didn't follow the script. He chopped Kimura in the neck, as hard as he could, knocking the judoka out and winning the contest via KO. There would never be a rematch, and by the end of the decade Kimura had returned to real combat. Rikidōzan went from strength to strength, beating Lou Thesz (who he had become good friends with) for the NWA International title in August 1958 at around the same time that wrestling on Japanese television was a runaway success. Rikidōzan would hold that title until his death.

Thesz and Rikidōzan respected each other massively, so Thesz was never portrayed as a foreign villain in the same way that other gaijin would be. Freddie Blassie and The Destroyer were huge draws against Rikidōzan, the former causing heart attacks among television audiences as he sunk his teeth into his opponent's forehead, drawing blood and the latter loading up his mask with a foreign object to seek an illegal advantage. All three gaijin would achieve legendary status in Japan thanks to being around at the inception of puroresu, going from being hated to appreciated by the loyal Japanese wrestling fans.

Everything changed on 8 December 1963. Rikidōzan had invested much of his money in property and businesses, but Tokyo had a seedy underbelly that he operated on the fringes of. Even now, it is not unusual to hear mentions of yakuza involvement in professional wrestling; in 1963, the involvement proved fatal.

Enjoying an evening in a nightclub, Rikidōzan was about to call it a night when he was stabbed by yakuza member Katsushi Murata. Initially, Rikidōzan brushed it off as a slight wound, refusing medical help. Murata was kicked out of the nightclub, and it was only at the insistence of friends that Rikidōzan even spoke to a doctor, being told that the wound wasn't too serious. However, Murata had soaked his blade in urine, a common yakuza tactic, which poisoned the wound and caused Rikidōzan to develop peritonitis. He would die in hospital a week later, and Murata would be sent to prison for seven years.

Rumours have always persisted that Murata was put up to the stabbing by Kimura, but nothing has ever been proved. Rikidōzan did live a brash lifestyle and had plenty of enemies, but we'll never really know the full story. The JWA lived on but was challenged by another company in 1966 and in 1972 lost its two biggest stars, who happened to be Rikidōzan's best students.

The first rival to the JWA monopoly was the AWA-affiliated International Wrestling Enterprise (IWE), established in 1966 by Isao Yoshihara. With Rikidōzan dead, IWE capitalised on the doubt over the Japanese wrestling landscape and did decent business in their initial years. But the 1970s would belong to two different companies, both led by former friends turned rivals: Shohei Baba and Kanji Inoki.

Baba was a former professional baseball pitcher, standing a massive six feet ten inches tall and with a head like an Easter Island statue. He would wrestle as Giant Baba and was immediately groomed as the successor to Rikidōzan when he started training in 1960. Being so massive meant that Baba was always seen as a star from day one. Inoki began training at the same time as Baba, but he was different: seven inches shorter and aged just 17, five years younger. An athlete, Inoki moved to Brazil with his family at the age of 14 and won All-Brazil titles in shot-put and discus.

Inoki took the first name of Antonio, based on his time in South America, and was a favourite of Rikidōzan's, but he was definitely in his peer's shadow, both physically and metaphorically. While Baba enjoyed excursions to the USA to take on Buddy Rogers and Bruno Sammartino in Madison Square Garden for Vince McMahon Sr, and was the first NWA International champion after the death of their mentor, Inoki grew impatient for his own glory. In 1966 he left JWA, joining up with Tokyo Pro Wrestling and becoming their biggest star for a year before the company folded. Inoki found himself back in JWA by 1967 and teaming with Baba, who held the NWA International belt from 1965 until 1972, with the exception of a couple of super-quick switches with Bobo Brazil and Gene Kiniski. They'd form a formidable tag team called B-I Cannon, holding titles and being built up as virtually unbeatable. But Inoki still wasn't happy. In 1971 he was fired by JWA after plotting a coup to put him in charge of the company, so he started his own. To draw attention to the fact it would be based around his modern ideas, he called it New Japan Pro Wrestling, which is pretty cheeky. They had their first show in early 1972.

A few months after Inoki left and had started putting on his shows, Baba made his move. With JWA struggling financially and knowing that he was the biggest star in Japanese wrestling at the time, he started up a new promotion with Rikidōzan's sons Mitsuo and Yoshihiro, forcing JWA to strip him of the NWA International title that had lineage all the way back to Rikidōzan's historic clash with Lou Thesz. Baba's company would be called All Japan Pro Wrestling (AJPW), with a name so similar to Inoki's promotion that it had to be a dig aimed at his former tag team partner. Wrestling is nothing if not petty from time to time.

Baba's style of promoting meant that gaijin like the Funk brothers and Mil Máscaras became legendary in Japan, while NJPW brought through Japanese stars with legitimate fighting backgrounds like Masa Saito and Seiji Sakaguchi, the latter being one of very few wrestlers who broke Inoki's stranglehold at the top of the NJPW card in the 1970s. Both Baba and Inoki booked themselves as their respective company's biggest stars throughout their first decade, something that would be leapt upon by wrestling fans these days; but truth be told, Baba was a genuine oddity, due to his height, and a decent worker before age caught up with him, and Inoki was charismatic and tough and had his aforementioned clash with Muhammed Ali to back up his own legitimacy as a fighter.

In 1984, Baba recognised that at the age of 46 he should be looking to the next generation of wrestlers to cement AJPW's legacy. Baba built up new superstars like Jumbo Tsuruta and Genichiro Tenryu while NJPW had Akira Maeda and Satoru

Sayama, working under a hood as the comic book character Tiger Mask. It was the norm for Japanese wrestlers to train under difficult conditions at a company dojo before being sent on 'excursions' overseas to make them better wrestlers before they made an impact in their home promotions. Tsuruta – originally a Greco-Roman wrestler – and Tenryu – a sumo – were sent to Amarillo to train and work under the Funk brothers by Baba. Maeda and Sayama were sent to the UK, working as Kwik-Kik Lee and Sammy Lee respectively, their martial arts skills played up on *World of Sport* because in the late 1970s and Eighties stereotypes were still all the rage.

History has an odd way of repeating itself, and as big stars were built up by Baba and Inoki they too tried to make a break for it and start out on their own, making themselves the marquee names. Sayama – as Tiger Mask – had a series of wonderful matches with Dynamite Kid in both Japan and America (their MSG match on 30 August 1982 still looks amazing to this day, both men doing things that crowd had never seen before). Sayama held both the NWA and WWF Junior Heavyweight titles and was a massive star when, out of the blue, he decided to retire from wrestling in August 1983. Sick of backstage politics and shenanigans, he wanted to walk away while he was at the top. The world of wrestling was stunned.

Sayama set up his own gym to train martial artists. He would soon be tempted back to wrestling of sorts by Maeda in the newly-established UWF, the Universal Wrestling Federation, which had an emphasis on submission moves and strikes rather than traditional professional wrestling, known as 'shoot-style'. It wouldn't take long for Sayama to fall out with the rather loose cannon Maeda, as a worked contest became a real fight. Maeda would become notorious for shooting on people throughout his career, including one time with Andre the Giant. He'd eventually set up Fighting Network Rings in 1991, which became a legitimate MMA company in 1995, so it was fine for him to kick people for real.

AJPW had a slightly less frantic 1980s. Tsuruta was the first AJPW Triple Crown champion and went on to become a fine company man. Of course, Inoki was the first IWGP (International Wrestling Grand Prix) champion in NJPW before starting to build up his next star, Tatsumi Fujinami, along with Riki Choshu and gaijin like Big Van Vader (called Vader because of the Star Wars link to the name; the 'Big Van' bit came because Leon White, the man playing the role, allegedly drove a big van).

The second-ever Triple Crown champion was Genichiro Tenryu, but he had dreams of becoming the biggest star elsewhere so jumped from AJPW in 1990 to form a new company, Super World of Sports (SWS). This was backed by, bizarrely, a massive glasses company called Megane Super who had initially hired Tenryu as a spokesmodel. A partnership with WWF was established but it never drew great crowds and was out of business within a couple of years.

With Tenryu jumping ship and convincing many of his peers to make the leap with him, other men had to make the step up for Baba. While NJPW had its Three Musketeers (Keiji Mutoh, Shinya Hashimoto and Masahiro Chono) dominating their brand, AJPW went one better, both in terms of number of superstars that the promotion was built around and on the cool name front. They had the Four Pillars of Heaven, and they're one of the reasons I got into wrestling in as nerdy as way as I have. It was watching their tapes that really made me appreciate it as an art form, having to concentrate purely on the stories being told in the ring as there were no promos that I could understand and no vignettes with wrestling being presented in Japan more as a serious sport than in the USA.

The Four Pillars were Mitsuharu Misawa, formerly Tiger Mask II, now a hard-hitting, unmasked grappler who the promotion was pretty much built around; Toshiaki Kawada, Misawa's nemesis who wielded incredibly stiff kicks; Akira Taue, a former sumo wrestler who used his height advantage for great impact moves; and Kenta Kobashi, probably my favourite wrestler of all time, a man who absolutely had it all.

For most of the 1990s, AJPW, mainly through combinations of those four guys, was putting on the best matches on the planet. And while you might think that's down to a subjective opinion, they were also the highest-rated matches at the time, thanks to rave reviews from Dave Meltzer in his *Wrestling Observer* newsletter which was growing in popularity. Meltzer has a match rating system, going from -***** for something absolutely awful, upwards through DUD for a poor match, * or ** for something acceptable, *** for a good match, **** for a great match and ***** for something absolutely must-see. During the 1990s, AJPW had a ridiculous amount of five-star matches, some of them just tag team matches between the Four Pillars. Those guys couldn't have a bad match.

Some great bouts for you to seek out from that era include Kenta Kobashi and Tsuyoshi Kikuchi v Doug Furnas and Phil LaFon from May 1992 (Kobashi had just returned from an injury and the crowd went absolutely insane for everything he did); Kawada and Taue and Masanobu Fuchi v Misawa, Kobashi and Giant Baba from February 1994; Kobashi and Misawa v Steve

Williams and Johnny Ace from March 1995; and every single time Kawada and Misawa faced off.

During one match in 1999, Kawada used something called 'The Ganso Bomb', kind of by accident. Wrestling with a broken arm (that he'd suffered early in the match), Kawada went to power bomb Misawa but instead dropped him square on the top of his head in a spectacularly dangerous move, also sometimes called the 'Kawada Driver'. It's so insane he's only used it another two times since. On a related note, Kobashi's 'Burning Hammer' finisher has only ever been used seven times, on particularly stubborn opponents, and has never been kicked out of. That's another reason to love Japanese wrestling.

The only group that could rival AJPW during that time for the quality of matches and in-ring product from anywhere in the world was also in Japan. It came from the world of *joshi puroresu*; women's wrestling. In most other nations female talent was used for a match or two on a card that would be dominated by men, but in Japan it was more normal for promotions to specialise in putting on *only* women's matches. The industry leader was All Japan Women's Pro-Wrestling (AJW), formed in 1968 after an explosion in women's wrestling in the country in the 1950s had settled down somewhat. That initial burst of excitement came after a tour from Mildred Burke.

Dominating the joshi scene until the company closed its doors in 2005, in the 1980s AJW had notable stars like Jaguar Yokota, Devil Masami, The Crush Gals (Chigusa Nagayo and Lioness Asuka) and the wonderfully named Dump Matsumoto. TV ratings were a massive success and arena ticket sales were brisk, but it was in the early to mid Nineties that joshi wrestling really took off with stars like Manami Toyota, Bull Nakano, Aja Kong and Megumi Kudo. The matches back then were stiff and innovative, with quite a lot of the moves that we see being used on the independent circuit and beyond these days having been invented by Japanese women. Toyota in particular is one of my favourite wrestlers of all time, male or female. She has been given an unbelievable 17 five-star matches for her work by *The Wrestling Observer* between 1991 and 1995, as well as being named most outstanding wrestler by the same publication for 1995. Seek out any of her contests with Aja Kong from 1994 or 1995; they remain stellar to watch even two decades later.

That gets us roughly up to speed with the rest of the world. The influence of Europe, Mexico and Japan would cross over more into wrestling in the USA as the world got smaller from the 1980s onwards. We'll return to developments in these nations in later chapters. Some of it I happen to have seen first-hand.

JIM'S TOP TEN: FEMALE WRESTLERS

I am certainly aware that this book, such is the nature of the history of wrestling, is somewhat of a sausage-fest. But women's wrestling has pushed some brilliant talents to the forefront of the business, and some of my favourite grapplers of all time just happen to be female. The industry these days is more equal than it ever has been, and that's absolutely for the best. Here's my top ten (and I know there's lots of great names that haven't made the list):

10. The Jumping Bomb Angels (Noriyo Tateno and Itsuki Yamazaki)
The first female wrestlers I remember being blown away by as a kid, after watching them team against The Glamour Girls (Leilani Kai and Judy Martin) in a two-out-of-three-falls match for the WWF Women's Tag Team Championship in an absolute classic of a match. They were hitting crazy tag team moves years before anyone else.

9. Lita
After training in Mexico and breaking into the business in ECW as Miss Congeniality, Lita's big break came in WWE, first managing Essa Rios and then, more notably, being part of Team Xtreme with Matt and Jeff Hardy. Her long-standing feud with Trish Stratus was an oasis in the desert of women's wrestling in WWE at the time.

8. Kyoko Inoue
One half of the tag team Double Inoue with namesake (but non-relative) Takako, Kyoko is notably the first woman to have won a men's championship in Japan (the DDT Ironman Championship, which is, admittedly, a slightly comedic title that has had 1,288 reigns at the time of writing and has been held by several inanimate objects). She's

also responsible for a flurry of fine matches in AJW between 1992 and 1995.

7. Awesome Kong

I went to see TNA in June 2008 in Coventry, and the match I remember loving the most was between Gail Kim and Awesome Kong for Kong's TNA Women's title. It only went five minutes or so but it was really stiff, and established Kong – who had a brief run as Kharma in WWE – as an absolute killer, full of power moves.

6. Aja Kong

Two Kongs in a row: Awesome got her name in Japan by replacing Aja on a show, eventually forming a team in the Gaea Japan promotion called W Kong. That was in 2004, by which point Aja already had a glittering career behind her. Still wrestling today, she is arguably the greatest-ever heavyweight women's wrestler, inventing countless signature moves and knocking foes out with her 'Uraken' spinning backfist. Aja had a brief run in the WWF in 1995, but it was back in Japan where her matches with Manami Toyota in 1994 and 1995 were really special.

5. Charlotte Flair

When you watch Charlotte on WWE television, two things hit you. One, it's obvious with her poise and in-ring skill that she is the daughter of Ric Flair. Two, it's astonishing how brilliant she has looked since the very start of her career, beginning fairly late on with her training and quickly making a name for herself in brilliant matches in NXT.

4. Bull Nakano

With face paint and huge, spiked hair, Nakano was always one of the most striking competitors in wrestling. She also had one of the best-named finishing moves – her 'Bull's Poseidon' piledriver. After nine years in AJW she spent time in the USA before retiring in 1997 due to injuries. Oddly enough, she went on to become a professional golfer for a short while after wrestling.

3. Asuka

Previously known as Kana and having enjoyed a great run throughout independent wrestling in both Japan and the USA, in 2015 Asuka was born, taking her hard-hitting style to NXT and quickly becoming women's champion there. Undefeated in her entire time there, it took a defeat in an amazing match with Charlotte Flair at *WrestleMania 34* to eventually halt her winning streak at 914 days, but not before winning the first-ever women's *Royal Rumble* match in January 2018.

2. Sara Del Rey

Now responsible for the training of exciting new talent at the WWE performance centre (where she is assistant head coach), Del Rey is one of the greatest wrestlers – male or female – to have never had a run as a competitor in WWE. Her work in Ring of Honor and Chikara is particularly brilliant, and the future of wrestling is definitely in very safe hands.

1. Manami Toyota

Not only the greatest woman to ever compete in professional wrestling, but one of the greatest-ever wrestlers full stop. Involved in a frightening amount of five-star matches, she has been brilliant from her debut at the age of 16 in 1987, to her retirement in November 2017, where she wrestled 51 one-minute-long matches against a series of opponents, before eventually losing over three falls to her hand-picked successor Tsukasa Fujimoto to end her career.

Chapter Nine:
Bigger, Better, Badder

WrestleMania III, the passing of Hogan's torch and the birth of 'Sports Entertainment'

The WWF was riding the crest of a wave in 1987, with business on the up and interest in the company so high that Vince decided to set up something really special. Buoyed by selling out three venues in three cities for *WrestleMania 2*, he knew that he could go one step further. *WrestleMania* broke new ground. *WrestleMania 2* broke new records. *WrestleMania III* had to be big. Massive. Enormous.

When 'Mean' Gene Okerlund came out during *WrestleMania III* to announce the attendance, it was an absolutely astronomical number; a number that stood as the record crowd for an indoor stadium until the Pope drew a bigger attendance; a number that was the record documented wrestling crowd for some time until a show in North Korea overtook it (and if we're being honest, maybe not everybody at that show wanted to be there); a number that I, first watching the show as a kid, could only equate with massive football matches in the 1950s: 93,173.

This monster crowd packed into the colossal Pontiac Silverdome on the outskirts of Detroit on 29 March 1987 to watch what would be the high point for wrestling in the Eighties. The entire industry had shifted from the hustlers in their own little territories to a massive, brightly coloured pop-culture phenomenon. When Vince wanted to go national he couldn't have imagined this in even his wildest dreams. Sure, people have said since that maybe there was only 78,000 people there, but I'll tell you this as a wrestling promoter: I absolutely would have taken that. I'm delighted with 700.

Before we look at the rest of the decade I think it's important to examine this show to see exactly why the public was so caught up in the enthusiasm for it. In hindsight, you can say it had arguably the biggest match and the best match of the decade, but they certainly weren't the same contest. Nearly every match had been meticulously set up by the WWF, and with 12 matches on the card that's a lot of prep work to do.

Only two matches went over ten minutes, an amazing statistic when you consider that Ric Flair in JCP/NWA was still routinely having matches lasting 45–60 minutes, and that a decade before even the most basic matches tended to always go over ten minutes. This was an echo of the culture that WWF had tapped into, attention spans getting ever shorter. Only one match would even get close to the 15-minute mark. By the time the 'Attitude Era' was in full swing just over a decade later, match times on televised shows would become even shorter in order to capture the goldfish minds among the prized 18–30 demographic.

Compared to the first *WrestleMania* two years prior, there was much less celebrity involvement even for a show of this scale, proof if needed that the wrestlers were now the celebrities. Hogan, Piper, Andre, Savage, Heenan, Steamboat, Roberts and so on were as recognisable to the American youth as any film or TV star. That said, compared to Gene Okerlund having to do double duty singing the national anthem at the first *'Mania*, this time around they had a star befitting of the scale of the venue, with Aretha Franklin singing 'America The Beautiful' to kick the event off.

The undercard was interesting, but not spectacular. Highlights included Harley Race, in the twilight of his in-ring career, going up against the immensely popular but out-of-his-league Junkyard Dog, and Brutus Beefcake, chum of Hulk Hogan, turning face after being on the losing side with Greg 'The Hammer' Valentine against the Fabulous Rougeau Brothers.

It took up to the sixth contest for things to get really memorable, though. That bout was between two gems of 1980s wrestling: One you already know all about, 'Rowdy' Roddy Piper, the fast-talking Scotsman (via Canada) who by *WrestleMania III* was a full-blown babyface and arguably the second most popular man in the company after Hogan. His opponent was the underrated superstar Adrian Adonis.

Sadly, Adonis would be dead just over a year after this match – back on the territorial circuit after being let go by the WWF, he was thrown from the window of a van as it swerved to avoid a moose on a road in Newfoundland and plummeted off a bridge. His performance in this match, and the feud leading up to it, is how we should remember such a brilliant talent.

Adonis began his wrestling life as an athletic, leather-clad biker character before becoming 'Adorable Adrian' during his WWF tenure, wearing tons of make-up, pink ring gear, scarves and dresses. Like Gorgeous George on crack, it was that effeminate, preening gimmick turned up to 11 for the MTV generation, made even more effective by the toughness of the man playing the role. Now overweight and out of shape, he remained one hell of a worker despite being around 350 pounds at his heaviest. New Yorker Adonis had been a WWF Tag Team Champion in the early Eighties, forming a North-South connection with fellow tough guy Dick Murdoch from Texas.

While Piper was on a break from the WWF of a few months in 1986, Adonis started his own rival to Piper's Pit, called The Flower Shop. This segment was a big part of WWF television, and was used to set up the feud between Hulk Hogan and Paul Orndorff during 1986 that drew good money wherever it went. With Piper stating that he would soon be off to Hollywood full time (he starred in the fantastic *They Live* and the terrible *Hell Comes to Frogtown*), this would be his retirement match and needed to be set up with the right amount of gravitas. And yes, you're right, of course he didn't retire after it. This is wrestling. You could never make a cops-type film starring wrestlers; nobody is ever really one day away from retirement.

When Piper returned to the WWF, he wanted to start his Pipers Pit segments again, leading to a clash between the two shows-within-a-show. This led to Adonis, with Bob Orton and Don Muraco, destroying the Pipers Pit set, beating down Piper and smearing his face with red lipstick. Later, Piper would destroy the Flower Shop set with a baseball bat, and the match was made with hair v hair stipulations. Whoever lost would have to have their head shaved. If you think about it, that should have revealed that Piper wasn't going to lose on his way out, unless he needed the shaven head for a film role.

(As a cool side note, Piper often wore a leather jacket during the 1980s; ironically, it had been given to him by Adonis during a Pipers Pit segment when Adonis first started moving away from his biker character – the two men were good friends outside of the ring. Ronda Rousey wore a leather jacket of Piper's for her WWE debut at 2018's *Royal Rumble*.)

For the match itself, Adonis was seconded by manager Jimmy Hart, known as 'The Mouth of the South'. Having made his name in Memphis, Hart was a bona fide rock star of sorts, having been part of the band The Gentrys in the Sixties, who had a hit single. By the late Seventies he was still working in music, but broke into wrestling thanks to his school friend Jerry Lawler, the biggest star in the Memphis territory. As well as being one of the most well-known managers in wrestling history, Hart is also famous for composing a huge amount of theme tunes for wrestlers in both WWF/WWE and WCW.

During the match, Adonis locked a sleeper hold on to Piper, believing he had forced him to pass out and celebrating before the referee had a chance to hold and release Piper's hand to test if he was conscious. As Adonis and Hart celebrated, the now babyface Brutus Beefcake came to ringside to help try and bring Piper round. He did, Piper locked Adonis in his own sleeper and Adorable Adrian went soundly to sleep. With Adonis still out cold, Piper tried to cut his hair but struggled; Beefcake took over, accidentally giving him the 'Barber' gimmick that would stick with him for much of his career. As Adonis woke up, there's a wonderful, almost cinematic shot of him seeing his face in the mirror and realising that his bleached blond locks had been shorn off. He left with Hart's jacket over his face as the crowd bid an emotional farewell to Piper.

The best match on the show, and arguably of the decade, was up next. After six months of feuding, Ricky Steamboat would challenge Intercontinental Champion 'Macho Man' Randy Savage for his title. The wild and unpredictable Savage had attacked Steamboat on TV, dropping him throat-first on a guard-rail, dropping an elbow on his neck and using the ring bell to crush his larynx.

Savage had arrived in the WWF from Memphis and was already looking like a megastar. The son of a wrestler (Angelo Poffo), he'd had a chance to play baseball professionally but went into the family business instead and his gruff voice and wild-eyed intensity made him stand out from the crowd.

Steamboat, in contrast, was the ultimate babyface, a handsome New Yorker of half-English, half-Japanese parentage who would famously never turn heel in his entire career, an incredible rarity especially as he was still performing in the 1990s. He had enjoyed a great run in JCP before being tempted to the WWF. Both guys could really go. This match would prove that.

Savage was accompanied by his manager (and in real life, wife) Miss Elizabeth, an almost-mute valet who would wear evening dresses and always look like she was on the verge of tears. Steamboat was seconded by a now babyface George 'The Animal' Steele, not teaching PE that week. This match went to nearly 15 minutes, but it feels like only five minutes. I watched it maybe two years after the original event, on a double-volume VHS tape and immediately watched it back again for a second time. The speed of the match, the technical skill, the intensity, it's all there. This is a great example of a match that was, apparently, incredibly rehearsed; I've mentioned that some wrestlers like to go out there and just work it out as they go, knowing what big moves or spots are markers that they need to hit. Savage was the opposite, obsessive about getting everything right, so both men had rehearsed every single thing several times by the time the match actually went ahead. This certainly wasn't the norm at the time, nor is it now.

Crucially, both men liked each other. Savage would enthuse to his brother Lanny how much he loved Steamboat and how he wanted to make him look a million dollars in this match. And he did so, just as Steamboat did for him. For there to be so many near-falls in that short space of time, all of them believable, is unheard of in matches of that era. There was still time for shenanigans too, with Steele stopping Savage from cheating with the ring bell during the match.

Steamboat eventually rolled Savage up with a small package to win the title to a massive ovation. Despite this, he wouldn't be around for much longer. After asking for some time off shortly after winning the title (his wife had recently given birth), he attracted the annoyance of WWF management who had put the title on him expecting him to be available to defend it across the USA. He dropped the title and was back wrestling for what was JCP by 1989, where depending on your point of view, he topped the quality of this match at least once (against Flair, as I'll come to later).

Then there was the main event: Hulk Hogan v Andre the Giant. This was also built fantastically, and not just by having no bouts on the day that could match up to its importance. Most of the first part of 1987 was given over on WWF television to making this seem as monumental as possible, but if you think about it, it had been building since Vince McMahon Sr gave Andre some advice way back in the 1970s. Don't ever lose. Don't go off your feet. Look absolutely unbeatable. Andre had always been a beloved babyface, but for this contest he was allowed to get mean and become a heel. It's hard to imagine such a massive man being a fan favourite for so long, especially as nowadays any giant wrestler tends to be booked as a villain for a good portion of their career because it's easy to make the crowd understand why they should hate them; after all, everybody has been bothered by somebody bigger than them in their lifetime.

The storyline between the two biggest stars in the WWF began on an episode of Piper's Pit in January 1987, with Hogan being awarded a trophy for keeping the WWF Championship for three years straight. Andre, one of his closest friends, came out to congratulate him. The following week, Andre was awarded a trophy himself for being the only undefeated wrestler in history. Now we know that isn't true, as even in the WWF he had lost matches via count out. He had certainly never been pinned in any contest for Vince though, or his father. He had been beaten in other companies, but they were outside the WWF bubble so didn't count. The important thing was that Andre's trophy was markedly smaller than Hogan's. This time, Hogan came out to congratulate Andre, but he quickly became the centre of attention. Annoyed, Andre left.

The key to any good heel character is that *they* have to feel justified in their actions, even if the crowd hate them for it. By sloping away during a celebration, Andre had sowed the seed in the minds of the fans that he was angry. And he had a point – Hogan was certainly being a bit of a dick.

In early February, a Piper's Pit was scheduled to get both men together and discuss what had happened previously. Hogan came out first, which should have signposted that something was afoot. Andre was next out, but not alone. He was accompanied by Bobby Heenan, who immediately accused Hogan of only being friends with Andre to keep him away from his title belt. Hogan tried to smooth things over, but Andre challenged him to a match, and in one of the most iconic images of wrestling in the 1980s, the massive Frenchman ripped the silver crucifix from around Hogan's neck.

Two weeks before 'Mania there was an edition of *Saturday Night's Main Event* where both men took part in a battle royal. Andre eliminated Hogan, in the eyes of the fans giving him an advantage over the champion. What fans *didn't* know is that Andre was constantly in immense pain. His gigantism had put tremendous pressure on his joints and back, and he was a shell of the man he once was. Hugely immobile and struggling with the constant travel required of a top professional wrestler, he had to be convinced by Vince to take part in this mammoth match while on set filming the classic *Princess Bride*.

A wonderful urban legend surrounds Andre and the back surgery that he had to have in order to even make it to this match, prior to his acting role. The assigned anaesthetist had no idea what dosage to give him to knock him out as he was so massive, so simply asked Andre how much alcohol it took him to get drunk in order to work it out. The answer was a lot; various wrestlers have told tales of him drinking over 100 beers in one sitting and referee Tim White (who often acted as his driver on the road) often had to tow a little trailer behind his car with Andre's booze in it.

When it came to the match, Andre made his long journey to

the ring in a motorised cart, raised a few feet above the crowd. They pelted him and Heenan with trash every single inch of the way. Hogan walked to ring, gesticulating wildly as always as the enormous crowd lost their minds at the very sight of him. It had built to this on the biggest show possible: a real-life superhero up against a colossal mega-villain.

The match, with Hogan's limitations as a worker and Andre's health issues, was by no means a classic. In football terms, it's the ugly 1–0 win that enables you to win the league title, with a sense of occasion and importance but nervy and only memorable for the roar of the crowd and a couple of key moments; yet it is hugely significant and will be remembered by so many more people than everything else that happened that year. Or decade. Or era.

A couple of minutes in there was the first big moment: Hogan went to slam Andre, trying to hoist him up, but like everyone before him (in the WWF at least), he failed. He collapsed under the considerable weight of his foe, prone as the referee counted a pinfall attempt from Andre. Legend has it that if he wanted to, Andre could have ruined the whole thing and not allowed Hogan to kick out, and it was the very closest of two counts. One of my biggest fears as a promoter is that a wrestler will not kick out of a planned near fall, and if I'd have been in Vince's shoes at that point my heart would have been in my mouth.

Hogan got in a few good flurries, but most of the match had Andre on the offence, which meant the match was slow and methodical rather than fast or exciting. Wrestling is all about moments, though, and the finish of the match would provide one that we're still talking about now as one of the most important ever. Andre went for a big boot, but Hogan ducked and smashed his opponent with a clothesline, knocking him off his feet for the first time in the match (and for the first time in a WWF ring in a very long time). The crowd was on its feet as Hogan hulked up, shaking his head and arms as he did so, sending droplets of sweat flying. He scooped Andre up for another body slam attempt, and this time the Giant allowed him to do it, helping Hogan to slam him to the mat. A few seconds and a leg drop from Hogan later, the match was over. Andre was finally defeated, after 15 years of slightly retconned WWF history. Hogan had been cemented as the biggest and brightest star of them all. It was going to take something unbelievably cunning to get that title from around his waist. (Luckily, Vince and his cohorts had a genuinely brilliant plan.)

The show itself had been a huge success: Savage and Steamboat had been an absolute classic; Piper and Adonis had delivered a contest full of character, humour and emotion; and while Hogan v Andre certainly wasn't a catch as catch can masterpiece, it felt suitably enormous in the cavernous Silverdome. $1.6 million in ticket sales, $10 million in pay-per-view revenue from viewers at home and even more on top from 160 closed circuit locations screening the show meant it had also been a financial bonanza. Best of all, the show had been built around that one final body slam from Hogan and that wasn't even the first time he'd slammed Andre. He'd done it in the early Eighties before he was a megastar. Nobody cared now though. The feud between Hulkster and Giant would rumble on, and in turn that would help the WWF create a new megastar.

WrestleMania IV in 1988 wasn't exactly the massive spectacle that the previous year had been, but it certainly had a lot of intrigue around it. It was the first time Donald Trump would be around the WWF with the show in Atlantic City, and it was the first-ever 'Mania without a certain chap called Hulk Hogan going into it as champion. In fact, nobody held the belt. It was vacant for the first time in company history thanks to arguably the greatest one-night wrestling angle ever.

'Mania itself was a mammoth 16-match show as a tournament was held in order to crown a new WWF champion. Booking any form of tournament is difficult, and thanks to double disqualifications a couple of matches became byes in order to keep things moving along and to give heel characters an advantage. A new champ was needed partly to keep things fresh, but mainly because Hogan was off to film the WWF-funded No Holds Barred. Rewind a few weeks and you can see how this was all set up, as Hogan went into his 1,474th (and final) day as WWF champion.

With Saturday Night's Main Event being such a ratings success, WWF was given a prime-time slot on network television on a Friday night for the cleverly titled The Main Event. Records were broken for the number of viewers watching wrestling that night, with over 30 million people tuned in. Five editions of The Main Event were made in total between 1988 and 1991, with the first three airing live on NBC. The show was only an hour long, so only three matches were shown and the match everybody was tuned in to see on 5 February 1988, Hogan v Andre, was the second of those three in case it got cut off by the strict TV time slot. It doesn't bear thinking about having the show end with an angle half-finished; the tag team title match between Strike Force and the Hart Foundation took the bullet that evening, going to black a few minutes in.

Hogan's feud with Andre had been rumbling on since

WrestleMania III, and now the massive Frenchman had 'The Million Dollar Man' Ted DiBiase as his benefactor and de facto manager, with lackey Virgil also helping him out. The simple story was that DiBiase, one of the best heels of the 1980s, wanted Hogan's title and was willing to bankroll anybody who helped him get it. For this encounter between Andre and Hogan, he wore what is possibly the greatest suit in the history of clothing, a sparkly silver number that made sure you knew his character was rich, even if he never said a word. Virgil wore something nearly as sparkly, but you know that he would be doing the dirty work as it was sleeveless. Wrestling is the only profession where you can get away with such a fashion choice.

With so many viewers watching the show, if you're going to run a crazy angle then you need to absolutely get it right at the first time of asking. The match itself was only nine minutes long. Andre, still suffering immense pain, was certainly not going to be able to wrestle an hour-long classic. But this wasn't about the match, even though the crowd was hot for anything that Hogan did and booed mercilessly every time that DiBiase and Virgil got involved.

Referee Dave Hebner was frequently distracted by the men on the outside of the ring, including not counting a pinfall after Hogan had knocked Andre down and hit his patented legdrop. When Andre was next on his feet, he grabbed Hogan and threw him with one of the ugliest moves in the history of wrestling, somewhere between a suplex and hip toss but certainly not enough to put a man like Hogan down. Andre made the cover, and Hebner counted to three despite Hogan clearly getting his shoulder up at two. Vince McMahon and Jesse Ventura on commentary sold the whole situation immediately, so everyone knew something was afoot.

Hebner took the title belt and handed it to Andre as ring announcer Howard Finkel told the live audience that they had a new champion. They seemed to be in disbelief, booing but at a volume that said they expected something else to occur. Andre then did an interview in the ring, accidentally calling his new belt the tag team title before giving it to DiBiase, strapping it around his waist and making *him* the champion, showing that he'd been bought off. The heel group left the ring, leaving Hogan livid within it, protesting that he kicked out and pleading with the fans to somehow help him reverse the decision. Eventually, like a drawn-out scene in a movie, he turned around (and the camera picked up) and saw that in the ring with him were two referees. Dave Hebner . . . and another Dave Hebner. Identical. Arguing with each other. And 30 million viewers screamed: 'What on earth is going on?'

What had happened was some seriously clever planning. Dave Hebner had not refereed the match at all; his twin brother Earl had. Dave had been in the WWF for a few years, while Earl had been working for JCP right up until this event. They'd never tried the twin gimmick before, but here it worked perfectly with Hogan even suggesting, post-match, that they weren't even twins and DiBiase's money had just paid for amazing plastic surgery. With Hogan grabbing both men, then letting them go, confused as to what had happened or what to do, the twins argued with each other, with Earl eventually hitting Dave and kicking him out of the ring, legitimately breaking his ribs (hey, they were referees; they weren't used to having to choreograph a fight). Hogan now realised that Earl, the aggressor, must be the impostor, so lifted him high above his head and launched him into the entranceway, on top of DiBiase, Virgil and Andre. With

Earl being so small, Hogan threw him way too hard, the tiny referee nearly overshooting the men he was meant to use for a soft landing.

WWF on-screen figurehead president Jack Tunney decreed that you can only win the WWF title, it cannot just be handed over, so Andre had actually vacated the title in giving it to DiBiase. The tournament for *WrestleMania IV* was set, but with Andre and Hogan meeting again in the second round and becoming the focal point for the advertising campaign for the show. Their match would end in a double disqualification to give DiBiase a bye in his semi-final match, keeping him fresh for his opponent in the final and making the lines of heel and face clearly drawn. DiBiase would be booed. The crowd would all be rooting for their new favourite: Randy Savage.

Savage had turned face during 1987, with fans starting to cheer him because he was so exciting and was accompanied by the glamourous Miss Elizabeth. When the Honky Tonk Man dethroned Ricky Steamboat to become Intercontinental Champion, he decided to declare that he was the greatest IC champ of all time, bringing out Savage and starting a feud. By October 1987, the final piece was in place to ensure that he would always be cheered. In the midst of Savage being beaten down by Honky and the Hart Foundation on an edition of *Saturday Night's Main Event*, Elizabeth ran backstage to get help, returning with Hulk Hogan. The Mega Powers were born, creating storylines that would populate the top of WWF cards for the next year and a half and ensuring that even when Hogan was away filming, his ties to Savage meant he was still the biggest star in the company.

The Savage v DiBiase main event of *WrestleMania IV* wasn't

exactly the title tournament final that would win match of the year awards, but Savage had already beaten three opponents that night. DiBiase had only needed to beat two. 'The Macho Man' would be victorious, winning the WWF title and becoming the first new champion for four years, but only thanks to the help of Hogan who neutralised the threat of Andre and Virgil and smacked DiBiase with a steel chair to allow Savage to hit his top rope elbow drop and get the victory.

Word has it that Vince wanted to pit Savage against Ric Flair at the first-ever *Summerslam* in August of 1988, but Flair remained loyal to JCP and the NWA. We wouldn't have to wait forever to see those guys go at it, however. *Summerslam* was the final piece of the 'Big Four' WWF pay-per-view shows, alongside *WrestleMania, Survivor Series* and *The Royal Rumble*. Savage did headline this show, albeit in a tag team match with Hogan against DiBiase and Andre, billed as The Mega Powers v The Mega Bucks. (The pedant in me dislikes that they used 'Mega' in two team names – somebody should have used a thesaurus.)

This huge tag match was the high point for The Mega Powers alliance, as Hogan wanted his title belt back around his waist, so some manoeuvring would need to be done. In this match, the moment everybody remembers is Elizabeth, always quiet and demure at ringside, jumping onto the apron and whipping off her skirt to reveal her red underwear, stopping everyone dead in their tracks and allowing the faces to pick up the victory via an elbow drop then leg drop combination. Heel commentator Jesse Ventura was referee, so when he counted to three slowly Hogan forced his hand down for the decisive third count.

The Mega Powers rapidly went downhill from there, with jealously starting to build on-screen between Savage and Hogan, mainly based around Hogan's relationship with Elizabeth, who had started managing both men. Their real-life marriage was never brought up on screen, for reasons you'll understand later on. Hogan would eliminate Savage from the 1989 *Royal Rumble* leading to friction before, to borrow a phrase, The Mega Powers exploded at the second *Main Event* prime-time special in February 1989. The break-up led directly to the main event of *WrestleMania* V, where Hogan would take on Savage who was now a heel again.

The other match of real note at the inaugural *Summerslam* only lasted 31 seconds. The Honky Tonk Man had been Intercontinental Champion for over a year, constantly cheating to keep the title around his waist or just walking away from a challenge, as the title couldn't change hands via a count out. He was scheduled to face Brutus Beefcake, but 'The Barber' was injured (thanks to a heavily censored attack by 'Outlaw' Ron Bass and his spurs on TV) and couldn't make it. With no opponent, Honky issued a challenge to anyone to come and face him. His plea was answered by a heavy metal track playing what sounded an awful lot like a facsimile of Black Sabbath's *Paranoid* and an incredibly muscular, vascular, face-painted man sprinting to the ring. His name was The Ultimate Warrior.

One slam, clothesline and splash later, and Warrior was the new champion. As a kid, I adored him. Sure, his promos made absolutely no sense whatsoever, his matches were rarely particularly great, and he was so unbelievably muscular that he looked like a condom filled with walnuts, but he was a star.

He had started in the territories as part of Powerteam USA, a group of very green bodybuilders who broke in when everybody caught up with what Billy Graham had started to popularise in the late 1970s. Alongside him in this group, and later in the tag team, The Blade Runners, was Steve Borden, later known as Sting and gaining the same level of popularity as Warrior in WCW.

Warrior had started to get some traction as Dingo Warrior in Texas for WCCW (World Class Championship Wrestling) before WWF came calling. He took the name 'The Ultimate Warrior' there, reasoning that would put him a notch above Kerry Von Erich, billed as 'The Modern-Day Warrior'. Warrior's birth name was Jim Hellwig, but as he started to become slightly more insane thanks to the ravages of fame in the 1990s, he changed his name, legally, to Warrior. He was just one of a glut of massively muscular guys starting to change what the industry looked like, alongside Rick Rude, Dino Bravo, The Warlord and of course, Hogan in WWF, and Sting and Leg Luger in WCW. Wrestlers were starting to look less like barroom brawlers and much more like living, breathing comic book characters.

WrestleMania V was subtitled 'The Mega Powers EXPLODE' around the main event of Randy Savage v Hulk Hogan. The two men put together an 18-minute match that was certainly one of Hulk's best of the era, mainly because of Savage being a step up in terms of a skilled opponent. Elizabeth was assigned a neutral corner for the contest, but Savage, acting the heel, would hide behind her when Hogan advanced towards him outside of the ring. Later in the match Elizabeth went to check on her real-life husband, but he pushed her away. She kept trying to help him until she was sent backstage by the referee. With her gone, Savage fell victim to the usual Hogan method: Hulk up, clothes-line, big boot, leg drop. Hogan was champ once more.

The feud continued though; first off, after the show had gone off air, Savage fired Elizabeth as his manager and replaced her with Sensational Sherri, a much more heel-orientated valet who used to scare the living daylights out of me.

With Hogan starring in *No Holds Barred*, he ended up in a feud with the actor Tiny Lister, who played his nemesis in the film: Zeus. This was dressed up as Zeus (he always went by that name) wanting revenge in real life for things that happened in the film, even though he was now feuding with Hulk Hogan the actor, not the character (Rip Thomas) from the film. Confused yet? You should be.

At *Summerslam 89*, Zeus and Savage went up against Hogan and Brutus Beefcake in a tag team match; there would also be a film tie-in wrestling show after a screening of the movie on TV in December 1989.

Hogan had a go at acting in a few films, but none ever really matched up with his performance in *Rocky III* that made his wrestling career skyrocket. *No Holds Barred* isn't as awful as people make it out to be, if only because wrestling fans can try to spot other wrestlers in the fight scenes. It's worth seeking out another Hogan vehicle, *Mr Nanny*, for one scene that most people missed but has been immortalised on the internet since. Hogan rides along the road on a Harley Davidson, and behind him at one point a man throws a dog into a river. That man was definitely *not* an actor.

With the challenge of Savage now nullified by Hogan, he needed a new challenger. This time, the WWF would go down a different route. Instead of turning someone heel or building up an existing villain, they decided to have the main event of *WrestleMania VI* between two babyfaces, the first time they had attempted this during the WrestleMania era. Throughout 1989, one man had gained enough traction to fit into this role, a man who had been shifting merchandise well and getting loud reactions from the fans: the Intercontinental Champion, The Ultimate Warrior.

WrestleMania VI was dubbed 'The Ultimate Challenge' and was the first *'Mania* I ever saw within a day of the original screening – I went backwards to watch the others after seeing this one. Nearly 68,000 people turned up for the show in Toronto on 1 April 1990, the first-ever *WrestleMania* from outside the USA (there still hasn't been one staged outside of North America).

As well as the main event that had captured the imagination of WWF fans, the show featured Andre the Giant's last televised WWF match, with him turning face after losing the tag team titles he held with Haku to Demolition. Andre would pass away in 1993, dying in his sleep in Paris after returning home to attend his father's funeral. Heart failure was cited as the cause of death, and his body was returned to the USA to be cremated, his ashes scattered across the ranch in North Carolina where he'd lived for many years.

The marquee match had been set in motion at the *Royal Rumble* that year, after the Warrior had come off a feud with Andre that he had dominated, often squashing him in incredibly short matches that both got Warrior over and protected Andre's many ailments. During the Rumble, Hogan was one of three men to eliminate Warrior, clotheslining him as The Barbarian and Rick Rude struggled to get him over the top rope. The reaction to this elimination told Vince that Warrior was certainly at main-event level, with Hogan seeking the challenge to see if it was Hulkamania or the Power of the Warrior that was the strongest force in the WWF.

The match itself was genuinely very good, despite neither guy being a worker at the level of Ric Flair, Randy Savage or Rick Steamboat. Their star power was enough to get them into the main event, and they worked their socks off for 23 minutes in what is arguably the best match of both men's careers. With Warrior's face paint washed from his face by sweat, he eventually splashed Hogan to get the three count after an epic back-and-forth contest. Warrior was the first man to hold both the World and Intercontinental titles at the same time (he would have to give up the IC belt, shortly to be won by 'Mr Perfect' Curt Hennig), and at the end of the match Hogan handed his title to his rival, passing the torch to the man now expected to carry the WWF through the Nineties.

It really felt like the end of an era, and to an extent it was: Hulkamania was never the same force again. Behind the scenes too, things were shifting. The word *wrestling* was in its first throes of being phased out following a 1989 court case in New Jersey, where Vince was seeking deregulation of the complicated State Athletic Commission regulations placed on wrestling. Going massively against what everyone in the business had done before, he flat-out insisted that wrestling was pre-determined, so they didn't need to have the same restrictions on their events that, say, a boxing match would.

He said: ' . . . participants struggle hand-in-hand primarily for the purpose of providing entertainment to spectators rather than conducting a bona fide athletic contest.'

With that, the phrase 'sports entertainment' was born. Took a while to catch on, but my infant son will probably want to be a sports entertainer rather than a wrestler when he's older.

With the 1990s in full swing, more change was coming. One event in particular was about to shape the next few years of wrestling more than you could ever imagine, and it happened outside of the ring, a chain of events set off by a man who had never wrestled and just wanted to be one of the boys.

JIM'S TOP TEN: MANAGERS

A manager can really make the difference to the gimmick of a wrestler, and some managers are such brilliant talkers and performers that you'd pay money to watch *them* over the wrestlers they represent. Here's my ten favourites:

10. Zelina Vega

The newest name on this list, Vega was previously a wrestler for TNA, working under the name Rosita. She's currently working as the business-savvy manager of WWE star Andrade 'Cien' Almas, and far from being portrayed as eye candy she's seen as the reason that the once out-of-control party animal became the NXT champion and one of the best wrestlers on the planet.

9. Gedo

A fine tag team wrestler with partner Jado, Gedo has an important behind-the-scenes role at NJPW where he actually books the shows. On screen, he remains very much visible as the manager of long-standing champion Kazuchika Okada, very rarely getting involved in matches but often delivering intense promos before or after contests to hype up his Chaos stablemate.

8. Truth Martini

Having trained dozens of wrestlers and being a decent in-ring performer, Martini formed The House of Truth in Ring of Honor in 2010, using his own gimmick as a self-serving, smug quasi-life coach to take wrestlers under his wing and help them achieve their goals. He managed both Roderick Strong and Jay Lethal to the RoH World Championship.

7. Paul Ellering

Best known for managing The Road Warriors during their rise to prominence in the 1980s, Ellering wasn't just their on-screen handler. He helped do all of their business outside the ring as well. He also managed the Disciples of Apocalypse during the 'Gang Wars' era in late-1990s WWF, and until recently managed the massive Authors of Pain in NXT.

6. Jim Cornette

I'll be honest, he'd be higher in the list if he hadn't had told his podcast listeners that I should be hung in a car park for being scruffy. Personal differences aside, I couldn't make a list of managers and not include Cornette; his work in both NWA and WWF was stellar, a highly-strung cheat who would stop at nothing to help his teams win. Plus, he managed The Midnight Express *and* blew his knee out falling to the ring during a scaffold match. Fair play to him.

5. Stokely Hathaway

I was at an Evolve show in Orlando in 2017 and watched Hathaway walk down the aisle introducing his client Timothy Thatcher, addressing the crowd with wonderfully delivered insincerity. A great talent with an acting background, it's a shame managers aren't more prominent in modern wrestling. If he'd have been doing his thing in the late Eighties he would be a household name.

4. Miss Elizabeth

Elizabeth is high on the list for managing Randy Savage as he exploded into mainstream superstardom in the 1980s, as well as being part of the storyline that split Savage and Hulk Hogan up ahead of *WrestleMania V*. A quiet, almost shy character, she didn't always do loads at ringside but when she did do something, it tended to be impactful and memorable.

3. Sherri Martel

Known as Sensational Sherri, Queen Sherri, Sister Sherri and at one point, Peggy Sue, Martel was a respected wrestler who took over from Miss Elizabeth to manage Randy Savage after he turned heel on Hogan. Hard as nails and willing to get physical if a match or story needed it, she also managed Harlem Heat in WCW and was Shawn Michaels manager during his first singles run in the WWF.

2. Paul Heyman

Currently the advocate for Brock Lesnar, the fast-talking former head of ECW is always a highlight whenever he is on *Raw* to talk for his client. But prior to that, in the late 1980s and early Nineties, Heyman (as Paul E Dangerously) had his own stable in AWA and then WCW called the Dangerous Alliance and it was a force to be reckoned with, featuring talent like Steve Austin, Rick Rude and Arn Anderson, plus giving Heyman the chance to occasionally break a large mobile phone over opponent's heads.

1. Bobby Heenan

'The Brain'. Heenan was, quite simply, the best manager of all time. A wrestler himself in the 1970s who was known for being part of many a bloodbath, his first major management role was taking Nick Bockwinkel to the AWA title. From there he jumped to the WWF and managed a who's who of their top heels, including Andre the Giant and Ric Flair. One fan in Chicago in the 1970s took such umbrage to Heenan that he shot at him, missing his target but injuring several bystanders. Now *that's* heat.

Chapter Ten:
JCP to WCW

**Jim Crockett Promotions, The Four Horsemen,
Ted Turner and Ric Flair's amazing year**

The NWA territory system was somewhat creaking under the strain as Vince continued to expand the WWF nationally. The biggest group under the umbrella was JCP – Jim Crockett Promotions – based in Charlotte, North Carolina and set up in 1931 by Jim Crockett Sr. Run by his namesake son by the Eighties, it was JCP that was the driving force and promotion behind *Starrcade,* even if it appeared to the untrained eye to be an NWA show. Jim Crockett Jr wanted to echo what Vince had been doing and give him real competition, buying up other NWA territories or merging with them to grow his company's reach and influence. You'll remember it was Crockett who purchased the WWF timeslot on WTBS cable for a cool $1 million, and he wasn't shy about splashing the cash.

At one point, Crockett had teamed up with Ole Anderson's new Georgia territory, Verne Gagne's AWA and Jarrett Promotions in Memphis to form the short-lived Pro Wrestling USA company, putting on the *Superclash* show in Chicago in September 1985. Arguments between companies quickly led to the group's demise, but Crockett wasn't deterred. He just bought out Ole Anderson's group and with Mid-South falling by the wayside after failing to secure the WWF cable timeslot themselves, Crockett and JCP found themselves in control of all the wrestling timeslots on WTBS, making them to all intents and purposes a national organisation, just like the WWF.

It also helped that Crockett happened to be NWA President, using the power in that role to ensure the best possible results for his company. With business on the up, he established *The Great American Bash* in July 1985, a massive show in the American Legion Memorial Stadium in Charlotte, attended by 27,000 and shown on closed circuit pay per view, capitalising on the swell of interest in that form of viewing that *WrestleMania* had kicked into gear. It was a stacked show to kick things off, arguably a better show for a pure wrestling fan than *WrestleMania*, where the hook for some viewers was celebrity.

The Road Warriors, Hawk and Animal (a pair of massive bodybuilder types with spiked shoulder pads and a gimmick straight out of *Mad Max*) went to a double disqualification with The Russian Team of Ivan Koloff and the terribly named Krusher Kruschev, who would later be part of Demolition, the WWF's knock-off of the super-popular Road Warriors (Kruschev was really a Minnesota native called Barry Darsow and he trained alongside the Warriors); Magnum TA defeated Kamala by disqualification to retain the NWA United States Championship;

Ric Flair defeated Nikita Koloff to retain his NWA World Championship; and in the main event, a steel cage match, Dusty Rhodes beat Tully Blanchard to win both the NWA Television title and the services of Blanchard's valet, Baby Doll.

By 1985 Dusty Rhodes was the head booker for JCP and wielded considerable power, as well as being one of the most popular wrestlers in the country. The battle scarred, overweight man from Texas with big black circles around his tired eyes was an absolute superstar, against all sensible odds. Speaking with a lisp, he managed to make that impediment work for him and transitioned from a rugged tag team wrestler in his early career to a true working-class superstar by the end of the 1970s, drawing massive crowds in Florida and Georgia and making some serious money. He was 'The American Dream', billed by commentators as the son of a plumber and the ultimate example of a man who could talk a crowd into an arena. He could take a sympathetic beating too, before firing back with his bionic elbow and a little bit of funky dancing. If he had caught on as well in WWWF (where he appeared a few times in the late 1970s) as he did in the NWA, he may well have spent years as a champion. As it stands, he had a few runs at being on top, but always gave way to the NWA way of having a heel champion. He'd end up being known as much for a finish that he invented for other people's matches as the elbow that he'd drop on fallen opponents. He also helped come up with the original *Starrcade*. His legacy in wrestling is enormous.

It was a sign of how over Rhodes was that he was the main event at the first *Great American Bash* for a lesser title than Flair's, although that might have had more to do with the practicalities of having to build and dismantle a steel cage.

He was also very good at putting together wrestling shows, with a knack of knowing exactly how to tug on the emotions of a crowd. His work in JCP behind the scenes is often focused on what became known as the *Dusty Finish*, a bait-and-switch where the crowd thought the babyface had won a title, only for the decision to be reversed shortly afterwards on a technicality. It was used fairly regularly during the 1980s, but it's important to remember that it wasn't always at the behest of Dusty, who is remembered fondly by almost everyone who met him.

An in-joke in the WWF that started in 1987 demonstrated how well known Dusty's talents were. As mentioned before, Ted DiBiase worked under the gimmick of being 'The Million Dollar Man', an arrogant, rich man who asked fans to perform humiliating tasks for him in return for money. He was accompanied by a bodyguard and lackey – a preliminary wrestler called Mike Jones, but who went by the name Virgil, Dusty's real name.

It's rumoured that Bobby Heenan came up with the original idea. In 1996, Jones turned up in Ted Turner's WCW at the height of the war between them and the WWF. His name there was firstly Vincent, after McMahon, then it was changed in 1999 to Shane, after Vince's son who was now in a prominent role in the family business. Poor Mike Jones probably wished he could have just come up with his own name at some point, rather than being used in a gag that lasted over a decade.

Also booked in a prominent position on the *Great American Bash* card was Magnum TA. The 'TA' didn't signify that he was in the Territorial Army (although that would have been one heck of a reason for him to miss the odd weekend show), instead it stood for his real name, Terry Allen. Everyone at JCP and within the NWA had really high hopes for Magnum, who took his ring name from the fact that he was a good looking, moustachioed chap just like TV star Tom Selleck in *Magnum P.I.* He was great in ring, could talk and best of all, had the mysterious ingredient of charisma that just made people want to cheer for him. He was, in JCP regions at least, approaching Hogan-like popularity. He was scheduled to be the one to take the belt from Ric Flair and carry the brand into the latter part of the 1980s.

In October 1986, Magnum was driving his Porsche in Charlotte, just a few miles from his home. He lost control of his car in the rain, smashing into a telephone pole despite forensic proof that he wasn't speeding. Left in the car for over two hours after the accident before anybody called for the emergency services, his back was smashed to pieces with two of his vertebrae destroyed. Not only would he never wrestle again, doctors believed that he would almost certainly never walk again. He was paralysed and remained in hospital for several months.

The accident meant that Rhodes had to think fast to create a new hero, turning the hated Nikita Koloff into a fan favourite by having him show sympathy and respect for Magnum after they had feuded with each other for much of the year. The plan worked, and soon Koloff was getting great responses, albeit nowhere near the level that Magnum was getting in his pomp. By 1987, Magnum would return to wrestling, walking with canes and assisted by referees, to embrace Koloff and Rhodes at the final of the *Crockett Cup* tag team tournament. It remains one of the most emotional moments in wrestling, with many members of the audience in tears just at the sight of Magnum being able to move again.

Despite losing Magnum TA, JCP and the NWA had another trick up their sleeve. While the WWF usually had a babyface at the top of their cards – Sammartino, Morales, Backlund and now Hogan – they always seemed to have a villain, so that babyfaces in the territories could go after the champion when he came to town. Ric Flair tended to move between babyface and heel every now and then, but in late 1985 his stock as a heel rose immeasurably with the establishment of the greatest stable that ever existed in wrestling; the reason that groups of wrestlers have been thrown together with a common cause ever since and a group that all wrestling fans will argue about the best incarnation of: The Four Horsemen.

Harking back to a storyline from the 1970s in Mid-Atlantic Championship Wrestling, Flair had been named as storyline cousin to the Minnesota Wrecking Crew, Gene and Ole Anderson. Gene wasn't wrestling anymore by 1985, so a wrestler called Marty Lunde, who bore some resemblance to Ole, was brought in to become Arn Anderson. The most hated and brilliant Tully Blanchard and manager James J Dillon formed what was technically five horsemen, but we'll gloss over that for now. The whole history of the group starts to get really complicated in a few years' time.

The Horsemen caused chaos wherever they went, being involved in several believable and incredibly violent angles, especially as part of their feud with Dusty Rhodes where they attempted to break his arm in the car park outside JCP's offices, and his leg inside the ring during a match at the Omni in Atlanta. These days they'd be cheered though, because as well as being villainous they were incredibly cool, living the lifestyle that their gimmick suggested: flying in jets, travelling in limos, partying all night and being surrounded by beautiful women. There's every chance they were claiming this on expenses.

The group wasn't even officially named as the Horsemen at first, it was Arn who referred to himself and his teammates by the name and it kind of stuck, suggesting that the last guys who created such chaos and misery were the biblical Four Horsemen. All five men in the group were cornerstones of JCP, contracted to the group despite often being NWA titleholders, this meant that Crockett had a huge stranglehold on the World title in particular, which Flair held, on and off, for most of the 1980s. It was, if we're honest, just a little bit unfair.

I'll recommend right now that you watch the Tully Blanchard v Magnum TA cage match from *Starrcade* '85 to get a real feel for how compelling, bloody and violent truly great matches within JCP/NWA could be at this time, a real contrast to what WWF had on offer. In that match, for Blanchard's NWA US Championship, you could only win by making your opponent say 'I quit'. Even by today's standards, where wrestling from over 30 years ago can seem slow, this match is a work of barbaric art, ending only when Magnum broke a wooden chair, took a piece from it and drove it into the forehead of Blanchard, forcing him to say the magic words.

WWF was a juggernaut by 1987. At the same time, Jim Crockett was in his third term as NWA president. He still had his dream of aping what Vince had done and going truly national; *WrestleMania 2* had been broadcast from three locations: New York, Chicago and Los Angeles, showing that the pull of the WWF had spread from its roots as a territory in the North East to becoming a truly coast-to-coast organisation. By this point, JCP controlled the St Louis, Central States, Florida and Mid-South territories in addition to those that they already controlled in Georgia and the Carolinas. To secure those territories, Crockett had been spending money like it was going out of fashion. It was becoming clearer that JCP may be using the NWA name, but was definitely a separate and growing organisation. All of the top stars were contracted to JCP, not the NWA and the title would only ever switch to JCP guys.

In buying the struggling Mid-South territory from Bill Watts, Crockett spent money that he didn't actually need to. The UWF was struggling massively due to the dire economic recession affecting its Oklahoma base. Fans simply couldn't afford to buy tickets, no matter how many great stars Watts was creating. If Crockett had waited another couple of months, he probably could have swept up the territory for nothing. He did gain talent like Sting, Steve Williams and Rick Steiner for his money though, all of whom would become big stars.

Watts had been running his organisation from an office in Dallas, and Crockett, presumably remembering that everybody had seen the dusty car park of the JCP offices during the Horsemen/Rhodes angle, decided to base himself there. Rhodes would join him, with the Charlotte office being kept on. Crockett would be shuttled between the offices and shows in his own private jet, and wrestlers like Flair would be allowed to live up to their gimmick on the company dime. While the WWF got lucky with the MTV link-up and then ran with the chances that they were given, Crockett seemed to think that the route to the top involved him living like a king before he'd even reached the summit.

With no Magnum TA to dethrone Flair, crowd interest wasn't at the level that Crockett needed to justify his spending. Furthermore, to ensure that his most prized wrestlers wouldn't jump ship to the bright lights of the WWF, Crockett was paying higher wages than ever before to keep people onside. By the end of 1987, things were rapidly becoming an awful mess. By 1988, JCP would be on the verge of going bust, untapped spending and dwindling crowds sick of Dusty Finishes forcing someone to step in and save the day.

Crockett and company were making a lot of mistakes. Not keeping a list of what they were burning money on was one of them, but an even bigger one was ignoring their fans. In their desperate bid to go national, they abandoned the crowds in the south who had always adored their brand of rasslin' over what WWF had to offer and tried to become successful in cities that had already been well and truly won over by Vince and Hogan. *Starrcade* had always been a success in Greensboro and Atlanta in front of rabid crowds, and yet it was inexplicably moved to Chicago in 1987, with a main event of short-term champion Ron Garvin against challenger Ric Flair. It doesn't take a genius to work out who went over there.

Even more inexplicably, the *Bunkhouse Stampede* PPV (pay per view) in 1988 took what had been a popular format at live shows in the JCP heartland for the previous few years and transplanted it without any adaptation to New York. The poster for the show even had a cowboy hat on it. The concept for the main event of that show was devised by Dusty Rhodes; a regular Bunkhouse Stampede was a battle royal where wrestlers dressed in their street clothes and brought a weapon to the ring with them (no, you weren't allowed to bring a gun). At the PPV version of the show, it had to be even bigger, so it was a steel cage bunkhouse stampede where eight men fought for victory by trying to shove their opponent out of the cage door or, even sillier, over the top of the cage. Considering that wrestling fans for years had been trained to see escaping the cage as *winning* a match, this really was a sight to behold. Dusty won the match, as he had done for the previous three years as well. In fact, he was the only person to ever win it.

This isn't a knock on Dusty, who remains one of my favourite performers of all time. For balance, I'll point out that he did come up with some amazing ideas, such as the multi-man tag team, double cage *War Games* matches that were a staple of the NWA and WCW for over a decade. Those gore-filled, incredibly long brawls remain the stuff of legend, as do Dusty's feuds with the Four Horsemen and the Road Warriors. But by 1988, Rhodes was tired, and you couldn't blame him. He'd given his all for the company, mentally and physically, but backstage was becoming a political minefield.

Despite JCP being nearly broke, thanks to its ties to NWA, it remained powerful. What it needed to do was absolutely smash into pay per view, just like the WWF had done. But Vince was one step ahead. *Starrcade '87* wasn't just a slap in the face to the southern fans who loved their rasslin' but couldn't travel to Chicago, it was also the biggest nail in the coffin of JCP. As a pay per view, the show was positioned to rival *WrestleMania* that year, being marketed as the NWA version of WWF's mega-show. To counter this, WWF came up with their first-ever *Survivor Series* on the very same day over Thanksgiving weekend. Cable companies, who already recognised that WWF was the hot ticket, were told to choose between carrying *Starrcade* or *Survivor Series*. If they chose the former, they would also lose other WWF programming.

Only five companies stayed loyal to Crockett, everybody else chose WWF. *Survivor Series* became an annual tradition, with matches often pitting four or five wrestlers against another team of the same size under elimination rules. *Starrcade '87* was a colossal failure. Remember those figures for *'Mania* that year: $10 million in PPV revenue, $1.6 million in ticket sales. *Starrcade* made just $80,000 profit after expenses, barely enough to scratch the surface of the company's mounting debts.

JCP was losing talent too. Some jumped ship for money; some did it because they felt they would have better opportunities away from the backstage political feud between Rhodes and Flair. An influx of talent did come in when Bill Watts's UWF became part of JCP, but despite some amazing talent at their disposal, JCP ran an 'invasion' angle where nearly all of the newcomers lost – booking built from ego rather than doing good business.

Things got even worse when the aforementioned *Bunkhouse Stampede* PPV did awful numbers as WWF again had a counter for it; their first-ever *Royal Rumble* show on free television. JCP would try this tactic themselves with some success, putting out their first free-to-air *Clash of the Champions* special on television at the same time as WWF's *WrestleMania IV*.

The *Clash* show did good numbers, but was just a plaster over a gaping wound. By November 1988, JCP was close to bankruptcy, and Rhodes and Flair's feuding meant that backstage was in turmoil as well. Dusty wanted Flair to lose the NWA title to Rick Steiner in five minutes at *Starrcade '88*, which was a quite ridiculous suggestion that had everybody taking sides and battle lines being drawn.

Massive changes were afoot though.

Ted Turner bought JCP for around $9 million in November 1988, keeping Jim Crockett on as a 'consultant' (read: on the payroll, not allowed to do anything damaging like spending money). Dusty would be fired soon after, as Turner tried to implement a no-blood policy and Dusty blatantly bladed in an angle with the Road Warriors after they unscrewed a spike from their terrifying shoulder pads and jammed it into his eye.

The company name also changed. It wasn't NWA, it wasn't JCP. Now, the company was named after the show it had been putting out for years: World Championship Wrestling.

1988 had been awful. In ring at least, 1989 was outstanding.

While JCP had changed hands and was gearing up for better things, and the WWF was making millions left, right and centre, other companies weren't quite so lucky. Verne Gagne's AWA was struggling, despite churning out huge stars from the territory like The Road Warriors, Vader (in the Eighties going by his real name: Leon White), Scott Hall, Curt Hennig and the Rockers. By 1987 and 1988, he'd start losing these bright young stars to the brighter lights of WWF and WCW.

In 1988, to combat the monopolies that had been formed elsewhere, the AWA buddied up with the Continental Wrestling Association (CWA) in Memphis, owned by Jerry Jarrett and starring the biggest name in that region, Jerry Lawler. 'The King' would win the AWA title from Hennig in order to promote this alliance.

WCCW in Texas was also struggling, so Fritz Von Erich and his territory came on board as well, to form the short-lived Pro Wrestling USA. In December '88, the conglomerate presented what they hoped would be a massive pay-per-view event, head-lined by Lawler against Kerry Von Erich. This massive show – dubbed *Superclash III* – drew only 1,600 fans and was a flop in terms of homes buying the TV show. Claiming he was owed money from the event, Lawler left with the AWA belt, refusing to return it. Verne had to make a new belt, which was hardly ideal when he was already strapped for cash. This wasn't the first time either; in 1986 Stan Hansen had refused to lose the title before a trip to Japan, as he'd been advertised on that tour as holding the belt and didn't want to upset his employers over there. Several arguments later, Hansen returned the belt by mail, but not before repeatedly running it over with his truck.

By 1989, the all-new AWA title was won by Larry Zbyszko, who was a decent hand but a fair few years removed from the hot streak that he'd hit during a feud with Bruno Sammartino in the early 1980s. Meanwhile, the AWA had a new guy working as an interviewer, some chap called Eric Bischoff. From this small opportunity, a very important figure would grow. Despite trying their best to bail out a sinking ship, by 1990 the AWA was inactive and filing for bankruptcy. Before this happened, Zbyszko saw the writing on the wall and jumped to WCW, never dropping the title on his way out. With no money and no champion, the company quietly folded, with many of its brightest stars from its final years now massive celebrities in the big two companies.

All was not lost in Memphis. Traditionally always a successful territory, mainly because of the draw of Lawler, who rarely ventured away from being a big fish in a small pond, it was no longer the company that it had been in the late 1970s and early Eighties. The storyline that everyone remembers most is the worked shoot between Lawler and comedian Andy Kaufman, since immortalised in the film *Man on the Moon* (and also in the documentary *Jim and Andy: The Great Beyond* that looks at Jim Carrey's portrayal of Kaufman). That whole arc between the two, starting with Kaufman declaring himself as the Inter-Gender Wrestling Champion of the world and taking on any female challengers during his act, became quite epic. Lawler would wrestle Kaufman at the Mid-South Coliseum after the comic had taunted Memphis residents with jibes about their cleanliness and so on, standard heel work but delivered by an incredibly committed showman; a guy who understood protecting the business through kayfabe more than a lot of wrestlers did.

Kaufman would have his neck 'broken' by Lawler's piledriver, and would then bring his Inter-Gender act to shows in Memphis too, always attracting massive heel heat and convincing the entire worlds of both wrestling and entertainment that he was genuinely crazy. Lawler and Kaufman would appear on David Letterman's show together in 1982, with Lawler slapping his nemesis hard in the face. The reality of course was that the two men were both friends, but this wasn't revealed until long after the comedian's premature death in 1984 at the age of just 35. A brilliant story about this whole era is that promoter Jerry Jarrett mailed cheques to Kaufman for two years during the feud with Lawler; they were for good money, but Kaufman never once cashed any of them.

Lawler was very much a nearly man throughout the Eighties; clearly a massive star in his region and charismatic enough to work heel or face wherever he went throughout the USA when he did venture outside of Tennessee. His reign with the AWA title was after it really meant something, brought about by the friendship and alliance between AWA and CWA. With CWA being an affiliate, he was often considered a viable NWA world title holder, but as the territory wasn't one of the JCP regions that was unlikely to ever happen as Crockett took more and more control of the title during the 1980s. You cannot overstate just how big a star Lawler was in his time though; he is easily one of Memphis' most famous sons.

As the cooperation with the AWA failed, Jerry Jarrett bought the ailing WCCW from Fritz Von Erich and merged the CWA with it, forming a new company: the United States Wrestling Association (USWA) in 1989. Grand things were planned for this company, but by 1990 the Texas part of the company pulled out, then by 1992 it was pretty much a developmental company for the WWF after Lawler signed up there as a talent, with wrestlers being sent there for short excursions to bump up ticket sales, often leading to short title runs. (In the nine years that the company ran, Lawler managed to be champion 28 times.)

1989 did kick off a bright new future for the now renamed WCW. Shoots of growth had been seen during the final knock-ings of the JCP era in 1988 as Ric Flair made a star out of Sting during their 45-minute draw on the first *Clash of the Champions* TV special, that went up against *WrestleMania IV* and drew great ratings. With Turner in charge during 1989 and Dusty Rhodes now an in-ring talent in the WWF, times were changing, and the in-ring product was about to see a series of absolutely world-class matches that fans still speak about today.

Ricky Steamboat had returned to the NWA/WCW side after his fall-out with the WWF, and this meant that he could resume his old rivalry with Ric Flair. This began at the end of 1988, following Ric Flair's defence of his title against Lex Luger at *Starrcade* (obviously, he hadn't lost in five minutes, as per Dusty's original idea). On WCW television on 24 December, Steamboat, as a mystery tag team partner for Eddie Gilbert, pinned Flair (who was partnered by fellow Four Horseman Barry Windham – I'd try to keep you up to speed with all the ins and outs of the Horsemen but by the end of the Nineties this book would run to a million pages long) and immediately asked for a title match. It was set for 20 February 1989, at the *Chi-Town Rumble* pay-per-view special.

The match itself was a classic, with two experienced performers at the absolute peak of their powers. Flair was a few days away from his 40th birthday, Steamboat close to his 36th. Nowadays, they'd be considered on the old side to be wrestling, back then it was the norm to have skilled veterans at the top of the card. This match certainly proved that point, with the work rate between the two a testimony to what good shape both men were in. Flair certainly liked to party outside the ring (the tales are legendary), but you couldn't question the man's cardio, even if he was probably constantly hungover.

Steamboat, after a referee bump for some intrigue, rolled Flair up with a small package to win the title.

This led to arguably an even better contest on the same day as *WrestleMania V*. While Hogan and Savage saw to their differences on pay per view, Steamboat and Flair had an epic 55-minute, two-out-of-three-falls contest on free television as part of *Clash of the Champions VI: Ragin' Cajun*. Flair took the first fall, as heels often do in these contests, with a cradle at the 19-minute mark. Steamboat levelled it up after 35 minutes, making Flair submit to a double chickenwing. Twenty minutes later, Steamboat went for the chickenwing again, but Flair fell on top of him. With both men's shoulders down, the referee made the count, but Steamboat got his shoulder up at the last millisecond. Flair's foot was underneath the ropes though, meaning the pinfall technically should not have been counted. This meant that one more match had to be signed.

At *Wrestlewar '89: Music City Showdown* in Nashville, the match was oddly not pitted as the main event, with two tag team title matches (one for the world titles, the other for the much less prestigious US titles) following it. Based on the quality of both the match and the angle following it, those guys were in a hopeless situation. I've done stand-up gigs where I've struggled because I've had to follow someone masterful; this was that experience magnified by a thousand.

Judges were set in place for the contest just in case the match went to the one-hour time limit and a winner needed to be named. The judges were all past NWA champions – Lou Thesz, Pat O'Connor and Terry Funk – giving the event even more prestige. The match itself didn't go to time limit but was a fantastic back-and-forth contest that lasted over half an hour, with Flair targeting the leg of Steamboat so he could go for his figure four leglock. Crucially, Flair wasn't his usual cheating self, taking less shortcuts and engaging Steamboat in as fair a wrestling match as the fans had seen from him in quite some time.

The work on the leg led to the finish, with Steamboat going for a slam on Flair but his knee giving way, and Flair cradling him for the pinfall victory. Steamboat, who was always the most sympathetic babyface in wrestling, helped turn Flair fully to the good side at the end of the match, exchanging a handshake as both men showed mutual respect.

With the crowd overjoyed at having seen such an amazing match and now being given reason to cheer for the charismatic Flair, Terry Funk took his opportunity to ask Flair for a title match. Flair turned him down and Funk went absolutely insane, battering Flair to within an inch of his life and, in an extreme spot for 1989, piledriving him on a table at ringside. This was immediately played up as a career-ending injury, as one great feud instantly segued into another.

In July 14,500 fans bought a ticket for *The Great American Bash* pay per view in Baltimore, with Flair meeting Funk in a tremendous match that had to follow a War Games contest. For some, that would be hard, but with Flair on top of his game and Funk rolling back the years (he was 45 at this point), it remains one of the best matches of the decade. Flair retained but the feud wasn't over, as Funk and manager Gary Hart (a fine manager; Hart doesn't get the credit that other great managers like Bobby Heenan do) brought in the mist-spewing, face-painted, mysterious talent from Japan, The Great Muta (Keiji Mutoh) to face off with Flair and his partner of choice, super-babyface Sting in a Thunderdome Cage tag match at *Halloween Havoc*. Hart would have to throw in the towel for a babyface victory.

Sting became part of the Four Horsemen, but that loyalty was tested at *Starrcade* that year. The main part of the show centred around an Iron Man Tournament, a round robin series of matches that took place throughout the show and included Sting, Flair, Luger and Muta. The main event was Sting v Flair, with the youngster picking up the victory to claim the Iron Man crown (Flair's title was not on the line). This meant he was due a shot, however, so the Horsemen turned upon him to try and keep the belt on Flair. At this point, WCW was doing well. Flair, Sting, Luger, the Road Warriors and the Steiner Brothers were all huge stars, so it finally seemed that the WWF had a decent national-level rival. Flair remained the crown jewel in the company, but WCW management got complacent. They didn't think he'd ever leave.

JIM'S TOP TEN: STABLES

This part of the book isn't a TripAdvisor guide to the best places to have your horse spend the night, but rather my favourite groups of three or more wrestlers with a common — and often villainous — goal.

10. The Wyatt Family

Led by Bray Wyatt, the cult leader who comes across as a villain from *True Detective*, this group started in NXT and made its way to *Raw* and *Smackdown* with Wyatt backed up by Luke Harper, Erick Rowan and eventually the massive Braun Strowman.

9. The Hart Family

When Bret Hart turned his back on America in 1997, tired of being screwed over (probably not the best choice of words given what followed in Montreal later that year), he was joined by family: brother Owen, brothers-in-law Jim Neidhart and the British Bulldog and friend Brian Pillman to form a stable that was the most hated in the world (if you lived in the USA) or one of the most beloved (if you lived anywhere else).

8. The Nation of Domination

Some stables have several incarnations; the finest of the Nation, for my money at least, was its second. After Crush and Savio Vega had formed their own groups, leader Faarooq was joined by D-Lo Brown, Mark Henry, Kama Mustafa and The Rock, the latter embarking on his first heel run on the road to becoming the biggest star in the business.

7. Generation Next

In 2004, Alex Shelley formed a stable in Ring of Honor that also included Chris Sabin, Austin Aries, Jack Evans and Roderick Strong. Quickly becoming the most hated heels in RoH, their path of destruction in this original form lasted for a year, before Sabin and Shelley were removed, replaced with Matt Sydal and another year of chaos ensued.

6. The New World Order

I know, I know. You're thinking that the nWo should be placed higher. If it was just their original three-man form, then I'd totally agree. Their legacy has been a little bit tainted by just how many members they had at one point, plus this is a list of *my* favourites. Take to Twitter to argue with me. (Please don't.)

5. D-Generation X

I prefer their original, most shocking form (Michaels, Helmsley, Chyna, Rude) over their second incarnation (which was also great, comprised of Helmsley, Chyna, X-Pac, Road Dogg and Billy Gunn), but I'm always impressed that they didn't keep adding members or overstaying their welcome. Plus their football jersey was the merchandise to be seen in during 1998.

4. Bullet Club

The top merchandise seller in the world right now, it seems, this is an odd one as it's a stable started by a friend (Finn Balor, when he was still known as Prince Devitt in NJPW) and one that in its current guise, has another friend in it (Marty Scurll). Easily the best stable of gaijin in Japanese wrestling history, the brand has gone global over the past year or so thanks to the skills of members Kenny Omega, Cody Rhodes and the Young Bucks.

3. Los Ingobernables de Japon

With a different, outsider feel to all the other stables in NJPW, LIJ (Los Ignobernables de Japon) are an offshoot of the original Los Ingobernables, set up in CMLL in Mexico. Led by Tetsuya Naito and including fellow members Evil, Bushi, Sanada and Hiromu Takahashi, they're easily one of the most striking groups to watch right now *and* they have the bonus of having three of the world's best wrestlers within the group.

2. The Age of the Fall

Mainly competing in Ring of Honor after their debut in 2007, I loved everything about this group: the odd dynamic of the original members (Jimmy Jacobs, Tyler Black and Necro Butcher); the cult-like nature of the leadership that Jacobs had; and the use of the internet to get their story across and develop angles, rather than just relying on the in-ring stuff. Even the death of the stable in 2009 is something special. I won't ruin that for you.

1. The Four Horsemen

Always likely to top this list, this stable gave rise to thousands of others, some brilliant, some awful. The Horsemen being such a phenomenon in the 1980s explains why it was reinvented so many times; before they came along, stables just weren't as brilliant and dominant. Fans will always argue over their favourite incarnation of the group; I'll go with Ric Flair, Arn Anderson, Tully Blanchard and Barry Windham.

Chapter Eleven:
Pills, Thrills and Bellyaches

The steroid crisis, Flair's WWF excursion
and the rise of the smaller man

In the midst of The Ultimate Warrior's run at the top of the WWF, another future star made his debut in the company. It's unlikely that this wrestler expected that he'd go on to dominate the industry in the way that he did; nobody could even agree on his name to start with.

His real name was Mark Calaway, and until 1990 he had led an unheralded existence within the squared circle. He enjoyed a brief reign as USWA Champion (one of the weeks that Jerry Lawler didn't hold the belt) as the ex-convict Master of Pain, then jumped to WCW and worked under the name 'Mean' Mark Callous, both as a singles wrestler and as part of the oft-changed Skyscrapers tag team. He certainly wasn't someone that you'd necessarily have your eye on, even if he was billed at six feet ten inches tall and had dark, sunken eyes and an oddly creepy, expressionless face.

Calaway had a WCW US title shot against Lex Luger in July 1990 and got word that people from WWF were watching. He dislocated his hip during the match but carried on, wanting to try and take his chance up north. Despite Vince passing that first time, in October he was signed up and given a gimmick for his first match at a TV taping: Kane the Undertaker. After that one contest, the 'Kane' part would be dropped (and saved for his storyline brother a few years later) and he'd just be known by his trade; in black and grey, dressed like something from the Old West, Calaway was now The Undertaker. Apart from changing his gimmick for a short while to make him some kind of Hell's Angel (dubbed by many 'Bikertaker') at the end of the decade, he would remain a supernatural presence and a massive draw for WWE until the so-called end of his career, even if 12-year-old me wasn't sold on him at the time.

Undertaker's debut came at *Survivor Series 90*, destroying opponents on the opposite team at the behest of his team captain Ted DiBiase, before being counted out as he was so hell-bent on going on a rampage. You couldn't help but pay attention to him as he looked and acted so different to everyone else at the time, no-selling moves to get across the idea that he was other-worldly and impervious to pain. Initially managed by Brother Love, a crimson-faced preacher man, he was soon matched up with Paul Bearer, a chubby manager who kept hold of the mysterious urn that 'Taker seemingly drew power from. Stuffing fallen opponents on TV into body bags and carrying them backstage, it managed to be both an incredibly cartoonish and oddly dark gimmick. Undertaker entered into a feud with The Ultimate Warrior in

1991, after starting his famous *WrestleMania* undefeated streak at *WrestleMania VII* by beating the now ageing Jimmy Snuka. The feud with Warrior wouldn't be over the title though, because by that point Hulk Hogan had it once again.

I was biased as a kid, because I thought The Ultimate Warrior was fantastic and as a Brit, didn't get the American patriotism whipped up by Hogan. Warrior was a decent champion, but it's fair to say that he wasn't hitting the heights that Hogan did. He also wasn't the easiest guy to work with backstage, despite his relatively short time in the business. Say what you want about Hogan, but he really put the yards in before he got to the big time. It made sense to get the belt back on Hogan, but to do that he needed to defeat a good heel. A plan was hatched to make the biggest villain that they could, using an established character returning, topical events and the good old stars and stripes.

Sergeant Slaughter returned to the WWF in 1990 after a stint in the AWA. He had been a big face character in the mid Eighties for Vince, an imposing drill-sergeant character who always looked like he was fortysomething, even during his younger years feuding with Pat Patterson and Bob Backlund. Upon his return, he was given the gimmick of a turncoat Iraqi sympathiser at the height of tensions in the Gulf; he adopted the Camel Clutch as a finisher and assigned veteran manager General Adnan, who bore the tiniest of resemblances to Saddam Hussein, if you squinted and had glaucoma.

Slaughter baulked at stunts such as burning the American flag in the ring, but he did still receive death threats and had to be accompanied by security wherever he went. This only escalated at *Royal Rumble 1991* when Slaughter won the WWF title, beating

The Ultimate Warrior in a massive shock thanks to the interference of Randy Savage who smashed his royal sceptre (he was now going as 'The Macho King') over Warrior's head. After Hogan won the Rumble match later in the show, the main event of *WrestleMania VII* was set for a show that was subtitled 'Superstars and Stripes Forever'. WWF hoped to fill the 100,000 capacity Los Angeles Coliseum with such a jingoistic blood feud, but the show ended up being moved. WWF said it was for security reasons with such a politically charged storyline at the top of the card; naysayers have held the belief for many years that it was down to sluggish sales with wrestling not at the heights in the USA it had been in the late Eighties. Obviously, Hogan regained the belt, on a show that featured an excellent match between Warrior and Savage where the loser had to retire. When Macho lost, his manager Sherri turned on him, only for Elizabeth to make the save. Savage turned face on the back of this, the moment where he held the ropes open for his former manager making many people in the crowd cry – and one pimply teenager at home in the Midlands too.

With Hogan now firmly back as champion, The Undertaker was catching on really quickly with the WWF fanbase. Because he was so massive and so genuinely different to other wrestlers (in fact, a lot of what he did in the ring would normally have been frowned upon as he seemed impervious to all pain, often just sitting up after taking a big move), it would have been impossible to *not* push him to the top.

At *Summerslam '91*, Hogan and Warrior were in a multi-man match on a show billed as 'A Match Made in Heaven, A Match Made in Hell'; they took part in the *hell* portion of the show, taking on Slaughter, Adnan and Colonel Mustafa (the returned Iron Sheik) in a two-on-three tag team match with patriotism and pride at stake. Warrior would be fired after this show; he demanded $500,000 before the event that he believed he was owed, threatening to no-show the advertised match if he didn't get it. Vince paid him to ensure the match happened and immediately cut him loose as soon as it was over.

The *heaven* part of the show involved the wedding of Savage and Elizabeth, even if they were already hitched in real life (and also, would not actually be married for much longer). Warrior was meant to be feuding with Jake Roberts going forwards, but because of his firing that feud was shifted to Savage, who made sure the feud would work as only he could; agreeing to be actually bitten by a snake during his own wedding reception. It's still absolutely awful to watch.

Hogan moved into a feud with the red-hot Undertaker, who was easily the biggest heel in the company, despite being pretty cool if you think about it. Their first pay-per-view encounter came at *Survivor Series '91* with 'Taker winning the title under controversial circumstances and the assistance of a man who had not long been in the company (more on that in a second). Six days later, Hogan regained the title at the one-off pay-per-view *This Tuesday in Texas*, again in a match full of controversy with Hogan throwing ash from the omnipresent urn into 'Taker's eyes to get the win. WWF president Jack Tunney vacated the title over all the hubbub, saying that the winner of the 1992 *Royal Rumble* would become champion. Would it be Undertaker, Hogan or Savage? Nope. Someone else who, at the start of 1991, was definitely absolutely out of left field.

Over in WCW, top babyface Sting had been haunted by a character called The Black Scorpion, a masked man from his past who kept appearing and causing him grief. To get a sense of how odd WCW booking could be during that era, nobody saw fit to decide who was actually going to play the Scorpion, with different workers donning the mask for different shows and the voice often provided by Ole Anderson. By *Starrcade 90*, Sting faced the Black Scorpion in a debacle of a contest where even the most gullible fan would have realised that the masked man that day was being played by Ric Flair. With that behind him, come spring 1991 Flair was WCW (and therefore also NWA) champion and respected by everybody in the company. Well, *nearly* everybody.

Running WCW at that point was a man called Jim Herd. Tight with Ted Turner's top brass, he had been the manager of the TV station in St Louis that produced *Wrestling at the Chase* and after that, a regional manager for Pizza Hut. Hired in January 1989, it is fair to say that he was absolutely in over his head. He saw that WWF was having a great time with colourful and cartoonish gimmicks, so tried to impose those ideas on WCW, such as having a tag team of hunchbacks who would never be able to have their shoulders pinned to the mat because of their odd-shaped spines. Yes, that really happened.

He also sanctioned a tag team called the Ding Dongs who had bells attached to them, and tried to turn ultra-tough, super-serious legend Stan Hansen into a comedic character. He caused the massively popular Road Warriors to jump to the WWF (where they became The Legion of Doom) and even wanted Flair to change his character. Not just a little bit, but wholesale.

Herd asked Flair to cut his trademark platinum blond hair, adopt some kind of Spartacus gimmick, get his ear pierced and also, while he was at it, take a huge pay cut. Herd had already removed Flair as WCW booker at this point, so this was the final straw for The Nature Boy. Arguments ensued. Herd, desperate to prove that he could handle wrestlers as well as he could handle a Margherita, fired Flair two weeks before the 1991 *Great American Bash*. WCW, behind the scenes, stripped the belt from Flair, but they never thought to actually ask for it back.

Despite advertising Flair v Luger for weeks leading up to the show, the main event now was Luger v Barry Windham, both solid workers but nowhere near as popular as Flair, who hardcore fans recognised as the best wrestler in the world at that point. The problems mounted up when WCW realised that they didn't even have a belt to give the winner of the match, having to attach a metal plate to a Florida title so they'd have something to hand over. Flair still had what was now known as 'the big gold belt' and was absolutely not giving it back. He, like all NWA and WCW champions, had to put up a $25,000 deposit when holding the title to ensure there were no shenanigans. As Herd hadn't returned the deposit, he took the belt and kept it. That would have been bad enough if he'd sat at home with it, wearing it to do chores or the food shopping. But he did something much more harmful to WCW and Herd's reputation: he turned up in the WWF with it.

The *Great American Bash* was a mess. From the first bell until the end of the show fans chanted, 'We want Flair'. Flair was still NWA champion, technically, until September when his signing with WWF was official. He was billed on WWF television as the 'Real World Champion' – WCW or NWA were never referred to by name but it was the first time that a world of wrestling outside of The WWF universe had really been referenced since seceding from the NWA. The belt was often blurred out during

TV broadcasts as WCW and NWA started getting active with their lawyers.

Flair was an instant hit in the WWF, accompanied by his aides Mr Perfect and Bobby Heenan. He didn't have to wait long for his stand-out moment in the promotion, after being the man that started the controversy between Hogan and Undertaker, he would be the man chosen to win the title during the 1992 *Royal Rumble*. Thing is, he didn't do it by entering at number 28, throwing a few guys out and taking the prize. Instead, as if to prove that he had been putting on hour-long matches left, right and centre while guys like Hogan had been having 15-minute main events every other month, Flair entered the Rumble at number three and lasted for over an hour before finally eliminating Sid Justice with help on the outside from Hogan. He'd been in the promotion for all of a few months, but Flair was already the top guy.

The feud that everyone in wrestling expected to see was Flair v Hogan, the two biggest stars from the two biggest companies finally facing off, but that only happened at a few house shows rather than being built up as a huge feud that could have drawn massive money. Instead, Hogan had a programme with the massive, muscular, curly-permed Sid Justice and Flair had a memorable and highly-charged feud with Randy Savage. Flair was insistent that he'd had a prior relationship with Elizabeth, promising to show photos of her on television, and the heated rivalry came to a head at *WrestleMania VIII* with Savage winning the title for the second time. Flair would regain it in September, before losing it once more a month later to Bret Hart. He'd be gone and back 'home' in WCW by February 1993, but certainly made the most of his run in WWF. And despite being in his forties by this point, he'd even have another run much later on, including the iconic match that this book is named after.

Herd was fired, like a pizza in a wood oven, by January 1992 while Flair was conquering the WWF. He was replaced by the splendidly named Kip Allen Frey, who was in turn replaced by Bill Watts. If Jim Herd knew nothing about wrestling, Watts was the opposite end of the spectrum. Arguably, he knew too much, bringing an old-school mentality with him that should have been admired for some reasons (trying to reign in company spending and asking wrestlers to keep kayfabe more) and was derided for others (asking all wrestlers to stay in the building until the end of every show; insisting that heels and faces should definitely never be seen together; and, best of all, banning top rope moves). Watts had done great things in the 1980s with his UWF in Oklahoma, building up stars that went on to awesome things and drawing great crowds until the local recession hit.

The top rope decision was quite baffling; after an absolutely amazing, genre-defining, years-ahead-of-its-time match between 'Flying' Brian Pillman and Japanese upstart Jushin 'Thunder' Liger (who wore a costume closer to that of a Power Ranger than wrestler), it seemed such a shame to stop these exciting youngsters from showing exactly what they could do, especially when wrestling has always appealed to kids. I know whenever I played a wrestling video game in my teens, the first thing I would always try would be to hop onto the corner turnbuckle.

Watts was very good at building up new stars though, and in particular African-American ones. He had helped make Junkyard Dog enormous in the Eighties and realising that the title lineage in WCW had never had a black champion, he decided to use that same formula to propel the talented former football player

Ron Simmons to the top of the tree. While this wasn't massive box office, it was a bold decision that made Watts' firing in 1993 even more head-scratching – Watts left under a cloud following accusations of racism based on an interview he had done previously. Lightweight wrestlers returned to the top rope rapidly, and presumably heels and faces crammed into cars together once again.

WCW in this period did have a ton of great talent though; Simmons, Pillman and Sting were all incredibly popular, but it was two heels that really stuck out, one more so in hindsight than the other. Cactus Jack had been one of wrestling's great wanderers, touring nearly every territory in the USA following his debut in 1983. Born Mick Foley, he was starting to get noticed for his oddly compelling promos, high-intensity in-ring style and most importantly, his willingness to get absolutely murdered for the entertainment of audiences and to make his opponents look great. The June 1992 *Beach Blast* contest between Foley and Sting was a falls-count-anywhere match that seemed utterly brutal at the time (and still stands up well today), poor Cactus Jack taking massive bumps while looking so deranged that he was a very real threat to Sting.

Someone else at the top of WCW cards as the Nineties wore on, and who also happened to have a lot of experience in Japan, was Vader. Not Darth; prefixes you can use are 'The Man They Call', 'Big Van' or 'The Mastodon'. Over 400 pounds of former pro football player, Leon White had started wrestling under his own name in the AWA, before making a name for himself as Baby Bull in Germany and Austria. In 1987, he debuted in NJPW in some style; taking on the legendary Antonio Inoki (who had just beaten Riki Choshu) and beating him, clean, in just nine minutes. He was only in NJPW as Baba had traded his AJPW contract; beating Inoki so early was a sign of intent and the reaction was insane, the partisan crowd at the Sumo Hall in Tokyo actually rioting. Never let it be said that Japanese crowds aren't passionate just because they don't all wear wrestler T-shirts, bring signs to shows or start chants. They'll riot so hard that you'll be banned from a venue, as NJPW were.

Vader once had a match with Stan Hansen in Japan that was so brutal that it's become the stuff of legend: Hansen was representing AJPW and Vader NJPW on a joint company supercard in early 1990. Vader's nose was broken before he even got in the ring, after being clobbered by Hansen's bullrope. Then following a series of stiff punches from both men, Hansen accidentally rammed his thumb into Vader's eye socket, causing his eye to pop out. While I would have screamed for my mother, Vader pushed his eye back in and used his eyelid to hold it in place before the match was eventually declared a no contest. He'd have to have a steel plate inserted in his face to stop it happening again.

Either side of Ron Simmons' run, Vader was a dominant WCW champion. An exceptionally agile man for someone so big, he'd think nothing of moonsaulting off the top rope as well as utilising brutal powerbombs to incapacitate his opponents. He would embark on an extended feud with Cactus Jack that led to some of the most terrifyingly stiff matches in wrestling history. Here's a quick run-down:

1. 17 April 1993: Cactus beats Vader by count out. Vader brutalises Cactus so much that he needs 27 stitches in his face – not for blading, for legitimate blows – and suffers a broken nose.

2. 24 April 1993: Vader beats Cactus by count out by power-bombing him on concrete outside the ring. Cactus loses some feeling in his hand and leg temporarily and suffers a concussion. WCW uses this for a terrible, cartoonish amnesia angle while Vader moves on to other things.

3. 24 October 1993: Vader beats Cactus in a Texas Death Match after Harley Race used a cattle prod to finally keep Cactus down. Before that, he had taken numerous stiff, dangerous moves to prove his toughness and establish himself as a legitimate challenger.

4. 16 March 1994: Cactus loses his ear in a match with Vader in Germany. Trying to hang himself in the ring ropes, Cactus didn't realise how stiff they were and pulled his ear off in freeing himself. The doctors at the hospital threw it in the bin and refused to reattach it.

Remember everyone, wrestling is 100 per cent fake.

Something much bigger than money squabbles or backstage politics was about to rock the WWF and – by virtue of them being the industry leader – wrestling as a whole. In 1991, a little-known doctor who worked as a backstage physician (mainly because he was a wrestling fan) at some WWF events was about to cause a lot of people embarrassment and accidentally change the business forever.

Dr George Zahorian was arrested and charged for the illegal distribution of steroids, with various wrestlers implicated in the criminal proceedings as part of the evidence. It wouldn't have been difficult to presume that steroids were being used around wrestling since Superstar Billy Graham first popularised that kind of body in the late 1970s, and with the comic-book muscularity of men like the Ultimate Warrior. But when stars like Hulk Hogan and Roddy Piper were named in the investigation, it shook wrestling from top to bottom. These guys were mainstream stars; Piper didn't even look like he was on the gas. For outsiders to the industry who always scoffed at wrestling, this was further fuel to their arguments of it being 'fake'.

In 1993, Vince was also indicted in the investigation, facing prison if found guilty of helping to distribute steroids. He always denied it, but people with grudges were queuing up to say that he was bang to rights; and given Vince's success in the business there were certainly those who had an ulterior motive to punish him. During the deepest depths of the crisis, Hogan went on the popular Arsenio Hall chat show and denied that he had ever done steroids at any point in his career, something that was immediately disputed by guys who had shared locker rooms with him. Billy Graham, for instance, alleged he had helped Hogan inject the drugs in the 1980s. If Hogan had said that he'd done them when steroids were legal he probably would have caught less heat for the interview, but his flat-out denial just made matters worse.

The WWF's business fortunes dipped noticeably in 1992 as the crisis rumbled on, the controversy leading to bad publicity for what had been a family-friendly company for the previous decade. When everything eventually went to trial, Vince would be acquitted of all charges against him, before issuing the classic statement: 'Just like in wrestling, in the end the good guys always win.'

Thing was, now he needed to create a whole new era of guys, good and bad, to keep the stain of the steroid crisis away from his company. That meant moving away from the land of the monsters and bodybuilders and pushing smaller, younger, more athletic talent. It's probably for the best that the Ultimate Warrior had already managed to get himself fired.

Ironically, during this time, Titan Sports decided to diversify its portfolio and start up a new company: The World Bodybuilding Federation (WBF), taking wrestling sensibilities and applying them to something that Vince was really into. The plan was to rival the main bodybuilding group at the time, the IFBB. Several leading names from the IFBB were signed up to lucrative contracts and competitions were to be screened on pay per view with regular television programming supporting those events. The competitors were given gimmicks and characters to make the shows more appealing to a crossover mainstream audience, but it failed as bodybuilding doesn't hold the appeal to kids and teenagers that wrestling always has. With poor buy rates, the project was abandoned in 1992 in the midst of the steroid mire.

While business took a noticeable hit, in-ring talent ramped up around this time as it was no longer in vogue to be so muscular that you couldn't throw a forearm without turning your entire body 90 degrees. Not that the big guys didn't still exist, they certainly did; it's just that some smaller guys started getting opportunities to take the ball and run with it . . . as fast as they could, away from the vascular goliaths.

From 1993, WWF made a concerted effort to push their 'New Generation' of wrestlers, with a couple of stand-out names at the top of this revolution. At this point they'd be friends, but later in the decade it would be a very different story indeed. First up was Bret Hart, a technical wizard who was only six feet tall and 235lbs, at that time considered small but these days would make him one of the bigger guys on the independent scene. Part of the legendary Canadian Hart family, Bret was the eighth child of 12. He grew up in a run-down mansion in Calgary, the son of wrestler and promoter Stu who would train hundreds of different wrestlers in the basement of the house, nicknamed the Dungeon because of the shoot stretches that the wily Hart patriarch would put his trainees in.

Hart was already in his thirties by the 1990s, and vastly experienced. He had his grounding, like all of his brothers who entered the business, in the family territory in Canada, Stampede Wrestling. One feud with the Dynamite Kid, in the late 1970s and early Eighties was particularly memorable and meant that Bret's stock was high in 1984 when the WWF purchased Stampede as part of their expansion. Initially asked to be a cowboy for his gimmick, Hart turned it down and instead was placed in a stable with his brother-in-law Jim Neidhart and manager Jimmy Hart (no relation, which is crazy when Bret had so many siblings). Dubbed the Hart Foundation, they were initially villainous, and Bret was always the workhorse of the team, Neidhart more the talker and powerhouse.

By 1988, the group turned face and ditched Jimmy. With their pink and black gear and Bret's gimmick of giving his mirrored wrap-around shades to a kid in the audience before each match (I waited for three months to order some of those shades from the WWF magazine), they were catching on well and Bret was rewarded with some high-profile singles matches. The team was broken up in 1991 to give Bret a singles run, and he won the Intercontinental title at *Summerslam* that year in a great match against Mr Perfect, using his new submission finisher, the 'Sharpshooter'.

From there, Hart dropped the title to Jacques Rougeau in his new gimmick as The Mountie, before he dropped it to Roddy Piper, his only major title in his WWF tenure. At *WrestleMania VIII* Hart and Piper would have a classic babyface v babyface encounter that really was Bret's coming-out party as a top-tier superstar, a wonderful match that had tremendous action and a compelling storyline. At *Summerslam 1992*, Hart was in the main event with his Intercontinental belt, defending it against home-nation hero The British Bulldog (another of Hart's brothers-in-law) in front of 80,000 fans at Wembley Stadium in London (in the UK we were slower to catch on to the WWF than most, and business here was still booming). That contest is one of the best ever, a great back and forth match that the Bulldog eventually won; upon reading Bret's autobiography you realise that the entire match was pretty much Hart's doing, with the Bulldog so nervous that he forgot everything early on and panicked.

Losing the IC belt just meant that bigger things were ahead for Bret. At a non-televised show in Saskatoon, Canada on 12 October 1992, he won his first-ever WWF World title, beating Ric Flair having only been told he was becoming champion that day. While it may have seemed odd to switch the belt like that, knowing that anything could happen on a house show was intended to help pump up ticket sales, as well as getting the belt off Flair who was, amicably, making noises about being unhappy and heading back to WCW. During that match, Hart dislocated his finger, but just popped it back in and got on with it. Hart would hold the title until *WrestleMania IX* in Las Vegas in 1993, but not before making good defences against fellow up-and-coming singles stars.

One of those names was Shawn Michaels, who would end up

always being intrinsically linked with Hart thanks to events in Montreal four-and-a-half years later. But at this point, Michaels was a hot singles star despite being just under six feet tall and no more than a cruiserweight. He had been in a super-popular tag team called the Midnight Rockers in the AWA with Marty Jannetty; they had jumped to the WWF in the late Eighties, got fired a few weeks into their first run for partying, then managed to get rehired and got their heads down and worked hard. Looking like they should have been in a Motley Crüe tribute act, they managed to win the WWF tag team titles once from the Hart Foundation in a two-out-of-three-falls match where the top rope of the ring broke, but because the match ended up being heavily edited and contract discussions with Neidhart which had stalled were resolved, the title change was never acknowledged.

In December 1991, Michaels and Jannetty, who had been having some storyline difficulties, appeared on Brutus Beefcake's *Barbershop* interview segment. In one of the most memorable turns of all time, a leather-jacket clad Michaels superkicked his tag team partner through a pane of glass (gimmicked glass, that is), ending their association with Jannetty covered – through blading – in his own blood. I know at the time it was meant to make Michaels super-evil, but to me it made him super-cool. He would become The Heartbreak Kid, or HBK for short, the nickname that would stay with him for the rest of his career, as well as his theme music that he sung himself. He was the man to take the Intercontinental title from the Bulldog just a couple of months after the huge Wembley show, and by 1993 he would start bringing a big bodyguard to the ring with him, another giant who, like The Undertaker, WCW didn't rate as highly as the WWF did: Diesel.

Alongside Diesel, who had been given a slew of awful gimmicks in WCW, WWF did still have its big lads. Hogan was still there, and Undertaker may not have been all ripped muscle, but he was a giant. Then there was Sid, called Sid Vicious in his WCW days, Sid Justice for his WWF debut, Psycho Sid later in his career and just Sid in some places – a monster from Arkansas who was tall, muscular, terrifying and could deliver an intense promo (even if, a bit like Warrior, you didn't always know what he was banging on about), but just wasn't very good at putting down roots. In the 1990s, he jumped from WCW to WWF over and over again, back and forth, often buggering off for a few weeks in the summer because he wanted to play softball. At one point, he was fired by WCW for stabbing Arn Anderson with a pair of scissors in a hotel in Blackburn, Lancashire. There has never been a bleaker sentence typed about wrestling than that last one.

Massive in a different way was the Samoan Rodney Anoa'i, a member of the famous Anoa'i family that is still producing top-level wrestlers today. After wrestling as Kokina Maximus in the AWA, he moved to the WWF in 1992 and was given the gimmick of a sumo wrestler, representing Japan and accompanied by Mr Fuji. He'd never actually competed as a sumo but could carry off the character with his massive size – he was billed as weighing over 600lbs at various points in his career. Initially agile for a man of such enormous bulk, he literally squashed competitors until he won the 1993 *Royal Rumble*, receiving a title shot against Bret Hart at *WrestleMania IX*, held at Caesars Palace in Las Vegas.

During their *'Mania* match, Hart would have the massive legs of Yokozuna tied up in his Sharpshooter submission hold, with the challenger ready to submit, when Mr Fuji threw salt in the eyes of the champion, enabling Yokozuna to pin Hart and win the WWF title just a few months after debuting in the company. He wouldn't hold it for long though; not even a day. Hulk Hogan came to the ring (he'd been in a tag team match earlier in the night) to help Hart and Fuji goaded him into challenging for the title. A few moments later, Yokozuna was accidentally blinded by Fuji's salt and Hogan got the win and the title. The crowd in attendance was pleased. Hardcore wrestling fans were less so, and the lustre was starting to come off Hogan as the golden boy (both metaphorically and tanned skin-wise) of wrestling.

The steroid crisis had affected Hogan. He was now visibly smaller in size, and the controversy around it – capped by his poor performance on TV denying any drug use – had weakened his pull with families. Also, the kids who worshipped him in the 1980s were now teenagers, and all of a sudden saying your prayers and taking your vitamins wasn't what they wanted to hear.

By *King of the Ring '93*, Hogan was on his last legs with the company. He allowed Yokozuna to kick out of his famous leg drop before a 'Japanese photographer' at ringside (actually manager Harvey Whippleman in a disguise) shot a fireball from his camera at Hogan, blinding him and allowing Yokozuna to beat him for the title. It was rumoured that Hogan didn't want to drop his title to a smaller man like Hart at *Summerslam*, so made the call on going out in that fashion. He walked away from the WWF, wrestling a couple of matches in NJPW and doing some acting work. It seemed like his time in the big league was over.

The next challenger to Yokozuna was Lex Luger, signed from WCW to be part of the World Bodybuilding Federation; when that folded, he was put to work as a wrestler, using the gimmick of 'The Narcissist'. He hadn't made huge waves with that, so was turned babyface in the most American of ways. Yokozuna and Mr Fuji, basking in the glory of ending Hulkamania, put forth a body slam challenge as nobody could get the giant Samoan off his feet. Many tried and failed aboard the *USS Intrepid* on Independence Day before Luger arrived by helicopter and managed the mammoth task. He was repackaged as 'Made in the USA' and given his shot at *Summerslam '93*, but didn't win the gold despite winning the match by count out, as titles weren't allowed to change hands under such circumstances. With a huge push behind him and a nationwide bus tour on his 'Lex Express' coach, legend has it that Luger boasted to strangers in a bar that he was getting the title at Summerslam. When word got out, plans were changed.

In 1993, WWF started something that still continues to this day, albeit in a much larger form. With business certainly not at its best, short of the anomaly of the European tours which were doing great, it was decided to revamp television for the product. What was dreamed up was *Monday Night Raw*, a prime-time show that broke from the usual WWF TV product of pre-taped squash matches and angles; instead, this would have competitive matches (albeit not quite pay-per-view level) alongside promos and angles all done in the one venue, in front of the same crowd. Sounds silly now to realise that this really wasn't the norm. The audiences for the first shows in the Manhattan Centre in New York were amazingly enthusiastic, enjoying the experience of being in a small theatre rather than a huge arena, up close to the action in the best way possible. At first the show was live each week, but this soon changed to taping three or four weeks' worth of shows at a time to save money, even if it did burn out the crowd a bit by the final recording of the day.

Raw showcased some fine matches in its first year, a handful of absolute classics that TV audiences were not used to getting outside of the now finished *Saturday Night's Main Event* specials. The evil clown Doink v Marty Jannetty in a two-out-of-three-falls match was spectacular, as was Jannetty winning the Intercontinental title from his former tag team partner Shawn Michaels. One of the very best angles from the time was within a great match; Razor Ramon was a tall, talented wrestler who had been in the WWF since 1992 and given a *Scarface* gimmick of chewing on a toothpick and speaking with a Latin accent, despite actually being from Georgia and once wrestling for AWA as 'Cowboy' Scott Hall, complete with moustache and mullet. Ramon was a top-tier star and had already challenged Bret Hart for the WWF title, so everybody expected him to beat the tiny jobber that he had been booked against, billed simply as 'The Kid'. In reality, this kid was Sean Waltman, a gifted high-flyer who had been working as 'The Lightning Kid' across the USA in small, independent promotions.

After hitting a moonsault on Ramon and getting a massive upset victory, Waltman was given the name of the 1-2-3 Kid, While Ramon offered him money to take him on again. This led to a face turn for Ramon as he was mocked for losing by Ted DiBiase, and a friendship developed in the ring as Ramon took The Kid under his wing.

Over the course of a few weeks it was genuinely compelling television that propelled the two men to stardom rapidly, rather than them relying on squash matches and hoping for interview time as had previously been the norm on TV. *Raw* also saw Ric Flair's last WWF match of this tenure, early on in the show's history, as he took on Mr Perfect in a great bout where the loser had to leave the company.

While *Raw* was a great idea and an initial success, it was ironic that after the war to become a national promotion that nearly all of the early tapings took place in old WWWF towns from back in the day.

Once Flair was back in WCW, he wasn't allowed to wrestle at first. Instead, he was given a chat show named *A Flair for the Gold* on WCW TV to capitalise on the hero's welcome that he received for going back home. By the end of 1993, at *Starrcade*, he would win the WCW title once again, defeating Vader in a classic David v Goliath encounter that he wasn't even meant to be in. WCW did terrifically well to build that match as rapidly as they did, because the slot was originally intended for Sid before him messing around with scissors in Blackburn put paid to that plan.

The match had such genuine emotion and a real fear that it would be Flair's last hurrah, with him putting his career on the line, that many view it as his greatest title win during his stellar career. Vader dominated almost the entire bout, with Flair taking his opportunity to attack the leg of the big man whenever he could. In the end, Flair would grab that leg, trip Vader over and roll him up after just over 20 minutes for the win. Many saw this as Flair's swansong, because at 44 years old, surely he wouldn't keep going for much longer, right?

Chapter Twelve:
E is for Eric and Extreme

The rise of Eric Bischoff, ECW and the Kliq

WCW continued to rotate its leadership, with former commentator Eric Bischoff taking the helm as executive vice president in 1993. His first year was an absolute nightmare as he struggled to implement his ideas and the booking direction of the company was coming from Dusty Rhodes and Ole Anderson, both with great backgrounds but running on empty and not coming up with great ideas. In that year the company lost $23 million and worse still, introduced a character called The Shockmaster. Played by Fred Ottman, formerly called Tugboat and Typhoon in the WWF, his debut went with a bang; clad in a furry gilet and wearing a glitter-covered Stormtrooper helmet, he burst through a door during a TV promo and immediately fell over, his helmet falling off and the other wrestlers trying hard to stave off laughter as Ole Anderson's sinister voice was piped in. You can clearly hear The British Bulldog say 'He fell on his arse' if you listen carefully. We laugh about this now, but at the time they had to retcon the character to be a blundering fool.

In 1994, Bischoff was determined to turn the business around. He went after the WWF, signing both Randy Savage and Hulk Hogan, despite the latter in particular being exactly what the fans that built the company *didn't* want back on Black Saturday. The Hulkster was the first to get his deal, and it was really something as Bischoff courted him as a free agent and splashed Turner's money. On top of his regular salary for working far fewer dates than he did in the WWF, Hogan would get $700,000 per pay-per-view appearance as well as 25% of the gross revenue from buys of those shows from viewers at home. He also demanded creative control over his character and role within the company. Bischoff agreed to this, and he'd come to regret doing so later on.

Hogan was unveiled by WCW with a staged parade at Disneyworld, using extras to show the enthusiasm for him joining their side. Actual fans still weren't that convinced; some loved him, but many were tiring of the gimmick. His first pay per view was *Bash at the Beach '94* and as well as picking up a whopping pay day, he also won the WCW title from Ric Flair, who had hastily been turned heel. That show did good numbers, but the company was still haemorrhaging money.

Over at the WWF, they had two contrasting *WrestleManias* in 1994 and 1995, X and XI. The former, the tenth instalment of the franchise, was held at Madison Square Garden on 20 March 1994 in front of 18,000 fans. It might not have been the heights of the Silverdome, but MSG was the right place to hold the anniversary (*WrestleMania XX* would be staged there as well). The opening contest may be one of the best ever on a pay-per-view show with brothers Bret and Owen Hart going at it as part of their ongoing family feud, Owen picking up the surprising win despite Bret being due to wrestle for the WWF title later on. This was because Bret and Lex Luger *jointly* won the *Royal Rumble* that year and both received title shots, but Bret had to wrestle earlier because of a coin toss. Complicated, isn't it?

Luger lost to Yokozuna by disqualification for pushing the referee, so the main event saw Hart win the WWF title by defeating the massive Samoan. But before that was a match that put even the battle of the two Harts in the shade, a fantastic ladder match between Shawn Michaels and Razor Ramon over the Intercontinental title. That contest came about because Michaels had been stripped of the title in autumn 1993 for not defending it enough and Ramon won it in a battle royal to decide the new champion. The feud was then built around the two real-life friends both making the claim that they were the rightful titleholder, with Michaels playing the heel role to perfection. The title belts were hung over the ring and the two competed to be the first man to climb a ladder and grab the gold; by today's standards of ladder match they take risks but nothing too excessive, but it's a brilliant, industry changing bout that propelled both men into mega stardom. As a side note, it's the first-ever WWF match that got the full five-star rating in the *Wrestling Observer*. The two men would have another ladder match over the same title at *Summerslam 1995* that was also fantastic.

WrestleMania XI was a different story, with the show built around the main event that featured two unlikely show-closers and not a title belt in sight. Set up by a confrontation at ringside during *Royal Rumble '95*, the marquee match on one side featured Bam Bam Bigelow, a heavily tattooed, remarkably agile big man who had returned to the WWF after a stint in Japan. With flames adorning his ring gear *and* tattooed on top of his head, he was an intimidating sight and an experienced hand who was part of Ted DiBiase's Million Dollar Corporation (I believe that most corporations are probably worth a million dollars, but that's an argument for another day). He faced off against retired NFL superstar Lawrence Taylor, who had been sat in the crowd at the *Rumble*, a man with no wrestling experience but who was renowned for being one of the greatest line-backers in the history of football; and also, for being a wild character off the field and for ending the career of Washington Redskins quarterback Joe Theismann with one devastatingly violent tackle. Bigelow and Taylor did an admirable job in the main event; while it wasn't the greatest match of all time, it was probably one of the very best to involve a non-wrestler (you might think that would be a short list, but by the end of the Nineties the number of such matches had increased exponentially).

Eric Bischoff, meanwhile, was making alliances to help strengthen WCW. As well as helping AAA put their *When Worlds Collide* show on US pay per view and having a talent exchange in place, he also courted Antonio Inoki and NJPW. In April 1995 this would bear fruit as WCW talent was part of a massive show that set the all-time attendance record for professional wrestling. Inoki and Ric Flair met in the main event of the second day of the *International Sports and Culture Festival for Peace*. You'll understand why the show had such an awkward name when I tell you that it was held at the May Day Stadium in Pyongyang,

North Korea. 165,000 people attended day one; day two had an unbelievable 190,000 fans there. You can look at attendances in the USA and often be told an attendance figure and a lower paid figure with it, so you can see how many fans were 'papered' or let in for free. I'm not saying that the crowd in North Korea were *forced* to go . . . but draw your own conclusions. Either way, it's a massive crowd that won't ever be topped.

WCW still wasn't making great money but was spending it hand over fist by acquiring ex WWF superstars to at least have an impressive-looking roster. Bischoff knew that the gun could be pointed as his head very soon, so he pre-empted this and requested a meeting with Turner himself. When asked why the company wasn't doing as well as the WWF, Bischoff replied by saying that the only way he could compete would be if he had prime-time TV, just like Vince did with *Raw*. He didn't expect to get it, but Turner gave it to him, in a slot that would pit WCW's offering directly against *Raw* on Monday nights.

Nitro debuted on 4 September 1995 as a one-hour show, but quickly expanding to two and then eventually to three hours' duration. Say 'Monday Nitro' fast and you'll see exactly why it was named that way. It wasn't done to appeal to Nascar fans.

The first *Nitro* came from the unusual setting of the Mall of America in Minnesota. and, happily for Bischoff, TV coverage of US Open tennis meant there was no *Raw* opposing it. That night, Lex Luger, who had appeared on WWF television not long before because of how their shows were taped, made his return to WCW. *Nitro* nearly always being live meant that surprises like this became a feature of what would shortly be dubbed the Monday Night Wars; this was the opening shot, and one delivered by a massive cannon.

By the end of 1995, Bischoff was doing all he could to rattle the cage of the WWF, including signing their Women's champion, Alundra Blayze, reverting her back to her previous in-ring name of Madusa and having her throw her WWF title belt into a bin on *Nitro*. From that point onwards, it was a dirty war.

Remember the late 1990s and how everything was 'extreme', the term applied to drinks and food and TV shows by executives who wanted to ensnare Generation X? The word gained relevance in wrestling in August 1994.

Rewind to when Ric Flair had returned to WCW in 1993 and won the NWA World Heavyweight title, taking it from Barry Windham. As his return was so popular, other NWA-affiliated companies (and a few still existed, now more as independent promotions than the territories of old) started demanding, under NWA rules, that the champion visited their groups and defended the belt there. WCW wasn't best pleased at this, then the NWA got very annoyed when Flair was due to switch the title at a taping at Disney without their permission to Rick Rude, WCW's choice to hold the belt next. With both sides getting huffy, WCW left the NWA in September 1993 and the rigmarole of renaming the big gold belt for a while began.

The NWA still needed a champion though, as it wanted to be a vital part of wrestling in the 1990s. Jim Crockett wanted back into wrestling in 1994 and chose to be involved with the NWA (ironically, the group that he had massively weakened in the late 1980s), and an affiliate company was chosen to crown the new NWA champion with a one-day tournament and a titleholder agreed by committee in the old fashion. The host company that they chose was based out of Philadelphia and was founded in

1989 by Joel Goodhart as Tri-State Wrestling, becoming Eastern Championship Wrestling in 1992 when Goodhart was bought out by business partner Tod Gordon. It quickly got a great reputation for hot crowds and exciting, often bloody action, with shows booked first by Eddie Gilbert and then, in 1993, by Paul Heyman, who had previously been working in WCW as motor-mouth manager Paul E Dangerously.

The tournament took place on 27 August 1994 at the ECW Arena, actually a former freight warehouse that doubled up as a bingo hall. ECW was chosen as it had the most eyes on it after a successful couple of years, so Crockett and Gordon got together to make it happen. NWA president at the time, Dennis Coralluzzo was worried that they'd then monopolise the NWA title like JCP had in the past, so he came along to oversee the tournament. Shane Douglas was scheduled to win the title, beating 2 Cold Scorpio in the final, but Gordon and Heyman had a very cunning plan indeed. They were aided by Douglas, who didn't care for Coralluzzo as there was animosity there over the NWA President bad-mouthing the soon-to-be-champ and word getting back to him.

After the final match, Douglas, who was also reigning ECW champion, was presented with the NWA title, which a decade before was the greatest honour in wrestling. Douglas, on the microphone, said, 'This is it tonight, Dad', a tribute to his recently deceased father who had drummed into him his belief in doing right by the people that do right by you.

Gordon and Heyman had looked after Douglas after he'd been let go by WCW; all Coralluzzo had done was cause him problems. He was absolutely on board with what his co-conspirators had suggested.

Douglas took a deep breath, before throwing the NWA belt down, saying to the partisan crowd that he had no intention of being the champion of a dead organisation. He then raised the ECW title, declared it as a World title, end of scene. The NWA was apoplectic with rage, with Coralluzzo immediately saying that he would strip Douglas of both the NWA title and ECW title; Tod Gordon responded by pulling ECW out of the NWA, reminding Coralluzzo that he had no jurisdiction over his hot, growing company, and changing what the 'E' stood for in ECW. No longer Eastern, now it was *Extreme*, reflecting the violence, cursing and blood that took place in that bingo hall.

The waves that ECW was making would soon reach both the WWF and WCW, but for now both companies remained mildly family-friendly. The workload was increasing too, with WWF adding cheaper pay per views called *In Your House* (starting in May 1995) to months that didn't have one of the 'big four' shows, increasing revenue but also removing some of the lustre from the massive shows. WCW took up a similar model, meaning more work for writers and bookers but making events blur into each other somewhat.

Neither company was short of raw talent at this point; the problem was both keeping hold of people as the war between the two heated up, and keeping them in line while they were under one umbrella.

The WWF was becoming dominated by a group of incredibly talented wrestlers who were aware of their market value and influence backstage: The Kliq. Formed in 1994, the initial line-up was Shawn Michaels, Razor Ramon (Scott Hall), Diesel (Kevin Nash) and the 1-2-3 Kid (Sean Waltman). Riding to shows together, partying together and prioritising each other's interests, they started influencing the booking of WWF shows, especially with three of the men – Michaels, Ramon and Diesel – being considered main-event-level talent. They were joined in 1995 by Paul Levesque, known in-ring as Hunter Hearst Helmsley (later in his career shortened to Triple H), who got on well with them but didn't drink. He initially broke into their group by being the designated driver.

Certain wrestlers that didn't see eye to eye with The Kliq would fall victim to their power, like Shane Douglas during his brief WWF stint who saw his push nullified, or Pierre Oulette who left the company because of them. Wrestling had always had its backstage alliances; indeed, The Undertaker and some of his friends (including Yokozuna, Savio Vega and the Godwinns) formed their own group called the Bone Street Krew (which is why 'Taker has BSK tattooed on his stomach); while Bret Hart was surrounded by family members, both through blood and marriage. A bit like prison, all of these groups had a working relationship with each other, but The Kliq was the most vocal and enthusiastic at getting its members' points across. In 1996, they'd be central to one event that kick-started chain reactions all over the place.

Over in WCW, Hogan had his group of compadres, as did Flair. Every now and again a great talent would fall through the cracks; one man was Steve Austin. A Texas native, he had been trained by 'Gentleman' Chris Adams and broken in through WCCW, taking the surname Austin instead of his birth name Williams to avoid confusion with the more famous Dr Death as that company became the USWA. By 1990, still a relative rookie, he signed to WCW and became 'Stunning' Steve Austin, quickly getting really good. He was part of Paul Heymans Dangerous

Alliance stable, then followed that in 1993 by being in one of the most underrated tag teams of all time, The Hollywood Blondes, with Brian Pillman. After that team was dissolved (far too soon, it could have run for years if it hadn't have been for the injury problems suffered by both men), he had a solid run as US Champion before losing it to Ricky Steamboat in 1994, then winning it back by default as 'The Dragon' suffered an injury; that was followed the same night by losing the belt in 35 seconds to one of Hogan's friends, Jim Duggan, who had recently joined the brand.

Austin then suffered some injuries in 1995; first a knee problem, then a triceps injury that he developed following a match in Japan. Eric Bischoff fired him while he was still laid up, lighting a fire underneath Austin that hadn't been seen before. Still injured, Paul Heyman hired him to appear in ECW as they were building their anti-establishment feel, mainly just to cut intense, funny, angry promos about Bischoff and Hogan, delivering vitriolic abuse that has become legendary as he took on the persona of 'Superstar' Steve Austin. Come on, we've all wanted to cut loose on an ex-boss that we've hated – Austin got paid to do it.

During his brief time in ECW, Austin would only have a handful of matches as he returned to full fitness, feuding over the ECW title with The Sandman and underdog champion Mikey Whipwreck. Whipwreck would give his Whippersnapper finisher to Austin, who'd rename it as the 'Stunner' and would go on to use it on wrestlers, celebrities and future Presidents of the USA. Austin never won the ECW belt, but built a massive buzz around himself, causing Vince McMahon – on the advice of right hand man and former WCW commentator Jim Ross – to hire him for the WWF.

At the WWF, he was given the gimmick of The Ringmaster, debuting in January 1996 as the charge of Ted DiBiase. By mid 1996, he had a different character and an all-new nickname that came about because of something that his British wife had said about a past-its-best cup of tea.

Even if you've been living under a rock, you know what that nickname is. A man with a shaven head, clad in plain black trunks was about to become the biggest thing in wrestling, helped by beer and the Bible.

Chapter Thirteen:
The Start of the War

The Monday Night War; the curtain call,
the New World Order and a loose cannon

As 1996 rolled around, the ratings war between *Raw* and *Nitro* was really heating up. The style of wrestling was initially still rooted in that of previous years, with WCW presenting family-orientated programming that was based around the fame of Hulk Hogan. The WWF had realised that the family audience was starting to dwindle and that *Raw*'s grittier feel had started to give the company a different, albeit smaller, identity. By the end of the year, the entire landscape would have shifted massively.

With WCW raiding his talent and pulling stunts like they did with Madusa and Luger, Vince had to hit back. Bischoff had also started airing segments on *Nitro* called *Where the Big Boys Play* at the end of 1995, taking pettiness to the next level as footage of former WCW wrestlers who had made their way to the WWF was shown, with their previous characters getting beaten and embarrassed, trying to illustrate that WCW was the better brand. Vince was understandably fuming at this, and it got worse as Bischoff, working as a commentator, started giving away endings to the matches due to air on pre-taped episodes of *Raw* while he was presenting live editions of *Nitro*. He was basically being that guy that we all know who can't wait to tweet spoilers for *Game of Thrones,* except this was making him money. The 2018 equivalent would be being a writer for *Buzzfeed.*

In January 1996, Vince started running segments on *Raw* entitled *Billionaire Ted's Wrasslin' Warroom* with actors playing stars who had jumped to WCW, with some mildly slanderous jokes mainly poking fun at the age of the chaps in question. Billionaire Ted was arch-nemesis Ted Turner, and he was joined by 'The Huckster', 'The Nacho Man' and 'Scheme Gene'. After a while, the USA Network asked for the sections to be dropped, but the fact that they ever existed shows you how rattled Vince was. I still don't think the name Nacho Man gets enough credit.

Luckily, WCW had let two more stars slip through their net and Vince quietly set about making them very different superstars to anything that had ever come before. The first was Dustin Runnels, the son of Dusty Rhodes, who had debuted in WWF in October 1995. During a decent run in WCW, he had been an upper-mid card player who always had to work in the shadow of his legendary father. He was fired by WCW in early 1995 after a ridiculous 'King of the Road' match at *Uncensored*. Ironically for a show with that title, Runnels and his opponent the Blacktop Bully were given their papers for blading during a match that took place on the back of a moving truck. With blood on screen and WCW being incredibly anti-plasma, what was an expensive gimmick match ended up having to be shown using mainly long-distance shots from a helicopter. After Dustin left WCW, WWF quickly picked him up and an outlandish gimmick was dreamed up, partially borne out of Rhodes and son no longer seeing eye to eye.

Dustin would become Goldust, clad in a shiny gold jumpsuit, long blond wig and face paint; he would deliver bizarre, innuendo-laden promos that pushed the buttons of the watching audience with over-the-top homoeroticism; and his name was a throwback to the lauded Gold Dust Trio of the 1920s. Fans had no idea how to take him, with Goldust instantly becoming one of the leading heels in the company, getting under the skin of Razor Ramon by essentially just clumsily flirting with him. At *WrestleMania XII* they were due to face off (more on that shortly) but Ramon was replaced by Roddy Piper, and they had a Hollywood Backlot Brawl match that managed to both parody the OJ Simpson slow-speed car chase and unintentionally resemble a hate crime as fans wildly cheered Piper beating up a character that they perceived to be homosexual.

Goldust would become Intercontinental Champion, eventually turning face by bringing his real-life wife Terri (initially named Marlena) into his storylines. The Goldust gimmick was, from the beginning, a brave, almost futuristic idea that helped Dustin step out of his father's shadow and enjoy a lengthy career. He would try to leave the gimmick behind a few times but always returned to it, having five stints in the WWF/WWE. He's still a roster member today, still wearing the face paint and a testimony to how different the character really was. A few years before, such a gimmick wouldn't have caught on, but in 1996 times really were changing among the wrestling audience.

Another guy started in the WWF in early 1996 with a very

different gimmick to what he'd been using before. He'd also had a good WCW run, but didn't have to step out of the shadow of his father. Mick Foley had been doing great things as Cactus Jack, but his time in WCW came to an end over money, and also because he spat on his WCW tag team belt during an excursion to the upstart ECW, trying to prove he could cater to hardcore wrestling fans who didn't care for Ted Turner's empire. Making his name on the independent scene, he would work mainly for the bloody, violent, adult-orientated ECW and the old-school, southern Smoky Mountain Wrestling, a company run by manager Jim Cornette. As I've already mentioned, he suggested that I be hung in a car park for the crime of scruffiness, I doubt we'll ever be best friends, but I'll say he was a great manager.

1995 was a crazy year for Foley, documented brilliantly in his first autobiography *Have a Nice Day: A Tale of Blood and Sweatsocks* which remains arguably the greatest wrestling memoir of all time, handwritten with pen on paper by a man who always demonstrated a special type of intelligence that contrasted with ECW's brand of extreme violence. In ECW, he would develop an anti-hardcore gimmick, refusing to use weapons and often sitting with a headlock applied to an opponent for as long as possible, as the fans in the ECW Arena in Philadelphia screamed for blood. During that time, he also put out two of the greatest promos ever recorded, the famous 'Cane Dewey' segment where he spoke about a fan's sign that implored opponent The Sandman to cane Foley's young son, meant as a joke but offending him massively, channeling his genuine rage into a tremendous piece; and also, a great interview where it looked like Foley was addressing a woman, making various rude comments, but he's actually talking to a steel chair ahead of a match with Tommy Dreamer.

On the flipside of this refusal to shed blood in ECW, that same year Foley spilled lots of his own (and others) in Japan for IWA (Independent Wrestling Association), in the now-legendary King of the Deathmatch tournament. In one August day, Foley went through three brutal matches: In the first round, he defeated Terry Gordy in a barbed wire bat and thumbtack deathmatch; in the second round, bested Shoji Nakamaki in a barbed wire board and bed of nails deathmatch and then in the final came out on top against good friend Terry Funk, still wrestling in Japan and reinventing himself to stay relevant, embracing the hardcore style (and also catching on well in ECW at the same time). That match was a – and brace yourself for this – barbed wire rope, barbed wire and C4 board, time bomb deathmatch. Every time either man would be thrown into the ropes, they would be cut to ribbons by the barbed wire; any time that either man hit one of the boards wrapped in wire and packed with explosives it would detonate, burning their flesh and deafening the crowd. The time bomb bit was less impressive, exploding after a countdown with both men down in the ring with a bit of smoke and a thud. Foley would retell the story of him being upgraded for his flight back to the USA because he was so badly burned from the C4 that he still smelled of smoke, his skin turning grey and flaking away all over his seat. He was paid $300 for that whole day's work.

As word got out of Foley moving to the WWF, ECW fans turned on him even more than his character had previously forced them to. They would chant 'You sold out' at him, while other wrestlers like Dean Malenko and Eddie Guerrero, bound for WCW, got 'Please don't go' chants during their final, epic two-out-of-three-falls match. After a few weeks of abject animosity, Foley was afforded a great ovation in his final-ever ECW match as fans begrudgingly admitted to themselves how much they would miss his talents, dancing out of the arena to the strains of *New York, New York*.

The WWF idea for Foley was to move him away from the Cactus Jack character that he'd been using for the previous decade and giving him a whole new character. Mindful of the initial unsuccessful Ringmaster gimmick that Steve Austin had been given, he made sure to give his opinion when his character was laid out to him: a masked madman called Mason the Mutilator. Foley didn't want to wear a mask, but that was amended to the now iconic leather strapping that was only half-mask and made him seem even crazier. He also suggested the name Mankind: Mason the Mutilator was dropped. On 1 April 1996, the day after *WrestleMania XII*, he made his debut on *Raw* in all-brown garb with a mysterious symbol embroidered on his back. His shrieking and heavy breathing in-ring made crowds sit up and take notice, his propensity for violence and taking extreme punishment really setting him apart.

Such was the level of insanity that Mankind demonstrated, he would soon become a viable opponent for The Undertaker, a man who had spent the previous few years nearly always taking on wrestlers around his size. Foley would embark on an on-and-off feud with 'Taker that lasted the best part of two years, being liked behind the scenes enough to score victories over 'The Deadman' and letting 'Taker show off in-ring work that he hadn't been able to for quite some time. Mankind and Undertaker would meet in Boiler Room Brawl (pre-recorded in the mythical boiler room that Mankind claimed to live in; the slight sticking point being it was always a different boiler room in whatever arena they were taping from) and Buried Alive matches, eventually involving Undertaker's long-term manager Paul Bearer and storyline brother Kane in the feud.

Mankind also had a wonderful match with Shawn Michaels at *In Your House: Mind Games*, a contest that showed just how well-conditioned Foley was despite his size and years of taking in-ring abuse. That match is one of the best to ever end in a disqualification, a work of art between two very different competitors. Another wonderful aspect of Foley's character at this time was he used two different theme tunes; one sinister one before he fought, then a soothing piano number after a match, that he would listen to while sat cross-legged, rocking back and forth and pulling his own hair out. Using a shrill 'Have a nice day' as his catchphrase, Mankind's character would be tweaked here and there, and occasionally replaced with alter-egos, but Foley would be a huge part of the next few years.

Speaking of Shawn Michaels, he had finally won the WWF title at *WrestleMania XII*, dethroning Bret Hart in an epic, brilliantly put together iron man match, where the winner would be the man with the most pinfalls or submissions after an entire hour of wrestling. This was an incredibly brave main event for a *'Mania* but showed you the trust that Vince had in his two most talented in-ring performers. Of course, they started slowly, conserving energy, but the scores were tied at 0–0 as the final 30 seconds of the match approached. Hart tied Michaels up in his patented Sharpshooter, really pulling back on it as the clock ticked down to zero and Michaels refused to give up. With no winner, the match went to overtime. Thirty seconds later, one 'Sweet Chin Music' from Michaels to Hart and it was all over. Hart waited around at the end of the match to pass the title to

Michaels and symbolically, away from storyline, pass the torch to his opponent, but The Heartbreak Kid screamed at the referee to get Hart out of the ring because it was his moment. This was the first big issue in a real-life rivalry that got increasingly messy.

The catalyst for business changing in the WWF happened in April 1996. It wouldn't immediately turn the company around, but it led to a chain of events that spiced up both sides of the battlefield. Razor Ramon and Diesel (Scott Hall and Kevin Nash) gave their notice to the WWF and signed with WCW, taking the huge contracts that Bischoff had dangled in front of them. On one hand, Vince couldn't compete with the astronomical figures that both men were offered; on the other, he didn't come back with too big a counter offer as he realised that losing Hall and Nash might well stop the monopoly on backstage power that The Kliq had. It was certainly a big risk to take. For a couple of years, it looked like letting them go had put a nail in WWF's coffin.

At Madison Square Garden on 19 May 1996, Hall and Nash had their last WWF matches at a house show. The main event put Nash up against WWF champion Michaels in a steel cage match. After Michaels had won, they were joined in the ring by fellow Kliq members Triple H and Hall (the 123 Kid was in rehab at the time so not part of this). All four men hugged in the middle of the steel cage in what became known as 'the curtain call', breaking their characters and more importantly, breaking kayfabe. This showed you how much power they wielded; not a single person stopped them from doing this. Hall and Nash wouldn't be punished as they were heading away from the company; indeed, Hall had already been suspended around *WrestleMania XII* for drug violations, the punishment possibly given partly because of his refusal to sign a new contract as well.

This left two men to take the fall for this, but one was the notoriously (at this point in his life) volatile Michaels who held the WWF title. Vince couldn't suspend him or give him any reason to breach his contract and end up on *Nitro*. Triple H could be punished though, and was de-pushed as much as possible, losing his chance to win the annual *King of the Ring* tournament and holding off his chance at being in the upper card for another couple of years. But that one hug between four friends managed to do two things: draw a buzz to the backstage business of professional wrestling as the internet started to catch on and more people looked for wrestling-based gossip online; it also meant that someone else would win *King of the Ring*. The guy they chose used that moment to invent a catchphrase that sold a million T-shirts. At least.

On 27 May 1996, unheralded grapplers Steve Doll and The Mauler were having a match on *Nitro*. All of a sudden, Scott Hall appeared from the crowd, an easily recognisable face to any wrestling fan. He climbed in the ring, got a microphone and said, in his faux-Latino accent: 'You all know who I am, but you don't know why I'm here.'

He would issue a challenge to WCW, alluding to other wrestlers soon joining him. At the end of the show, he grabbed Bischoff from his position on commentary and told him to tell Ted Turner to choose three wrestlers to represent WCW for a war. The following week, he continued his guerrilla tactics interrupting the show, promising a big surprise. That surprise would be Kevin Nash, joining up with Hall the next week. Dubbed 'The Outsiders', it was implied from their first entry into WCW that they were still working for the WWF. With Hall still acting like Razor Ramon (Nash's Diesel character wasn't so well-defined and away from his normal demeanour), Vince was understandably annoyed as he felt that WCW were running storylines with characters that he had developed, not to mention the suggestion that they were actually representing his company. Legal action was taken.

As The Outsiders caught fire in WCW, the WWF response was to take the very unusual step of still using the characters of Razor Ramon and Diesel, with more background stuff being alluded to as Jim Ross introduced the new versions, revealing that he had a backstage role outside of just being a commentator. Ramon would be played by Rick Bognar, who had previously worked in Japan as Big Titan. Diesel would be played by Glen Jacobs, who had previously played demonic dentist Isaac Yankem within the WWF and was well liked. He would eventually go on to play The Undertaker's brother, Kane, initially under a mask. The all-new versions of Ramon and Diesel did not succeed, but this is wrestling – maybe that was always the plan, killing off their legacy while they built a new career in WCW.

The 'war' between The Outsiders and WCW came to a head at *Bash at the Beach 1996*, in a main event dubbed the 'hostile takeover'. WCW was represented by Sting, Lex Luger and Randy Savage, the latter an odd choice as he'd been in WCW for a couple of years but before that was in WWF for a decade. The Outsiders hinted at having a third man, but started as a duo, quickly incapacitating Luger so he was carried out on a stretcher and making the contest a level two on two. After a low blow on Savage by Nash, all four men were down in the ring, when out came Hulk Hogan. The crowd went wild, presuming Hogan was there to protect the honour of WCW.

As the crowd popped, Hogan strode to the ring, pointing and looking angry. He climbed inside the squared circle, tore off his shirt as he had done thousands of times before, the fans screaming for him to help his stricken friends. Then, out of nowhere, he hit his leg drop on Randy Savage, turning heel for the first time in 15 years. With the crowd in absolute disbelief, he dropped another leg drop on Savage and celebrated with Hall and Nash, throwing the referee out of the ring so the match was called as a no contest. With trash raining down on the ring from the genuinely distraught crowd, Hogan cut a promo with his new friends, dubbing the group the New World Order of Professional Wrestling. That group name would be shortened to just the nWo, even if Hogan accidentally called it the less impressive 'New World Organisation' at one point, making it sound like a telemarketing company. The best part of the whole turn was how commentator Tony Schiavone sold it: ending the broadcast by saying 'Hulk Hogan . . . you can go to hell'.

Bischoff came up with the idea for the nWo after attending NJPW's *Battle Formation* show at the Tokyo Dome, an event built around the invasion of New Japan by upstart shoot-style promotion UWFi. Founded by, among others, Nobuhiko Takada, it followed on from what both incarnations of the UWF tried to do in the 1980s and was initially very successful, drawing good crowds with matches that *looked* real but remained pre-determined, using Lou Thesz in a commissioner role and declaring their title to be the 'Real Pro Wrestling World Heavyweight Championship'. Takada would challenge champions of other companies in Japan, calling their forms of wrestling 'fake'. But after an initially super-hot period, the company was getting stale and losing money. In late 1995, it was proposed that they co-promoted shows with NJPW.

Unfortunately for everyone at UWFi, NJPW booker Riki Choshu negotiated that his company would have full control of the booking of the 'invasion'. Aside from Takada having a run with the IWGP Heavyweight Championship, the UWFi guys were nearly always booked to lose to their NJPW rivals, making only one company look like a big deal. Once the angle had run its course, UWFi only lasted for a few more months before closing its doors. But Bischoff saw the genuinely innovative idea of having one company invade another as a really cool concept, and he wanted to utilise the animosity between WCW and WWF to fuel speculation and rumour, even if he knew he wouldn't actually be able to work with the WWF.

Once he had signed up Hall and Nash and turned Hogan, the nWo would have a different aesthetic to their segments on *Nitro* and pay per views, filming their promos in black and white and even inserting fake commercials into TV broadcasts for their 'brand'.

Taking the name 'Hollywood' Hogan, the former Hulkster quickly became the central figure of the nWo, even if the initial buzz was built off The Outsiders. He started wearing black, in line with the group's monochrome colour scheme. At *Hog Wild* in August 1996, he won the WCW title from former rival The Giant (who was, upon his debut, billed as the son of Andre the Giant to kick-start a feud with Hogan), who was now a babyface, taking the historic big gold belt and spray-painting 'nWo' on the front of it. *Hog Wild*, which became *Road Wild* the next year was a strange PPV show, presented at the Sturgis Motorcycle Rally in front of a crowd that paid nothing to get in and often didn't care too much about the wrestling. Eric Bischoff sure loved bikes though, so those shows happened for four years.

The New World Order soon started to expand; slowly at first before getting wildly out of hand. At the *Nitro* after Hogan's title victory they were joined by another WWF convert, Ted DiBiase who took up the nickname 'Trillionaire Ted' to be a better version of his 'Million Dollar Man' gimmick, acting as spokesman and financier for the group.

Next to join was The Giant; if I listed every time the big man really known as Paul Wight has turned from face to heel or vice versa during his career in WCW and then WWF in this book then it would run to many, many more pages. Having recently feuded with Hogan, his arrival really jarred with logic.

Next was Fake Sting, a wrestler called Jeff Farmer who was following the *real* Sting by copying his gimmick, even as it was evolving from blond surfer dude to black-clad goth guy who had watched *The Crow*. Sting's new character would become a really cool part of WCW, as he barely wrestled, doubted everyone around him and attacked people at random.

Fake Sting would do his thing while the real one vanished for a while, then the sixth member of the nWo returned us to the WWF invasion theme. Kliq member Sean '123 Kid' Waltman jumped over to WCW to be with his buddies, taking the name Syxx in honour of his number on their roll call.

At this point, it did all seem to make sense. Then the silliness started to kick in. The group gained Nick Patrick as their own biased referee; Miss Elizabeth as *another* manager figure, mainly to accompany Hogan; and the artist formerly known in WWF as Virgil, now called Vincent as a dig at McMahon. No disrespect to the guy, but he wasn't exactly a top-tier addition and was labelled as 'security', having the odd match here and there.

Every heel group needs someone to oppose them, but with Sting not around the WCW side didn't have much going for it and no real leader. They got one in Roddy Piper who became the chief thorn in the nWo's side, despite nobody pointing out that he'd basically been a WWF talent for years as well. Even now I can't believe that nobody noticed that.

On *Nitro* on 18 November, Hogan and his cronies spent much of the show harassing Eric Bischoff. At the end, Piper and Bischoff were arguing in the ring and the nWo saved their back-stage boss; he then revealed that he was always in the group (bear in mind he had been beaten up by them repeatedly for weeks) and became an egomaniacal company boss. He was, to be fair, absolutely great in that role.

Yet more joined the nWo towards the end of 1996 as Bischoff told his WCW employees (in character) that they had to choose a side. Those that did included Buff Bagwell, Mr Wallstreet, Big Bubba Rogers, Scott Norton and Masahiro Chono who began spin-off group nWo Japan. The main foe for the company on the WCW side was Diamond Dallas Page, previously a manager who had belatedly developed into a great and charis-matic wrestler in his thirties. The whole storyline really propelled him into the main event and helped him build an impressive career. In a strange turn of events, his yoga and self-help company *DDP Yoga* has been instrumental in saving the careers of many wrestlers, but most notably saving the actual life of his former nWo foe Scott Hall, who he helped to kick alcohol and get into better shape. DDP is legitimately one of the nicest people on the planet.

Oh, and of course, by the end of 1996 The Giant was kicked out of the group.

Sure, the nWo storyline had been doing great business, but for me there was an even more interesting storyline during this period, one that took one of the most talented in-ring workers and blurred the lines of storyline and reality in a quite extraordinary way. Brian Pillman had built a career on having hard-hitting, high-flying matches with opponents like Jushin Liger earlier in the decade, before teaming with Steve Austin and showing what a great talker he was with his raspy voice, affected by dozens of surgeries on his throat as a child. Pillman had enjoyed a quick excursion to ECW in 1994 as a result of a brief talent exchange, and he stored that experience for later use. He wrestled in the first-ever *Nitro* match against long-time foe Liger, before being part of a great incarnation of the Four Horsemen with Ric Flair, Arn Anderson and Chris Benoit, recently signed from ECW and having made an impressive name for himself in Japan.

By the end of 1995, he had started running a gimmick that he called the 'Loose Cannon', wearing leather and shades and acting absolutely crazy. Not just 'wrestling crazy', but living the gimmick, acting like it all the time and going so far when he was on TV that his own stablemates didn't even know what to do with him. He became the master of the *worked shoot*, performing promos that seemed to tell the fans inside information when he was actually working in as scripted a way as everyone else. On a *Clash of the Champions* show in January 1996, he wandered over to Bobby Heenan on commentary and grabbed him by his neck without warning. Heenan, who had injured his neck earlier in his career, blurted out, 'What the fuck are you doing?'

At *Superbrawl VI* in February, Pillman was booked into an 'I Respect You' strap match with Kevin Sullivan, who was actually running much of the behind-the-scenes workings of the company. It was a regular strap match, the men bound together at the wrists with a leather strap and the winner being the first to touch all four corners of the ring in turn. The twist was that the loser would have to say in public that he respected the victor. Before the match could even begin, Pillman took the microphone and said, 'I respect you, booker man' before leaving. This was genuinely mind-melting at the time, a wrestler calling someone the *booker* on screen. The growing internet community of smart fans went crazy for this, and Bischoff fired Pillman, for breaking the fourth wall. For real. Except this firing was just to make the whole storyline, which Bischoff was in on, look more convincing. Bischoff approved of Pillman heading to ECW to do even more crazy stuff and develop his character and notoriety. At no point did Bischoff think this might backfire on him in any way. Pillman was about to work many more people than just the fans.

At ECW's *Cyberslam* in February 1996, Pillman appeared and cut a promo in the ring, calling Bischoff a 'piece of shit' and then trying to urinate in the ring before being dragged away. During the melee getting him back to the locker room, he stabbed a planted front-row fan with a fork. The buzz around Pillman was now massive, and Bischoff presumably sat back in his office waiting for the ratings he'd draw when he recalled him to WCW. But Pillman, for the sake of that much-needed realism, wasn't Bischoff's employee anymore. Vince wanted him and signed him up to the first guaranteed money contract in WWF history, with Bischoff unable to do anything about it.

Pillman was due to head to WWF after a short feud with

ECW's Shane Douglas, but in April 1996 he fell asleep at the wheel of his car and was in a quite awful accident. He remained in a coma for a week and had to have his shattered ankle fused into a walking position. Because he'd already signed for the WWF, he initially used his charisma to work as a commentator. Sadly, he died prematurely in October 1997 following a heart attack from a previously undiagnosed condition, but not before he had his part in a brilliant angle and one of the most controversial episodes of *Raw* ever.

Chapter Fourteen:
The Birth of Attitude

Austin 3:16 to the Montreal Screwjob

Brian Pillman's former tag team partner Steve Austin wasn't happy with how he'd started off in the WWF. His Ringmaster gimmick wasn't exactly setting the world on fire, so he started trying to come up with something more suitable and memorable than just being good at wrestling and representing Ted DiBiase. Inspired by various people including serial killer Richard Kuklinski, he wanted to be a tough, no-nonsense loner; a ruthless, cold-blooded killer. He was apparently given new potential names by the creative department at the WWF that included Chilly McFreeze and the absolutely terrible Otto Von Ruthless. In the end he kept his original in-ring name but added the prefixed nickname 'Stone Cold' after hearing his English wife say the phrase when talking about her cup of tea.

Once switched into his new gimmick, he then started to catch on, despite being a heel. He'd cheat, stick two middle fingers up to the crowd, hit low blows, use weapons and generally be a massive, angry tool of a human being. But there was *something* there that made people boo him with a smile on their faces. They wanted to see him wrestle, win or lose; every time he hit his new finisher, the 'Stone Cold Stunner', the crowd would pop.

With Triple H still the only member of The Kliq who could be chastised for the Curtain Call incident, with Michaels WWF champion and Hall and Nash in WCW, a new planned winner of the *King of the Ring 1996* tournament was required. With Austin starting to make waves, he was chosen. It would end up being one of the best decisions in wrestling history. Only the semi-finals and final were part of the pay-per-view show; in his semi Austin beat Marc Mero, also recently signed from WCW, who had been working as a flamboyant Little Richard-based character called Johnny B Badd, making his entrances there with a device called the 'Badd Blaster' that would fire confetti into the crowd. In the WWF, he had a gimmick of being a wrestler crossed with a boxer, playing into his legitimate background. He'd eventually be overshadowed by his wife, Sable, who had been signed at the same time as Mero.

In that semi-final match, Austin received an injury to his mouth that later required stitches. While he was being sewn up, he started thinking about things he could say later on that night when he'd be crowned as King of the Ring. He wasn't about to make being the King his gimmick like Harley Race did back in the 1980s, but he knew this would be a huge moment. The final match pitted Austin against Jake Roberts, who was back in the WWF after some time in the wilderness battling the demons of drink and drugs, and also finding religion. Both of these aspects of his life were being used as part of his gimmick. Austin won the match in less than five minutes, and then when he was being crowned as the King he spoke about Roberts and uttered the catchphrase that launched his career into the stratosphere and sold about a million T-shirts:

'You sit there, and you thump your Bible, and you say your prayers, and it didn't get you anywhere. Talk about your Psalms, talk about John 3:16; Austin 3:16 says I just whipped your ass!'

Just a week later, signs saying 'Austin 3:16' started springing up throughout arenas for *Raw* tapings. As he was still a heel, it took a while for Austin to start getting his own merchandise. When he did, he became a multi-millionaire just from that, with the iconic black '3:16' shirt worn everywhere the eye could see in some venues. Austin started to be booked as something of a tweener; not face or heel, acting very much like a villain but getting cheered just because he was incredibly cool.

He got into a feud with Brian Pillman that culminated in Austin visiting the injured Pillman at his home during an episode of *Raw* in November 1996. With wrestling meeting reality television and resembling an episode of *Cops*, Austin forced his way into the Pillman household only to be confronted by the Loose Cannon holding an *actual* cannon (of sorts); with Pillman pointing a handgun at Austin and screaming, 'Get out of the fucking way!', the feed cut out and the screen faded to black. While the WWF would apologise for the language and violent nature of the segment, it certainly was memorable.

The Pillman/Austin feud was built around how 'Stone Cold' didn't like how his former partner was taking the side of Bret Hart. 'The Hitman' had taken a fair part of 1996 away from wrestling, and Austin kept using TV time to try and goad him into returning. After weeks of insults, Hart made his comeback and a fantastic match was set up for *Survivor Series 1996* that Hart won with the same sleeper/roll-up combination that he'd beaten Roddy Piper for the Intercontinental title with at *WrestleMania VIII*. Both Hart and Austin were then in the final two at the *Royal Rumble* in January 1997, with Hart eliminating Austin but the officials not seeing it, before Austin picked up the victory. They would then be part of the four-man, elimination rules main event at *In Your House: Final Four* with Vader and The Undertaker, with the now *vacant* WWF title at stake. But why had the belt been held up?

On 13 February 1997, a special edition of *Raw* aired on a different day to usual. Called *Thursday Raw Thursday*, it came from Lowell, Massachusetts, and is remembered mainly for one interview. Shawn Michaels had been WWF champion for much of 1996 after winning the belt at *WrestleMania XII*. He lost the title to Sycho Sid at *Survivor Series* but won it back at the *Royal Rumble*. Just two weeks later, he would walk out on TV and hand the title over to Vince McMahon, seemingly leaving wrestling forever. Michaels' in-ring style had certainly taken its toll on him; he was known for being one of the best sellers in the game and he had suffered a genuine career-threatening knee injury. That's not what most fans remember the interview for though; it's more for him 'losing his smile'.

What he actually said was as follows:

'. . . I have to go back and fix myself, and take care of myself, and I have to go back, and I have to find my smile because somewhere along the line I lost it . . .'

Michaels came across as genuinely emotional and very nervous throughout the interview. But somewhere backstage, Bret Hart was watching a TV screen and lost his mind. He was convinced that Michaels wasn't all *that* hurt and was simply giving up the title rather than lose it to him at *WrestleMania XIII*, as had been mooted. As Michael's speech played out in front of him, this was another factor in developing the ongoing legitimate mistrust and bitterness between Michaels and Hart as the two most popular men in the company continued to butt heads backstage. It wasn't over between the two of them yet, not by a long shot.

Hart didn't win the WWF title at *WrestleMania XIII*, but he was part of the best WWF match of the 1990s, an absolutely spellbinding contest that didn't even have a title at stake. Hart met Austin in a submission only match, with UFC star (and soon to be WWF superstar) Ken Shamrock as guest referee. This match showcased one of the trickiest storyline points to carry off, something that has been done so rarely in the history of wrestling and certainly never to the level that it was done here: the double turn.

Going into the event, Hart was *in theory* the babyface, and Austin was *allegedly* the heel. For a double turn to work, you've got to be able to read what the crowd is starting to do; in the case of Austin, they desperately wanted to cheer for him. In the case of Hart, he was starting to be positioned as a little bit of a whiner, screaming 'Bullshit' at Vince McMahon on an episode of *Raw* when Austin and The Undertaker interfered in his business and factored into him not winning the WWF title. Hart had been on top for a few years and he and the WWF management realised that the tide was starting to turn. Traditional babyfaces – much like Hogan when he started in WCW – just weren't as appealing to an audience anymore.

They wanted cool anti-heroes like Austin. They just needed to officially change the face and heel dynamic and had one match to get it right for both men.

As the match was submission only, it meant that there could be no disqualifications. So instead of just getting mat-based technical wrestling, the crowd in Chicago got a lot of brawling and hardcore violence, with Hart getting more and more angry and being keener to resort to underhanded tactics in order to get the job done. Austin was bloodied by Hart (0.5 Muta) and locked into the Sharpshooter at the end of the match, valiantly refusing to submit, screaming in pain as blood poured down his face and the crowd started chanting his name. He passed out in the hold, giving Hart the win but the fans had chosen *their* winner. As Hart left the ring, the vast majority of the audience in the arena booed him, while Austin received a standing ovation. For pretty much the rest of 1997, neither man looked back.

After *'Mania*, Hart's in-ring business picked up even more with a modern take on national identity. He was reunited with his family members – brother Owen, brothers-in-law The British Bulldog and Jim Neidhart, and also Brian Pillman – and started denouncing crowds in the USA, playing up his Canadian heritage and using the bitterness that had already seen him turn heel. This led to nuclear heat at any show in the US and waves of genuine love at all shows within Canada. This rivalry between two countries came to a head at a pay per view – *In Your House: Canadian Stampede* – that is overlooked by many, but had some wonderful contests on it: Mankind against Triple H, now accompanied to the ring by 'the ninth wonder of the world' Chyna, a female bodybuilder who was as tall and muscular as many of the men on the roster; The Great Sasuke, a masked high-flyer from Japan against his compatriot Taka Michinoku; and in the main event, The Hart Family against Austin, Shamrock, Goldust and The Legion of Doom in a ten-man tag team match that was accompanied by an atmosphere that has rarely been topped since, the Harts victory treated like a Stanley Cup triumph.

Austin and Owen Hart would go on to a feud, and that rivalry would nearly end Stone Cold's career. At *Summerslam* in a match for the Intercontinental title, Owen dropped Austin on his head with a piledriver but performed it in a way that Austin wasn't used to, keeping slightly too much of his head exposed and severely injuring his neck. Unable to initially move but knowing he had to win the match, Austin somehow weakly rolled up Owen to get the win before being taken out to be treated. The injury changed his in-ring style, meaning he had to brawl more for the rest of his career rather than be as technical as he initially was, and limiting the risks that he put himself through.

Behind the scenes, Bret wasn't enjoying himself anywhere near as much though. Shawn Michaels returned to wrestling fairly quickly after having knee surgery, as Bret suspected he would, and was very much back to his best. The two men kept aiming barbs at each other both backstage and in-ring, Hart bringing up Michaels posing for *Playgirl* in one promo and then Michaels hitting back by saying that he'd heard his rival had been enjoying a lot of 'Sunny days' lately. That might have sounded like an odd insult to anyone who wasn't party to backstage gossip, but Michaels was referring to the manager Tammy Sytch, known as Sunny, one of the most popular women during the early years of the internet. By throwing out a thinly veiled suggestion that the married Hart was seeing Sunny (who, in turn was married to wrestler Chris Candido; Hart has denied these accusations in his own autobiography), Michaels found himself in a very real fight backstage with Hart, having some of his long hair pulled out before walking out of a *Raw* taping. From a comedy point of view, it's a great gag, especially if Shawn improvised it; from a sensitivity point of view, a little bit less so.

The animosity between the two wasn't helped by Bret's contractual status. He was by far and away the best paid member of the WWF roster. In 1996, he had negotiated with both WWF and WCW to see what the best deal he could get would be. Bischoff was desperate to sign him, offering him a massive $8 million, three-year deal that would have seen him at home with his family a lot more (presumably in a solid-gold mansion). But staying loyal to Vince was important as it was he who made him the star that he was, and he chose instead to sign a deal for less money per year but the job security of spending the rest of his career with the WWF; he agreed a 20-year contract that made him the highest paid wrestler in the company so long as he was still an active member of the roster, then he would transition to a senior managerial position upon retirement.

The prompting for guys like Hart and Michaels to bring backstage issues in front of the cameras came in part from Vince Russo, who was appointed head writer for the WWF in early 1997. He was hired in 1992 to work on the official WWF magazine, then climbed the ladder until he found himself with huge influence over the direction of the televised product. He loved worked shoots and put a lot of emphasis on sudden turns or swerves and a distinctly less family-friendly product. Somewhat reflective of the watching generation's attention span, *Raw* started having less wrestling and more segments, things moving quickly in a style of television that was eventually dubbed 'Crash

TV'. Hart wasn't a fan of Russo, but the writer knew the value of appealing to the growing legions of smart internet fans and his style of writing started pushing Michaels to the forefront again.

While Russo was helping change WWF television, WCW was still winning the ratings war thanks to the successful nWo gimmick. But it was starting to get a little bit silly, with Randy Savage feuding with the group for months and then inexplicably joining up with them. International stars like Konnan from Mexico and Hiroyoshi Tenzan and The Great Muta from Japan were added to the bulging group roster. And then, for some reason, basketball star and general oddball Dennis Rodman joined up with them, even teaming up with Hogan for a wrestling match against Lex Luger and The Giant. Well, I say 'wrestling' but Rodman mainly looked a bit out of it on the apron. Ridiculous as this will sound, that was not even the stupidest celebrity involvement in WCW at this time.

With the nWo doing undeniably great business, the WWF started introducing factions galore to see what caught on, leading to an era known as 'Gang Warz' where everybody apart from Austin seemed to be aligned to one group or another. Obviously, you had the Harts, then in June 1997 The Nation of Domination, led by Farooq (the artist formerly known as Ron Simmons), got rid of a couple of members, leading to them setting up other stables in their wake and Faarooq reinventing the Nation-of-Islam-inspired group.

Savio Vega and Crush were the two men that Farooq cut loose; Vega brought in a group of fellow Hispanic wrestlers and became Los Boricuas, while Crush teamed up with Chainz, Skull and 8-Ball to become biker gang D.O.A. The Nation in its new form had Farooq, D-Lo Brown, former Olympic weightlifter Mark Henry, Kama Mustafa (formerly Papa Shango, soon to be the Godfather) and some guy who really couldn't catch on as a babyface, Rocky Maivia. He'd now be known as The Rock.

The three groups would feud throughout the year, but they're not the stable that everyone remembers the most from the WWF at that point.

Feuding with the Hart Family as autumn 1997 rolled in, Shawn Michaels had accidentally got himself a stable. With most of The Kliq now in WCW, he still had his allies. Triple H and Chyna joined up with him, making their real-life friendship part of the storyline, and the group would be managed by Rick Rude, back in the WWF after some time in WCW and a great little stint in ECW. Only two members of the group wrestled, Rude having retired from in-ring activity through injury and Chyna not yet fully trained as a wrestler. On every edition of *Raw*, Michaels and Triple H would get up to various childish, innuendo-laden antics, even stripping on one edition of the show. Hart would call Michaels a 'degenerate' in one interview, leading to the name of the group: D-Generation X. It was expected that DX and the Harts would feud for the next few months, maybe the next year. But one night in Canada quickly stopped that.

In mid 1997, the WWF was struggling financially after a few years of sluggish ticket sales and pay-per-view buys. While business seemed to be turning around, it needed an injection of cash, so Vince made the decision to try and float the company on the stock market. In order to do this, he needed to eliminate any long-term financial commitments that the company had. One of those commitments that the accountants flagged up was Bret

Hart's 20-year contract, a few payments of which WWF had deferred on due to their cash-flow issues.

While it was true that Bret was still a huge star, he was starting to be eclipsed by guys on less money than him: Michaels, The Undertaker and especially Steve Austin. Vince spoke to Bret and told him that he would honour their deal but didn't necessarily have any huge plans for him; he also said that Hart would be free to talk to WCW if he wanted to, just to see what they had on offer. Bischoff offered Bret a *lot* of money: $3 million per year to do fewer dates than he was doing in the WWF. It was too good for Hart to refuse, and he signed the deal. He would become a WCW wrestler from 5 December.

But there was an issue. Hart was, after *Summerslam 1997*, the WWF champion. Going into *Survivor Series*, Hart's final WWF pay per view, the number one contender was Shawn Michaels. These two men already didn't get on and their relationship worsened after a backstage meeting between the two in October that was supposed to clear the air. At first, Hart told Michaels that he would be professional and lose to him if instructed to do so, with Hart knowing that he had some degree of creative control in his contract. Michaels apparently replied that he wouldn't do the same if he was told to, leading to any hope of a resolution between the two being abandoned and Hart then insisting that he would never lose the title to Michaels. Hart was a proud man and although technically speaking a title is just a prop, winning one is usually the reward for being at the top of the business. The animosity between him and Michaels was at such a level that it would be a blow to his honour and pride in dropping the belt to The Heartbreak Kid.

Michaels had of course lost cleanly to Hart before, but this was before The Kliq had the power that they did and before he personally was such a main-event player. Vince was in a pickle as he needed Hart to drop the title before he left; he couldn't risk having another star jump to WCW and throw a title in a trash can like Madusa did. Bret knew this – all he wanted to happen was to be represented well on his way out of the company that he'd served for so long. He certainly never threatened to resort to the usual dirty WCW tactics.

Survivor Series was in Hart's native Canada, in Montreal. Hart offered to drop the title in the USA prior to the show to anyone other than Michaels, or to vacate the title on *Raw* in Ottawa the next evening. He even offered to stay a little longer to drop the title in a way that suited before he started in WCW, with the gap between his contract ending in one company and starting in the other.

The tension between WCW and WWF no doubt played on Vince's mind during all of this. *Nitro* was now a three-hour broadcast to *Raw*'s two hours, starting an hour earlier. There was a chance that Bischoff could kick off *Nitro*'s first hour, unopposed by WWF, and announce to the world that he had signed Hart, or give away that he would be dropping the title with his move imminent. Vince felt something needed to be done. He sat in a hotel room in Montreal the day before *Survivor Series* and planned out events with Michaels and Pat Patterson. Hart had already agreed to allow Michaels to put him in his own 'Sharpshooter' move at some point when the referee would be knocked out. The supposed end for the match, as agreed with Hart, was meant to be a double disqualification, no-contest deal as D-Generation X and the Hart Family came in and brawled as the referee came back to consciousness.

Other wrestlers close to Hart, however, warned him to watch out for being screwed.

Much of that night is documented in the superb documentary *Wrestling with Shadows*; the match itself started with intense heat for both competitors. Michaels came to the ring and picked his nose with the Canadian flag, before going on to do much worse to it, playing up the US v Canada rivalry that had been running for months. Hart came out to a hero's welcome initially, but you could still hear chants of 'You sold out' from pockets of the crowd. The ring was surrounded by an unusually large amount of match agents, explained away as being needed because of the volatile situation in storyline between Hart and Michaels and their warring factions. In reality, it was to ensure that Vince's carefully constructed plan to protect his championship went ahead without a hitch.

Vince wasn't on commentary for the match and was instead on his feet at ringside, something that Hart thought was odd at the time. The referee, Earl Hebner (of wonderful Andre and Hogan angle fame), took his bump as planned and Hart relaxed, allowing Michaels to put him in the Sharpshooter, presuming the planned finish was coming up in a few minutes. Hebner was meant to stay down to allow for the planned interference, but Hebner was soon up on his feet, shouting at the timekeeper to ring the bell. Vince did the same, and the bell was rung. Hebner made a sharp exit from the ring; Michaels was declared champion but didn't look happy about it, in order to ensure he didn't look in on the plan.

Hart was incredibly angry, spitting in Vince's face and painting out the letters 'W' 'C' 'W' with his hands. With Michaels ushered backstage, Hart smashed up the ringside area out of sheer rage.

Something like this hadn't happened on as large a stage since Stanislaus Zybysko screwed the Gold Dust Trio.

By the time Hart got backstage, Michaels was in tears insisting that he didn't know a thing. The Undertaker, by now the respected locker room leader, told Vince that he needed to apologise to Hart or risk a mutiny. McMahon made his way to Hart's locker room to speak to him; when he refused to leave at Hart's request, Hart punched him in the face, knocking him to the ground.

There was a potential revolt in the locker room. Hart was a respected veteran and popular with his fellow wrestlers; furthermore, it made everyone worry that a similar thing could happen to them. Neidhart, Bulldog and Owen all left the arena with Bret; Owen couldn't get out of his contract so remained working for the WWF while the other men gradually moved over to WCW. Some wrestlers wanted to make a stand for Bret; Mick Foley didn't show up for *Raw* the next night, but Hart convinced him to go back to work, knowing that it was the best job he'd ever had. Vince also took the time to explain to his locker room why he did what he did.

Rick Rude did quit, jumping immediately to WCW and showing up on a live *Nitro* that was opposite a recorded *Raw*. They used this to showcase the live nature of WCW TV by Rude having a moustache on *Nitro* versus a full beard on *Raw*. This may have been one of the first times that facial hair was used to prove a point.

As more fans became smart to what had happened, now dubbed 'the Montreal Screwjob', the knock-on effect was that Vince became the Mr McMahon character that would be an integral part to WWF turning the tide in the ratings battle over the next couple of years. It would be acknowledged that he ran the WWF and wasn't just a commentator, stating at one point that 'Bret screwed Bret' and taking the heat he was getting and turning it into *wrestling* heat. The screwjob would be used in storylines going forwards, most notably at *Survivor Series 1998*. Bret wouldn't hit the heights he expected in WCW, soon joining the massed ranks of the nWo and sadly being finished in-ring by 2000 after having a stroke.

Fans will always speculate whether Hart was actually in on the screwjob or not. A film was made about it, books have been written about it and Hart and Michaels have long since kissed and made up. Hart's an old-school guy; if he was in on it, he'll never tell us. Over 20 years later, wrestling fans are still debating it as enthusiastically as they did when it first happened.

The old-school style of wrestling was starting to become much less prevalent as the top of the WWF card was all about guys like Michaels, Austin, Undertaker, Triple H, The Rock and more adult-orientated violence and mature storylines. The in-ring style in the USA was evolving thanks mainly to one company drawing the eye of both WWF and WCW: Paul Heyman's ECW. This was a company that in 1997 was absolutely on fire. Sometimes literally, so a man could be thrown through it.

What most fans at the time didn't realise is that ECW had a very close relationship with WWF in particular, with Vince secretly helping out with some money here and there and wrestler loans. ECW had its first pay per view in April 1997, but it nearly didn't get to that stage because of money, censorship and a kid getting stabbed in the head.

ECW was *meant* to debut on pay per view in December 1996 with its *Barely Legal* show, but that plan was derailed after a match on a house show in Revere, Massachusetts. The Gangstas – New

Jack and Mustafa – were due to take on D-Von Dudley and Axl Rotten, but Rotten couldn't make the show for family reasons. A young man called Eric Kulas introduced himself to Paul Heyman and offered to replace Rotten, claiming to be 23 years old and having been trained by Killer Kowalski. He had the gimmick of being a bus driver and, being a large chap, worked under the name 'Mass Transit'. That would be a brilliant joke if the rest of this story wasn't so horrible.

The match would involve very little wrestling and mainly weapon shots, so Kulas would need to bleed. He'd never bladed before, so he made the very silly decision of asking New Jack to blade for him.

Now, I have met New Jack. He was perfectly pleasant to me but did call me a pussy for refusing to drink with him at a show in Miami. When I insisted I couldn't drink as I used to have an alcohol problem, he patted me on the back, told me he respected my sobriety, then laughed, stopped suddenly and told me I was still a pussy. Even if the next part of this story had never happened, New Jack would still have a reputation for being a bit crazy, having got into shoots with other wrestlers and at one time working as a bounty hunter.

The match was supposed to be a massacre, with D-Von left on the outside and the Gangstas beating Kulas down with weapons in the ring for the victory. They hit him with, among other things, crutches and a toaster. When the time came for Jack to blade Kulas, he didn't lightly graze him with a sliver of a razor. He used an actual knife and sliced Kulas so deeply that he cut through two arteries in his forehead. Blood actually sprayed upwards from the face of Kulas as he lay on the mat, screaming. The Gangstas kept beating down Kulas as the ring became covered in blood (yes, it was 1.0 Muta) and all of a sudden, a voice was heard from the crowd. It was Kulas' father screaming, 'Ring the fucking bell! He's 17!'

New Jack was painted as a villain by the Kulas family on the TV show *Inside Edition*, focusing on the violence in the match and what he'd said on the microphone after the match: 'I don't care if that motherfucker dies'. As Kulas was presented as the innocent victim, what they *didn't* discuss all came out during criminal proceedings three years later, when New Jack was tried on charges of assault and battery with a dangerous weapon.

Firstly, if you watch the footage (the show was shot on a camcorder and was a hot property for tape traders back in the late 1990s), you can see New Jack clearly ask Kulas if he's okay after blading him. The reason he did it so deep is that the overweight Kulas had thick, virgin skin on his forehead. It was an accident. The whole 'motherfucker' speech was both in character and also to fill time while Kulas got medical attention. As Kulas was carried out, he raised his middle finger to the crowd, and he was seen to puff his cheeks out in order to make the blood flow even more. The criminal case was thrown out and the Kulas family were told they could not file civil charges either.

The Mass Transit incident may have caused the first planned ECW pay per view to be pulled, but it also added to the aura of the outlaw promotion. The rescheduled *Barely Legal* was actually plugged on WWF television, with ECW wrestlers 'invading' editions of *Raw* and stars like Sabu and Taz starting to get formidable reputations. Vince certainly noticed the reactions that ECW was getting with an adult crowd and applied much of that style to his growing 18-plus audience.

On 15 December 1997, *Raw* began with Vince himself, in a

studio, delivering a pre-recorded speech. He addressed the audience directly, wearing a rather natty combo of a beige checked blazer and yellow shirt. He referenced fellow late-1990s pop-culture touchstones like *Jerry Springer* and *Seinfeld* and said the following:

'We, in the WWF, think that you, the audience, are quite frankly tired of having your intelligence insulted. We also think you're tired of the same old simplistic theory of good guys versus bad guys.'

He encouraged parental discretion from that moment forwards, stating that the company was from that point onwards under a new direction. Of course, it had been heading that way already with D-Generation X and Austin and the writing of Russo. He acknowledged without referencing the whole Monday Night War situation that more people were watching wrestling than ever before. The second hour of *Raw* was now called *The Warzone* to suggest even more violence. He then added this line: '*Raw* and the *Warzone* are definitely the cure for the common show.'

And with that, a thing called *Attitude* was officially born. It would be injected into everything that the WWF did, and it would take a while to really pulse through the veins of the whole organisation. But when it really kicked in, it was a game-changer. WCW wouldn't be winning the ratings war forever. Bischoff was sat in Atlanta thinking that he'd already won.

Poor Eric couldn't have been more wrong.

Chapter Fifteen:
Putting Butts on Seats

Austin, Foley, The Rock and Triple H;
Hell in a Cell and Owen Hart

At the start of 1998, everything in the WWF was built around Steve Austin, the blue-collar, beer-drinking hero that everybody could get behind thanks to a shared sense of empathy. After all, who *doesn't* hate their boss and wish they could kick him in the stomach and drop him with a 'Stone Cold Stunner'? I don't have a boss, so presumably I'll have to do this to myself like Graham Chapman did when he wrestled himself on *Monty Python*.

We've recently seen the 25th Anniversary of *Raw*, and it began with a segment where Austin came out and hit the Stunner on Vince, mainly because it feels like the one thing the show is most well known for. It first happened before Montreal, on 22 September 1997, with Austin taking exception to being told by Vince that he cared about his physical well-being after his neck injury. Vince wasn't really a heel at this point, but Austin's sudden act of violence resonated with the crowd and drew a tremendous pop. It definitely wouldn't be last time the two men would get into it; if anything, it was this one event (and Austin's defiant 'arrest', replayed over and over for years afterwards) that started the whole Austin v McMahon war that would more than just turn the tide in favour of the WWF.

It made a lot of sense to get the WWF title around Austin's waist. He had been in main events and title matches before, but building to something at *WrestleMania XIV* he was striding out as a true main-event player. He was easily the biggest babyface in the company, with WWF Champion Shawn Michaels the biggest heel. All of a sudden there was nothing resembling a traditional, wholesome fan favourite anywhere in the upper card. The Bob Backlund of 1979 would have been slaughtered by the baying crowds (indeed, Backlund had made a comeback a few years previously as a deranged heel).

Austin won the *Royal Rumble* in January 1998, meaning that he was the number one contender to Michaels title, surviving the 30-man battle royal with every single other competitor going after him, the poster and video cover for the event showing a target on the back of Austin's bald head. The *Raw* the night after kicked the 'Mania hype into high gear as Vince brought out Mike Tyson, feting him as 'the baddest man on the planet'. Austin stormed out, taking exception to this, raising his middle finger at Tyson, who shoved him. The place came unglued. Vince publicly stated that he would not tolerate Austin as his champion, a man who could not be trusted to toe the corporate company line.

Tyson would be named as the guest enforcer for the main event at *WrestleMania XIV*, an interesting parallel with Muhammed

Ali doing a similar job at the first-ever 'Mania: one man the most respected heavyweight champion of all time, someone to cheer for in the clear-cut good guy v bad guy dynamic of the 1980s; the other, the incredibly polarising Tyson, a man loved by some, vehemently hated by others, the perfect metaphor for the shades of grey and anti-heroes that were now populating wrestling.

Iron Mike aligned himself with Michaels and his D-Generation X group, the sight of him awkwardly doing their crotch-chop taunt still makes me giggle 20 years later. The match itself wasn't a technical classic but was a masterpiece in terms of heat. Austin adapted his style because of his recent neck injury; Michaels, meanwhile, was carrying a dreadful back injury where one of his vertebrae had pretty much exploded after being slammed on a coffin during a match with The Undertaker at the *Royal Rumble*. And yet, knowing how important the match was, both men still went all out.

The finish came as Austin blocked Michaels superkick finisher, span him around and hit the Stunner, with Tyson making the three count. When Michaels protested to Tyson after the match, he was knocked out with one punch and Tyson revealed an Austin T-shirt underneath his DX one; that's how you show what side you're on in wrestling angles: jerseywear.

Evil Mr McMahon was now kicked into high gear. The *Raw* after 'Mania had Vince telling Austin he can do things 'the easy way or the hard way', meaning he can be his corporate puppet or find his own path. Of course, this meant that Vince got a Stunner for his troubles. The following week, Austin turned up in a suit and tie, seemingly ready to join the dark side. Of course, Vince copped another Stunner. Austin needed a new opponent after beating Michaels, the swaggering Heartbreak Kid, the master of Sweet Chin Music. His next opponent would be a tie-dyed hippy, an alter-ego of an alter-ego, the master of Sweet *Shin* Music: Dude Love.

The Dude was another persona for Mick Foley, but it was always acknowledged that The Dude was the same man as Mankind and indeed Cactus Jack. All three characters had been part of the *Royal Rumble* that year, with the idea of Foley having separate personas introduced in a series of ground-breaking interviews a year earlier, just after *WrestleMania 13*. Not having the chance to demonstrate the talking ability that made him such a hot prospect in ECW while playing the role of the often-shrieking Mankind, these sit-down interviews between Foley and Jim Ross looked at the path that he had taken to get to the WWF. The death matches in Japan, the fandom as a kid, and old home videos where a teenage Foley played a character called Dude Love, throwing himself off the roof of his garage in order to entertain his friends. Fans took to this side of his character, presumably seeing a lot of themselves in Foley; it's certainly the reason he's one of my favourite wrestlers. He was never super muscular, he just seemed to be a regular guy who loved wrestling, could talk and take unbelievable punishment.

As Mankind, Foley had reached the final of *King of the Ring 1997*, losing to Triple H, who was now past being in the doghouse for the curtain call incident and carving out a good WWF career, especially with female bodyguard Chyna helping him to a lot of victories. Steve Austin needed a new tag team partner after Shawn Michaels had left the company following his backstage fight with Bret Hart in July 1997; both men held the tag team titles at the time. Facing Owen Hart and the British Bulldog to decide who would go forward with the titles, Austin turned down the help of Mankind; Foley then appeared as Dude Love and the duo won the titles, abandoning them when Austin suffered his neck injury. Foley would then feud with Triple H, appearing for a falls count anywhere match as Cactus Jack, which was sold as if Helmsley had seen a ghost. (I have used the booking instruction of 'Triple H Cactus Jack sell' on more than one occasion to convey how surprised and frightened I want a wrestler to look.)

Cactus Jack stuck around for a while, forming a tag team with old friend Terry Funk, who for some reason decided to not be called by his real name and became Chainsaw Charlie, with a stocking over his head and with the insanity of both men turned up to 11. At *WrestleMania XIV*, they would beat The New Age Outlaws (Billy Gunn and Road Dogg Jessie James, two former midcard acts who had abandoned earlier gimmicks to be part of a brilliant heel tag team) in a dumpster match, where your opponents had to be placed in a dumpster. They would lose to the Outlaws the following night in a cage match, the match ordered because Foley and Funk had violated the little-used 'wrong dumpster' rule the night before. The Outlaws, along with the returning Sean Waltman (now called X-Pac) formed a new version of D-Generation X with Triple H, revamping the stable as Michaels was now in retirement (he wouldn't be seen in a WWF ring again until 2002).

Initially heels, the often very funny DX became babyfaces thanks to Road Dogg's catchphrases and the desire of an audience of 15–35-year olds to shout 'Suck it'. They also pulled some brilliant stunts, including turning up to *Nitro* in a jeep (often mistakenly called a tank) and baiting WCW at every turn. By the middle of 1998 they were quite ridiculously popular.

This irked Foley's characters; Cactus Jack abandoned the fans and Dude Love turned heel, the pawn of Vince McMahon in his war with Steve Austin. The two had a couple of great main-event matches on minor WWF pay per views, with Vince and his 'stooges' (backstage assistants and agents like Gerald Brisco and Pat Patterson) frequently getting involved. After the stint as heel Dude Love, Foley returned to being Mankind, now choosing to wear a tatty shirt and tie to wrestle in. His next big match would be the reason I returned to wrestling at the age of 20. It is either the best wrestling match in history or the absolute worst, depending on your viewpoint. It was certainly incredibly important, even if many people wouldn't have cared to see Mankind v The Undertaker yet again. At least this match had a gimmick: Hell in a Cell.

People don't tend to remember WWF's *King of the Ring '98* for the main event, but it saw Steve Austin drop his WWF title to the masked 'brother' of The Undertaker, Kane, in a first blood match. You're a smart person, you'd realise that Kane would be unlikely to lose that match as he's wearing a mask; it was another part of the growing Austin v McMahon storyline, another hurdle thrown in Stone Cold's way to keep his reign fresh. He'd win the title back the next night on *Raw*.

Everyone who watched that show remembers it for one match. I can remember exactly how I saw it for the first time, literally switching to *Sky Sports* during a replay of the show the next day a couple of seconds before one of the most relevant incidents in the bout. The contest saw Mankind against The Undertaker, a match that had happened a fair few times before. Nobody expected much going in to the show; it would be a good match as both men had great chemistry together, but Undertaker had a broken foot and Foley was always banged up thanks to his in-ring style. While fans may have greeted the match announcement with a shrug, at the end of the contest The Undertaker was back to being considered as a brooding, malevolent monster of a wrestler, the human embodiment of a villain in a slasher film. Foley was elevated, as signs in the audience often said, to a god.

The bout was the second-ever Hell in a Cell match, where the action took place inside a steel cage that is different to the traditional type. It had a roof, some space around the ring rather than the cage being flush to the ropes, and the only way to win was by pinfall or submission, not escape. The first Hell in a Cell match in October 1997 at *Badd Blood: In Your House* saw The Undertaker take on Shawn Michaels in an absolute bloodbath, with the smaller Michaels allowing Undertaker to throw him around like he was nothing. During that match, Michaels took a bump from the side of the cage, maybe ten feet up, through one of the ringside announce tables, dangling then dropping into it. Michaels only managed to win thanks to the debuting Kane, who hit The Undertaker with a tombstone piledriver. That match, universally beloved by nearly every fan, was the reason that Michaels ended up being in the main event at Montreal the following month as victory made him number one contender to Bret Hart's title.

Foley and Undertaker weren't sure if they could top the previous Hell in a Cell and knew that it set such a high bar that they had to do *something* amazing right off the bat. Mick Foley has said that Terry Funk initially suggested that he should let 'Taker throw him off the *top* of the cage to beat Michael's ground-breaking (literally) bump from the year before. Foley replied to that by saying that he'd then climb back up and do it again. Undertaker apparently didn't want to go through with Foley's suggestions but trusted him and they went through with it. My words won't do it justice, so if for some reason you've never seen this match, go and watch it right now. It's the reason I'm writing this book. If Undertaker had Foley in a head-lock when I flicked on to that channel that night, I wouldn't have fallen back into wrestling so hard. I wouldn't have a tattoo of Mick on my right arm.

Foley, in his tweaked Mankind garb, made his entrance and immediately climbed up the side of the cage, waiting on the roof for his opponent. The Undertaker took his time making his entrance, then also climbed up the structure to meet Foley head on. They brawled briefly on the roof of the cage, fans reacting with oohs and aahs, expecting both men to tease a big bump but not doing anything silly so early in the match. Just as nearly every person in the arena had that thought, 'Taker grabbed Foley and threw him off one side of the roof of the cage.

From 22 feet up, Foley landed back-first on the Spanish announce table, flattening it and disappearing from view, his legs under a steel guardrail and his head under splintered wood. Jim Ross made one of the all-time great calls on commentary, screaming: 'As God is my witness, he's broken in half.'

To all intents and purposes, the match was over. The crowd didn't know what to do. Vince, Funk and backstage doctor Francois Petit came out to ringside to tend to Foley, placing him on a stretcher, with the cage being lifted to allow the medical staff to get Foley out on it, The Undertaker ominously stayed on the roof as it was raised.

Then, as the stretcher got halfway up the entranceway, Foley dragged himself off it and, with a crazed look on his face and without his leather mask, took himself back to the Cell. He climbed up again, remarkably rapidly for a man who had dislo-cated his shoulder during his massive bump a few minutes previously. Once again, 'Taker was there to greet him, choke-slamming him on the mesh roof of the cage, which had already buckled under their weight earlier. This time it would do more than bend a little; when Foley hit the cage the roof panel swung open, sending him unexpectedly into the ring below. A chair that had been used as a weapon previously came down with Foley, smashing him in the face. It was either that or the impact from the fall that knocked him out cold.

While the first bump may have looked more insane to the fans, the unexpected nature of the second fall was much rougher on Foley. There's a great camera shot of The Undertaker looking down through the hole in the cage at Foley, looking like a man who realises he's just murdered someone. With Foley out cold for a while and then trying to get his wits about him, Terry Funk took a chokeslam from The Undertaker who had by this point wisely decided to leave the roof of the cage. Meanwhile, Foley was awake and mugging for the camera, a tooth smashed out of his mouth and near his nose, his jaw dislocated and a hole in his lip that he was sticking his tongue through, obscured by his beard.

Foley would even start to mount a fightback, bringing thumb-tacks into the match and taking bumps on them before finally being pinned with a tombstone piledriver.

Foley had bought elements of ECW and his time in Japan to a mainstream WWF ring, added in even more high risk and helped create even more power at the top of the WWF roster. The Undertaker's aura only grew; it took a little longer for Foley to catch on as a megastar, but it did happen, especially when he combined his hardcore brawling with elements of comedy and his ability to talk. The next few months in the WWF would be among the most exciting in its history.

McMahon kept up his campaign to get the title away from Austin. At *Breakdown: In Your House* he put Stone Cold up against both Kane *and* The Undertaker, insisting that the brothers could not pin each other, so both pinned Austin and Vince left with the title himself. The next night, Austin crashed *Raw* on a Zamboni, keeping up his habit of mechanised assault (nothing beats his attack with a beer truck in 1999, spraying everyone in the ring). At *Judgement Day*, Kane took on Undertaker with Austin forced by McMahon to be the referee. Paul Bearer came to ringside and hit Kane, previously his charge, with a chair. Austin refused to count the pin, clocking 'Taker with a chair himself after a Stunner, pinning both men and declaring himself the winner. This caused Vince to finally fire him, only for Austin to be rehired by Vince's son Shane. With nobody holding the WWF title, a tournament was held at *Survivor Series 1998* to crown a new champion.

Austin, Kane and The Undertaker were all favourites going into the tournament. Mankind was getting over too, with Vince reluctantly choosing him as his pick to win the tournament, more to get the silly, bumbling Foley out of his hair. Mankind had always used a finishing move known as the mandible claw, shoving his fingers into the mouth of his opponent and pushing down, causing them to pass out. During some hilarious skits with Vince, he introduced Mr Socko, a sock puppet that he tried to entertain his boss with; he would now perform the claw with Socko wrapped around his hand. It sounds daft written down, but it really worked.

Also, in the build-up to the show, The Rock was becoming a massive star, getting a babyface reaction by being good in the ring, great on the microphone and eminently quotable. The reactions he was getting had taken a while to come around, with his initial push in 1996 and early 1997 almost derailing his career before it got started.

A third-generation wrestler, Dwayne Johnson was the son of Rocky Johnson and grandson of 'High Chief' Peter Maivia. With a black father and a Samoan mother, Johnson was part of a massive wrestling family. After playing college football in Miami, Johnson broke into the business in 1995, first performing as Flex Kavana in the USWA.

When he signed with the WWF in 1996, he was given his debut at Madison Square Garden at *Survivor Series*. Given a name that combined his father and grandfather, Rocky Maivia, he was pushed off the bat as a super-clean-cut babyface, dubbed 'The Blue Chipper' and full of smiling, generic fire and basic catch-phrases. Fans immediately took a dislike to him, with crowds in 1996 starting to favour anti-heroes like Steve Austin. By the time he won the Intercontinental title in February 1997, you could hear fans chanting 'Rocky Sucks' and more worryingly, 'Die Rocky Die'. He disappeared after dropping the title and suffering a knee injury, resurfacing in August 1997 with a slightly tweaked look. He would join the Nation of Domination, fired up by the genuine hatred he had received previously from the fans, turning it back on them. He became 'The Rock', referring to himself in the third person and being a dick to audiences, opponents and interviewers alike.

He feuded with Austin over the Intercontinental title at the end of 1997, then was part of the Nation v D-Generation X feud for much of 1998. By *Breakdown: In Your House* he was in a three-way match with Mankind and Ken Shamrock and was getting cheered so loudly that he started referring to himself as

'The People's Champion', using his 'People's Elbow', one of the daftest finishing moves of all time. It made Mr Socko seem almost brutal. He'd stand over a prone opponent in centre ring, ceremonially remove his elbow pad, throw it to the crowd, run the ropes a couple of times and drop a regular elbow drop that his opponent would sell as if it had killed them. Crowds would lap it up. He went into *Survivor Series* as joint crowd favourite with Steve Austin.

That show itself will never be remembered for the quality of the wrestling on show, but as a spectacle it's magnificent, especially for the number of stories told in one evening and the wonderful twist at the end of it all. If we fast-forward to the semi-finals, Mankind surprisingly beat Austin in a match that had a lot of moving parts. Vince, at ringside in a wheelchair, punched the referee, and Austin seemed to have the match won after a Stunner to Mankind. With no ref to count the fall, in slid Shane McMahon, recently demoted to referee by his evil father. He counted one . . . two . . . and refused to count. Austin had been screwed. Incredulous, he was then taken out by a chairshot from Vince's cronies and Mankind advanced to the final. The Rock won his semi over The Undertaker by disqualification.

The final summed up what a lot of WWF main event matches were like at this time; it had a brawl around ringside. Chairs got involved. Naturally, the Spanish announce table was destroyed by falling bodies. Then, as the crowd cheered on his every move, The Rock twisted Mankind into a Sharpshooter and, one year on from Montreal, Vince had the bell rung, awarding the title to The Rock and revealing that was his plan all along. The Rock would become his Corporate Champion, screwing over poor, gullible, lovable Mankind and raising the ire of the fans and, of course, Steve Austin. At this point Stone Cold hit the ring, brawling with The Rock and then, proving that he didn't trust anyone, hitting Mankind with a Stunner at the conclusion of a quite breathless three-hour show.

It was booking and writing like that which had seen the WWF recover from the beating it had been taking from WCW in the ratings war and start to pull ahead. After some back and forth throughout 1998, from 2 November *Raw* won every single ratings battle until the end of the Monday Night War. The WWF became absolutely untouchable during 1998, led by Austin, The Rock, D-X, Mankind and the McMahon family. Not that they didn't make mistakes, I'm sure they'd be the first to admit that they did, like the ill-fated *Brawl For All* tournament that pitted mid-card wrestlers against each other in *real* fights, just as UFC was really taking off. It led to a lot of injuries, not least to 'Dr Death' Steve Williams, who was expected to win the whole thing.

After *Survivor Series* '98, The Rock reigned over everybody, easily stepping into the role of top heel in the company as part of Vince's villainous Corporation stable. It made sense to feud The Rock with Steve Austin, but that was reserved for the next *WrestleMania*. Before then came one of my favourite feuds from that era, and one of the most successful rivalries in the WWF that didn't involve a beer-drinking feller from Texas.

After being screwed out of the WWF title at *Survivor Series*, Mankind became a full-blown face character once again, winning everyone over with his blend of taking a hiding for our entertainment and being one of the very best talkers around. At *Rock Bottom: In Your House* he had a shot at The Rock for the belt and managed to win the match with his Mr Socko covered mandible claw; but as The Rock had passed out rather than submitting or being pinned, Vince ruled that the title couldn't change hands. Then on *Raw* on 4 January 1999, a show that was taped a week earlier, Foley would get something that a lifetime of getting beaten up to make other people look great had earned him.

At the start of the show, Foley demanded a title match by putting Shane McMahon in a submission hold he learned when doing amateur wrestling as a schoolboy, telling Vince he'd break his son's arm if he didn't get his way. Going up against The Rock in the main event that night, fans were treated to two of the loudest crowd pops in history: the first for the glass-shattering beginning to Steve Austin's music, returning after a short absence to hit The Rock with a chair; and the second for Mankind, let go and treated badly by WCW and covered in scars from working death matches for little money in Japan, getting the victory and winning the WWF title.

On *Nitro* at that same moment was the 'fingerpoke of doom' (more on that in a while . . .), but a lot of fans didn't see it. Announcer Tony Schiavone, working at a live show against the recorded *Raw*, was told to give the result of the match away over commentary. He didn't want to, but did as he was told, spoiling the result for everyone and even adding 'that'll put a lot of butts on seats'. 600,000 people switched the channel from *Nitro* to *Raw*. Babyface wrestlers charged the ring and held Foley aloft with his new belt, a genuine outpouring of joy for someone who had worked hard, while on the other channel two guys at the top of WCW were just using a belt as a prop within their own power games.

Foley wouldn't hold the title for long, but would have more

than one reign. At the *Royal Rumble 1999*, he met The Rock again in a 'I Quit' match that was immortalised in the documentary *Beyond the Mat* as it seemed things went a bit too far, Foley's willingness to take punishment being taken a little too literally and leading to him taking a few unprotected chair shots, while handcuffed, to the back of the head before he was screwed out of the title again, a recording of him saying 'I quit' being used instead of his actual voice. The shenanigans here – as well as plentiful violence – then led on to an Empty Arena Match during the halftime break of the Super Bowl, with Foley regaining the title by using a forklift truck to keep The Rock down for the count. Foley would retain the belt at the *St Valentines Massacre* pay per view as that match ended in a double knockout in a last man standing contest, before losing it the next day on *Raw* in a ladder match. While the old days of extended uninterrupted title reigns were now long gone, this feud elevated The Rock to megastar level and certainly didn't do Foley any harm either – indeed, a couple of years later Foley was a bestselling author.

The winner of the 1999 *Royal Rumble* match was not, as you would expect, Steve Austin. It was his boss, Vince McMahon, with both men being the first two to enter the match, and the last two remaining in it. McMahon threw Austin over the top rope after The Rock had come to ringside, taunting Stone Cold with his WWF championship. Vince spent most of the match hiding from actually competing, providing commentary after slipping out of the ring without going over the top rope. The next night on *Raw*, McMahon forfeited his title shot at *WrestleMania XV* that he had earned by winning the Rumble, only to be interrupted by WWF commissioner Shawn Michaels informing him that the title shot would then go to the runner-up,

Austin. This led to Vince being goaded into a match with Austin at the next pay per view, *St Valentine's Day Massacre*, where the two would meet in a cage match to decide whether Austin would get to main-event *'Mania* or not. That match, where Vince put a shift in, taking bumps galore as Austin beat the living daylights out of him, was memorable for the finish. Paul Wight – the artist formerly known as The Giant and soon to be called The Big Show – had jumped from WCW and debuted by emerging from beneath the canvas, ripping his way through the mat and grabbing Austin, launching him with force into the cage. The wall swung open with the impact, letting Austin drop to the floor to win the match. At *WrestleMania XV*, Austin regained his WWF championship by beating The Rock, but it wouldn't be the last time they'd headline on the grandest stage of them all.

McMahon's Corporation would eventually combine with another faction, The Undertaker's Ministry of Darkness, which seems a bit daft now but in the days of nu-metal was actually pretty cool. In fact, nu-metal is a perfect metaphor for the Attitude Era in that we can all be snobby about it, but if Limp Bizkit comes on in a club you're transported back to the late 1990s and you're having the time of your life.

The Ministry originally feuded with the Corporation, with Undertaker constantly talking about a 'higher power' (and at one point, a 'hower power') and using McMahon's daughter Stephanie to incur his wrath further, as both of Vince's kids started making their own names on screen and behind the scenes. On the first-ever edition of *Smackdown*, WWF's new weekly TV show to rival (and easily beat) WCW's *Thunder*, the Ministry combined with Shane's Corporation (Vince was out of the picture) to form the Corporate Ministry, which sounds like a church for insurance brokers. The higher power was eventually revealed to be Vince, pulling off a hood in the ring one day and screaming 'It was me, Austin! It was me all along!' in a bit of footage which I get tweeted at me as a meme at least once a day.

A note on *Smackdown*: it made perfect sense to have another TV show as ratings and arena attendances were so good. If you had any doubt of The Rock's star power, this new two-hour broadcast was named after a word he repeatedly used in one of his many catchphrases. Starting on a Thursday night, it has been shifted around in terms of its broadcast day and channel a fair bit since but remains an attraction. It was originally a taped show, recorded the day after *Raw*, shown on UPN. The added pressure of two hours more television a week would affect some things backstage, as well as changing things in-ring over the next few years.

Not everything in the WWF was going fantastically well during this time though. On 23 May 1999, a fine in-ring performer and beloved backstage character was lost to a tragedy that played out in front of the eyes of millions of wrestling fans. Owen Hart had remained with the WWF after Montreal, feeling that WCW wouldn't match his WWF salary or use him properly. Still under contract, he got his head down and carried on. He was always a very solid hand to have in-ring and was known for ribbing his co-workers but being a down-to-earth family man, well-liked by pretty much everyone.

Over the Edge was held at the Kemper Arena in Kansas City, and Owen was due to compete for the Intercontinental title against The Godfather, a clash of characters as his foe was a pimp, coming to the ring with his ladies of the night. Owen was playing the character of the Blue Blazer, his masked persona that he used earlier in his career. By 1999, that character was portrayed as a bumbling fool, being used for comic relief as anyone wholesome and righteous was usually booed by the anti-hero-loving crowds of the time. Owen was meant to be lowered from the rafters of the arena on a harness, then as he got near to the ring he would pretend to be tangled up in the cable and his cape, struggle and fall to the ring face-first.

Something went very wrong. As the pay-per-view audience watched a vignette, Owen fell from a height of 78 feet, landing on the top rope chest-first and rebounding into the ring. He died from his injuries despite frantic efforts to save him.

Immediately following the fall, a very serious Jim Ross told the TV audience that what had transpired was not a storyline; Owen Hart had been badly hurt in the ring and was being tended to. The cameras didn't show what was happening in the ring, making it all seem more surreal. I was watching the show live and instantly felt very uneasy about it; Ross and co-commentator Jerry Lawler were clearly incredibly shaken up. The crowd were not told about what had happened; those at ringside would have been aware that it was clearly a horrific accident, but those further back didn't know if it was real or just a stunt.

Controversially, the show continued. The WWF received a lot of negative press for this, but to play devil's advocate for a second, I don't know if anybody knew what to do for the best. The shock of what had occurred hit everyone and none of the matches after the accident had any real verve behind them, every single member of the roster was affected by what happened. The accident occurred because Owen's harness had a quick-release trigger, so he could do his pratfall upon getting near to the ring; it is thought that he triggered it by mistake when adjusting his cape and costume up in the rafters. His family won a large amount in an out-of-court settlement, using some of the money to set up a foundation in his name.

The next night on *Raw* saw something very unusual; ratings and storylines were abandoned to put on *Raw is Owen*, a two-hour tribute to Hart that I remember recording off the TV, watching once and never being able to view the programme again as it was so heartbreakingly sad. The show consisted of real interviews with wrestlers, out of character, speaking about their late friend, and matches that were just intended to be fun and light-hearted, with absolutely no angles. Talent was given the choice of whether to work or not – most did. The show began with a ten-bell salute and all of the interviews were full of genuine emotion. Mick Foley used his time to say that Owen was his son's favourite wrestler, while Jeff Jarrett was so upset he could barely speak. Crucially, nobody had a bad word to say about Owen; nobody was playing politics, and everybody was keen to pay a tribute to him in their own way. The Undertaker was absent, but for a good reason; he went to visit Bret Hart to show his support, the two men remaining friends after Bret had left for WCW. The show ended with Steve Austin toasting Owen in the ring with a can of beer, raising it to his image on the big screen and symbolically leaving a can in the ring for him.

By the end of 1999, Triple H had risen to the level of a main-event performer, winning his first WWF title from Mankind the day after *Summerslam 1999*. By the time of *Royal Rumble 2000*, one of my favourite top-to-bottom shows of all time, he was a mega-star. That show featured the Hardy Boyz (yes, spelled with a 'z', it was 2000 after all . . .) beating the Dudley Boyz (also a 'z') in a tag team tables match that featured crazy bumps galore. The recently debuted Kurt Angle was choked out by the debutant – and New York native – Tazz (an extra 'z' from his ECW name), his surprise entrance getting a massive reaction at Madison Square Garden.

Tazz had been a star in ECW for several years, and despite his small stature made a career out of suplexing opponents in every possible way. Like many of the ECW mainstays, he also worked for the company behind the scenes. Angle was very different; he had won a gold medal for freestyle wrestling at the 1996 Olympics in Atlanta and was coveted by many professional wrestling companies. As soon as he had signed with the WWF he was sent for about a year of seasoning in their various developmental territories before debuting at the 1999 *Survivor Series*. If he'd have started his career in the 1980s he would have initially been a massive babyface, an American hero with a legitimate background. But times had changed and in 1999 he was a heel, booed by fans from the start and developing into a pompous, arrogant villain who would talk about his 'three I's': Intensity, Integrity and Intelligence and wear his gold medals around his neck to enter the ring. It's hard to find anyone who got as good at professional wrestling as quickly as Angle did.

The main event of the *Royal Rumble 2000* put WWF champion Triple H against Mick Foley, in his Cactus Jack form. This is one of my favourite-ever matches, again proving the ECW influence on the in-ring style of the WWF with it being a bloody, hardcore street fight with no rules. To set the match up, Foley as Mankind had been fired from the WWF by Triple H and Stephanie McMahon. During 1999, The Rock had turned babyface and had been part of a team with Foley called The Rock and Sock

Connection, with one of their segments on *Raw* breaking all ratings records; Foley presented a 'This is Your Life' show for The Rock that was genuinely quite ridiculous. They had great comic chemistry and after Foley had been 'fired', it was The Rock who gathered together all of the other WWF superstars on *Raw* to insist that they would all walk out if Foley wasn't reinstated.

Triple H would attack Foley with the ring bell during a multi-man tag team match at the end of that same show, and after the contest had concluded Foley symbolically removed his Mankind mask and attacked Triple H in return. With a street fight already signed for the *Royal Rumble*, on *Smackdown* three days later Foley emerged as Cactus Jack, ramping up the violence in his matches and bringing back memories of his earlier contests with Triple H as that persona. I couldn't have been more excited for the match when it came around, and it really delivered.

Both men fought around the ringside area, and even into the crowd at one point, with weapons being liberally used and Triple H selling every advance of Cactus Jack as if he was dealing with an unbeatable monster. A barbed wire two-by-four was brought into the equation, with both men getting hit with it. As it was 2000, of course the announce tables were destroyed and there was some interference (The Rock attacking Triple H as Foley was handcuffed, enabling them to be unlocked). Thumbtacks were involved too, but in the end Triple H got the win. I remember being genuinely annoyed that Foley hadn't won as he'd given it everything, but Triple H was carried out on a stretcher rather than Foley at the end of the contest.

It was a quite beautiful ballet of brutality, and a match that still stands up to rewatching today. I'm happy that I've managed to tell both men involved how much it means to me as a fan.

Chapter Sixteen:
Hotshotting and Hubris

Goldberg, the 'fingerpoke of doom' and the downfall of WCW

Over in WCW, business was seemingly going so well that a second weekly television show was added on a Thursday evening. Called *Thunder*, it was the idea of Ted Turner rather than Eric Bischoff, who was initially against the idea, but used it as leverage during the planning stage to be able to finance the deal that he signed Bret Hart to at the end of 1997. Beginning on 8 January 1998, it spread the creative team behind WCW very thinly. In terms of talent, WCW happened to have loads of it. They just didn't seem to know how to utilise it. Having already let Austin, Foley and Triple H slip through their fingers, seeing nothing for them, they had an astounding undercard of cruiserweight wrestlers who would all start to tire of being held down by the bigger boys at the top.

Most WCW pay-per-view shows or episodes of *Nitro* would have the latest nWo shenanigans around the main-event scene, but every show would have at least one cruiserweight contest on the card, popping the fans with death-defying moves from talent who had spent their formative years in Mexico and Japan. At *Halloween Havoc 1997* Eddie Guerrero and Rey Mysterio Jr had an unbelievable match which pitted Guerrero's Cruiserweight title against Mysterio's mask, Guerrero continuing on as a brilliant heel in the mould of his old tag team partner in Mexico, Art Barr, Mysterio setting the world on fire after doing wonderful things in Mexico and then in ECW. Standing only five feet four inches tall, Mysterio was establishing himself as one of the best high-flyers in the world. Also, in the division was his ECW nemesis Psicosis, Juventud Guerrera, Blitzkrieg, the almost old-school grappler Dean Malenko, already well-travelled Chris Jericho and Japanese star Ultimo Dragon. These guys were all great reasons to watch WCW.

By 1998 the nWo didn't seem to be slowing down at all. The concept wasn't indestructible though; on the *Nitro* before *Starrcade '97* the whole show was rebranded as nWo instead of WCW, with the plan for the soon-to-start *Thunder* to be the WCW show. Ratings tanked during the episode, so the idea was dropped. *Starrcade* itself had a huge main event of Sting v WCW Champion Hogan, the brooding Sting becoming hugely popular by appearing from nowhere every now and again to attack his enemies and hanging out in the rafters of arenas like a bat (or a goth who likes to climb things).

Earlier on that show, Bischoff wrestled Larry Zbyszko, as Eric started to push himself as an in-ring talent. Vince would do similar, but his pushing of himself came as an organic result of the reactions that the WWF was seeing for evil Mr McMahon. In the main event, referee Nick Patrick was meant to make a fast count at one point when Hogan had Sting pinned, but he forgot. Bret Hart came out to protest the fast count, that wasn't *actually* fast. Then Sting caught Hogan in his 'Scorpion Deathlock', the same move as Hart's Sharpshooter, and Hart had the bell rung in a reference to the Montreal Screwjob. What should have been a monumental contest was reduced to a farce. The title would be held up and then won by Sting before he lost it to Randy Savage at *Spring Stampede*.

Poor Randy got to keep the title for one day, with dissension in the nWo being the reason that Hogan (surprise, surprise) regained it. During a match between the two on *Nitro*, Kevin Nash interfered by attacking Hogan, sick of him being out for himself rather than the nWo (according to the storyline, but the reality could also have applied). Then Hart interfered, attacking Savage and enabling Hogan to regain his belt. This caused a split in the nWo, which aided storytelling for a while and presumably also assisted merchandise sales as people had to choose a side. Now using a black and red colour scheme, nWo Wolfpac was Nash, Hall, Savage, Konnan, Curt Hennig, Elizabeth, Rick Rude and Dusty Rhodes. nWo Hollywood kept custody of the black and white palette and was made up of Hogan, Bischoff, Scott Steiner, Scott Norton, Brian Adams (formerly Crush in the WWF), Vincent and the Disciple (Brutus Beefcake's latest gimmick). Hart wasn't on either side, apparently. The Wolfpac arm was the first babyface incarnation of the nWo and seemed like a good idea at the time, but as we'll see, the company would have been better served by actually coming up with much fresher ideas and new stars.

The Giant would rejoin with Hogan, keeping up the pattern of his regular turns, the most schizophrenically booked character in wrestling. Scott Hall would soon turn on Kevin Nash and join the Hollywood side. Lex Luger and Sting joined the Wolfpac, meaning the whole WCW roster felt like it was aligned with one side or the other in the nWo battle, far less exciting than when it was warring with WCW itself. It all got really confusing; you shouldn't need notes to watch a wrestling show when you've missed it for a couple of weeks. My head hurts from just writing about it.

Stagnating creativity wasn't WCW's greatest worry. Bischoff was obsessed with TV ratings, and WCW had enjoyed 83 weeks of winning the war with the WWF. The streak had started on 17 June 1996, just before the nWo was officially formed. It ended on 13 April 1998 as *Raw* ran the angle of Dude Love being Vince's hand-picked man to take on Austin. The ratings would still switch between the two companies for a while, but the WCW side was getting messy – it was losing money every single day, plus, Bischoff was starting to lose the locker room, in particular falling out with Ric Flair after refusing to let him take a day off to go and see his son Reid in an amateur wrestling championship. Flair had asked in plenty of time for the time off and Bischoff had either forgotten or hoped that his employee would cave in to his pressure. Flair went to watch his son.

All was certainly not lost for WCW though, because they had another ace up their sleeve. A man by the unassuming name of Bill Goldberg, a former pro footballer who had retired following an awful injury that saw part of his abdominal muscles torn off his pelvis. While on the mend from that, he started mixed martial arts and powerlifting and happened to bump into Lex Luger and

Sting in a gym. They convinced him to give wrestling a try, and he started training at the WCW school in Atlanta known as the Power Plant. Initially he wrestled a few untelevised dark matches, fine-tuning his character while remaining unheralded until he actually started on TV, making his debut on 22 September 1997 on *Nitro*, beating Hugh Morrus, a decent mid-carder, incredibly quickly. He then started squashing opponents every week, something that hadn't been seen in a while since wrestling TV shifted emphasis towards hosting more competitive matches. Fans popped for it, the powerful Goldberg destroying foes with a spear and then his jackhammer finishing move (a hanging suplex turned into a powerslam).

Goldberg looked a little bit like Steve Austin, which can't have hurt. While definitely larger than him, he had the goatee beard, the shaven head, the black trunks and boots. But unlike Austin, he barely spoke, merely saying 'Who's next?' after beating yet another opponent. His win count did start getting a little bit silly – eagle-eyed fans noted that his stats would improve each week by more than the actual number of matches that had taken place! – but he was getting over massively. He won the US title from Raven and started having slightly longer matches. His next target was easy: Hogan. This should have drawn huge business. It could have broken pay-per-view records. But Bischoff was so obsessed with ratings that he did something very foolish indeed: he put the match on *Nitro*, proving a point but not making an extra penny in doing so.

Forty thousand fans packed into the Georgia Dome in Atlanta for *Nitro* on 6 July 1998, with Goldberg immediately given a roadblock in his quest to get to Hogan; he would have to beat Scott Hall first. He did, and then went on to the main event where he beat Hogan to a stunning, deafening reaction from the crowd, winning the title less than a year after his debut. It was some ascent, but his meteoric rise rattled the veterans who virtually ran WCW; and the fact that his title win wasn't on PPV meant that it could be suggested that he couldn't draw money.

After he lost his title, Hogan threw himself into pro-celebrity matches, often in the main event over Goldberg defending the WCW title. He teamed up with Dennis Rodman again to take on Diamond Dallas Page and Utah Jazz power forward Karl Malone at *Bash at the Beach* 1998, then even more ludicrously tagged with Bischoff at *Road Wild '98* against DDP and TV host Jay Leno. At least Rodman and Malone were athletes. It did get sillier still, with WCW bringing in The Ultimate Warrior, now just called the Warrior for copyright reasons, for a match at *Halloween Havoc*. At least this was the actual Warrior, rather than some poor chap called Rick Wilson.

In 1995 WCW had hired Wilson, who had been working as Rio, Lord of the Jungle and bore a slight resemblance to the Warrior, who at that point had fallen off the face of the earth. Making his TV debut, his silhouette was used as Hogan talked about his 'Ultimate Surprise'. Wilson was given the name The Renegade and worked in a fairly similar way to the Warrior, proving that even with Turner's money WCW had the ability to be as carny as a show in a leisure centre that puts lookalikes on a poster. Renegade would become TV champion fairly quickly, but his push was killed when the Warrior came out of the wilderness and started doing interviews again.

In short order, The Renegade was just a jobber. He was let go at the end of 1998 and, depressed at how things had turned out, shot himself in the head in February 1999. He was only 33 years old.

Rumour had it that Hogan was desperate to make sure that he got his win back over the Warrior, who was paid top dollar to come in and do the programme. Warrior would debut on *Nitro* with a rambling promo, forming his own stable, the One Warrior Nation. He kidnapped and brainwashed the Disciple, who was probably worried he'd be getting another new gimmick. He would appear and disappear in clouds of smoke, which were actually used to disguise the fact he was appearing from a trap-door in the ring. That same trapdoor caused a horrific back injury to The British Bulldog, leading to the spiral of painkiller addiction that eventually led to his premature death. The story between Warrior and Hogan was so hokey that at one-point Hogan saw a mirage of Warrior in his dressing-room mirror. You can genuinely hear the live crowd laugh.

The match itself may well have been one of the worst of all time, so markedly awful that it takes away from how good their encounter at *WrestleMania VI* was. The finish was meant to see Hogan throw a fireball at Warrior, using the old magician's flash paper trick, but Hogan got it wrong and ended up singeing his own moustache and eyebrows as the fireball erupted in his own face. A new ending was improvised, with Hogan's nephew Horace hitting Warrior in the back with a chair shot so weak that it wouldn't have put my infant son on his back. Warrior would retire soon afterwards, his three-match run in WCW symptomatic of how they spent money at the time.

Hogan himself appeared to retire too – on Thanksgiving during an interview with Jay Leno on his chat show, both men now friends again despite 'fighting' a few months before. With Jesse

Ventura seeing legitimate political success after being voted governor of Minnesota, Hogan wanted some of that glory too. So, he shot higher; throwing his hat in the ring to run for president at the next election. He even held a press conference on *Nitro* to really make it seem real, and let's be honest, recent events in the USA have taught us that anyone can have a go at the top job there. It would have been fun if Hogan had won, with him insisting in every trade deal that he had creative control over the outcome.

Goldberg's streak was at 173–0 when he finally lost, dropping the WCW title to Kevin Nash (by that point, head booker) at *Starrcade '98*, thanks to Scott Hall (yes, him and Nash were friends again) using a Taser. Nash and Goldberg were due to wrestle again in a rematch on *Nitro* on 4 January 1999, but Goldberg was arrested at the start of the show for allegedly stalking Elizabeth. With Kevin Nash lauding it over the fans in attendance, Hogan showed up to take the title shot instead. The bell rang, and Hogan walked up to Nash, poking him in the chest with his finger. Nash went down like he'd been shot, letting Hogan pin him for the three count, the nWo reformed and we were treated to the veteran stars blending reality with fiction in the worst possible way, laughing at both the fans and everyone in the locker room. Wrestling didn't matter anymore. The lunatics well and truly ran the asylum.

This event was dubbed 'the fingerpoke of doom'. It cannot be overstated just how stupid it was, a move that was meant to win a ratings battle but meant that WCW would never win it ever again. Worse for WCW, as previously mentioned their own commentary team would plug something that was happening on the other side, where one man's hard work was rewarded with a title win. Loads of people would change channel to see it. They'd never come back.

Click.

The start of 1999 was as awful for WCW as it had been brilliant the year before. Fans had been appalled by the 'fingerpoke of doom' and the mocking of Mick Foley in the same broadcast, and now they'd also lost The Giant after years of seemingly turning him face or heel every other month. The final ratings win for WCW came on *Nitro* after their *Halloween Havoc* pay per view in October 1998, the one with the oft-maligned Hogan v Warrior match. The main event on that show was Goldberg defending his title against Diamond Dallas Page but most viewers didn't get to see it as the feed cut out with the show going over its allotted timeslot. The match was then shown in full for free on *Nitro*, meaning that their last-ever ratings victory ironically came from something pre-recorded that many people knew the result of already, after years of Bischoff pushing that as a massive negative because of how the WWF taped their shows.

Once Goldberg's streak had been ended, creatively WCW was spent. A great gimmick that had happened by accident hadn't been properly capitalised on, the opposite of WWF taking Steve Austin's rise and running with it. Talented up-and-coming under-card wrestlers weren't happy, knowing that no matter how hard they tried they probably wouldn't be able to reach the top of the company. While they were demotivated from a lack of oppor-tunity, the stars at the top of the cards were collecting massive guaranteed pay cheques, so they didn't need to kill themselves week in, week out. The booking committee, possibly driven slightly by fear of the wealth of talent on the undercard in

WCW – and failing to learn the lesson from letting Steve Austin, Mick Foley and Triple H slip through their fingers in the mid Nineties – decided that guys like Eddie Guerrero, Chris Benoit, Chris Jericho, Rey Mysterio Jr and Booker T didn't have what it took to become huge stars. All five of those men would go on to be main-event-level performers for WWE further down the line.

Goldberg's swift slide from invincibility showed you just how well the WWF had protected Andre over the course of a decade. Sure, there wasn't as much TV exposure back then, but he was always kept super-strong until him getting beaten meant something. Goldberg's charm was that he was a monster, everything built around the '0' in 173–0. After the streak ended, he didn't have the personality to immediately climb back to the top (although he did go on to have two memorable and successful runs in WWE).

At one point, WCW had 250 wrestlers on their books, all on guaranteed contracts. As well as having a massive roster, it was constantly bringing in celebrities to bolster their cards, paying them over the odds for limited involvement when wrestling fans tended to want to watch, you know, wrestling. By this time, wrestling was mainstream and cool enough to not need stars from the world of entertainment to draw in new viewers. What worked and was important in 1984 didn't matter a bit now. On top of all of this, in 1998 WCW was ordered to be more family-friendly by Ted Turner, just at the point that WWF's violent, profane, over-the-top Attitude Era content was really getting over with the fans.

Shows continued to be built around old stars with clunky angles while *Raw* felt vibrant and new. Despite paying countless wrestlers a fortune and knowing that certain guys were ready to break out and take their opportunity, more money was wasted on even *more* celebrity involvement, like hiring rapper Master P to head up a stable of babyfaces (the No Limit Soldiers) who were quickly and universally rejected by WCW's southern fanbase, turning their rival stable the West Texas Rednecks babyface by accident thanks to them making a song called 'Rap is Crap'. Master P was paid $200,000 every time he appeared on TV, which he only really did to get his cousin (who wrestled as Swoll) a job. With deals like that, no wonder Master P amassed a fortune of $350 million.

Bischoff also sanctioned a character called the Kiss Demon, played by Dale Torborg and based upon Kiss bassist Gene Simmons. This was meant to be part of a Kiss-themed stable, and a huge push for the character who would then headline a special New Year's Eve pay per view, featuring a concert from Kiss. Part of the contract said that the Demon would get a main-event match; once the character bombed he was put in a 'Special Main Event' at *Superbrawl* in 2000 to get around that. It was the fourth match on the card. The Demon lost.

Ratings were down, and WCW was managing to lose $5 million a month, having barely made a profit at any point during the Monday Night Wars. Sure, they'd been ahead in the TV ratings for a long time and had enjoyed great attendances, but they'd been stung by guaranteed contracts for stars like Hogan, giving away matches for free instead of thinking about pay per view, and holding back stars, not thinking about the future. In September 1999, Bischoff was fired.

The month before his sacking, an incredibly charismatic man had made his debut on *Raw*, getting a great response to one of the most memorable first appearances of all time. Chris Jericho had been given runs with the Cruiserweight and TV titles in WCW but was never allowed near the big time, despite his undeniable charisma. Jericho had spent his formative years in Mexico, Japan and Germany as well as all over the USA and his native Canada. He'd been responsible for two of the best segments in *Nitro* history; one time trying to prove he was a better wrestler than Dean Malenko – dubbed the man of a thousand holds – by insisting that he knew one thousand and *four*. He produced a list, written on a roll of printer paper and started reading it in ring, mentioning the word 'armbar' more than once and introducing the world to move names like the three-handled moss-covered family credunza (which Perry Saturn would name his finisher after). Even more hilarious was his parody of Goldberg's entrance, prowling through backstage looking all serious before taking a wrong turn and locking himself out of the arena.

Bischoff just didn't see Jericho as a star though, and the old guard thought he was too small. He signed with the WWF and made his debut on 9 August 1999; a countdown clock that had been appearing from time to time on the show interrupted The Rock as he was delivering a promo in-ring, counting from ten to zero and heralding the appearance of Jericho, now nicknamed Y2J ahead of the turn of the millennium, sporting a ludicrous top-knot and silver shirt. He declared that from that point onwards, 'Raw is Jericho' and would quickly ascend to being Intercontinental Champion. He'd be a solid upper-carder until 2002 when he became the first-ever Undisputed WWF Champion and he'd main event *WrestleMania X8*. In other words, he proved WCW very wrong, very quickly.

The replacement for Bischoff was, quite rightly, an accountant. Somebody needed to reign everyone in and be able to work an Excel spreadsheet. In what looked like a pretty sensible first recommendation, Bill Busch hired the man that many felt was responsible for WWF winning the ratings war: Vince Russo. With fellow writer Ed Ferrara in tow, Russo left WWF in October 1999, annoyed at the increased workload on his plate after the launch of *Smackdown*.

Now I'm not exactly going to paint Russo in the best of lights over the next few pages, so I'll say this now: he was a huge part of the Attitude Era, and his approach to writing wrestling television was revolutionary and often absolutely brilliant. He knew exactly how to hook in the most casual of channel-hopping viewer with his brand of fast-paced 'Crash TV' and he should, rightly, be given credit for what he achieved in the WWF. Ferrara too, who I'm likely to say even less bad stuff about as I've met the guy and he's an absolute sweetheart. Hey, I'm not a journalist.

The key thing when Russo started working at WCW was that he wasn't really accountable to anybody. While he was often brilliant in the WWF, there he'd had the likes of Vince and Pat Patterson to reign in some of his crazier ideas. They knew how to make the wrestling part of things work, and Russo could be relied upon for segments and promos and as a team, everything was drawn together perfectly. In WCW, with no one to answer to, his first move was to make shows ruder and more violent, with less wrestling involved on any episode of *Nitro* than before and loads of customary shock turns and insider internet-fan language. You could argue that rescuing WCW at this stage would have been like turning around an oil tanker; it was going to take a long time, and everybody hits a creative wall eventually.

Russo did at least start to push younger wrestlers, almost to stamp his authority on the company and irritate the old guard, many of whom he had worked with in the WWF and had been in competition with for the previous few years. He did, however, bring back the nWo, which kind of defeated the object of that. He then lost Bret Hart to a concussion that ended his career, and Goldberg to a seriously lacerated arm, caused by punching it through a car window in an on-camera stunt that went rather wrong. That put Goldberg on the shelf for five months.

Russo was often 'seen' as an on-screen presence, albeit from the back or as a disembodied voice, blurring reality with wrestling as he used insider terms and had the tag team Creative Control (the Harris Brothers) do his bidding for him. Nothing was bringing viewers back though, no matter how much his character banged on about ratings. Then early in 2000, everything started coming undone. Ahead of the *Souled Out* pay per view, he was contacted by Bret Hart (at the time the WCW World Champion) and Jeff Jarrett (the WCW US Champion) who both said they were injured, unable to compete and would have to vacate their titles. With both men part of the revamped nWo storyline, this meant a lot of rapid rebooking. Russo suggested that the world title be put on Tank Abbot, the controversial former UFC star, despite him not catching on with audiences at all and being firmly mired in the midcard. The next day, Russo was asked to be part of a booking committee and not the head booker; he turned that down and left WCW, with the new booking committee being headed up by Kevin Sullivan.

While Sullivan was incredibly experienced and had been around WCW for many years, he wasn't exactly well liked by a lot of the talent. In order to keep the locker room happy, the new champion – to be crowned at *Souled Out* in a match against Sid Vicious – would be Chris Benoit. Nicknamed 'The Crippler' after accidentally breaking Sabu's neck in ECW, Benoit had a stellar career in Japan before gradually becoming a star in WCW, his in-ring intensity getting him over with crowds even if he wasn't the greatest of talkers. Crucially, he didn't care for Sullivan, and was in a relationship with his ex-wife Nancy, known in wrestling circles as Woman. That had come about as Benoit was booked in a feud with Sullivan in 1996 where an affair with Woman was implied; to keep up the pretence they would spend a lot of time together and eventually actually fall in love, marrying in 2000.

Having had a few years of being ignored and backstage uncertainty, Benoit asked for his release from WCW on the day of *Souled Out*, even after being told that he was winning the title. As soon as he'd beaten Sid, he went backstage, handed the title belt over and went to the WWF with Eddie Guerrero, Dean Malenko and Perry Saturn, where they formed The Radicalz stable. Two out of the four Radicalz would become world champions in the WWF.

Mid 2000 for WCW was frankly awful. Ratings were at an all-time low, and the only sensible thing seemed to be to bring Eric Bischoff *and* Vince Russo together. Both men had such a good track record, so surely this couldn't go wrong, could it? The first big storyline that they put together was The New Blood against the Millionaires Club. The former was meant to be newer, hungrier wrestlers; the latter the older guys who had already made all their money. However, for some reason the New Blood were the heels in this equation. Plus, the company still didn't have a strong championship, with the WCW title being vacated for a third time by April that year for what was actually described on-screen as a 'reboot'. When you're admitting that the company isn't doing well on television then it's hard to convince fans that you'll ever turn it around.

By the end of April, there would be three more WCW title switches. Jeff Jarrett lost it to Diamond Dallas Page, who then in turn lost it to David Arquette. Yes, that's right. The actor who was married to Courtney Cox. Definitely not a wrestler. The least famous person in his own house. All to promote the film *Ready to Rumble*, which off the back of this became a massive success. Just kidding, it absolutely bombed and doing this angle pretty much killed off WCW. Even Arquette, who was a lifelong wrestling fan, implored Bischoff and Russo to not do it.

Even the way Arquette won the title was utterly stupid. In a tag team match with WCW Champion DDP, the title was on the line for whoever got the pinfall in a match against Bischoff and Jarrett. As Arquette pinned Bischoff, he was awarded the title, which DDP seemed oddly okay with. This set up *Slamboree* where Jarrett regained the belt, which then kept switching hands. In some cases, wrestlers would win it and then just hand it over to a mate. It meant absolutely nothing. Then we got to *Bash at the Beach 2000* and everything got super weird.

Jeff Jarrett was the champion going into this show, and Russo wanted Hulk Hogan to lose to him. Allegedly exercising the creative control clause in his contract, Hogan refused. Infuriated, as the match began Russo told Jarrett to lay down for Hogan, who did, and the Hulkster pinned him. Russo petulantly threw the belt at Hogan, and then it all goes a bit shades of grey, the kind of stuff Russo always loved.

Hogan said, 'Is this your idea, Russo? That's why this company is in the damn shape it's in, because of bullshit like this'.

Hogan then left, and up until this point it was probably all a work. WCW had been talking of people 'going off script' on commentary and trying to work the internet fans for ages, so it makes sense that they'd do it again. However, once Hogan had left Russo reappeared, stripping him of the WCW title and stating about Hogan that: 'I can guarantee you that this is the last time you will ever see that piece of shit', going on to explain the whole creative control thing to the crowd who genuinely couldn't have cared less.

Later in the show, Booker T would beat Jarrett for the *new* WCW title, and Hogan would be gone from WCW.

It feels weird constantly telling you, dear reader, that it got worse, but it really did. Two-and-a-half months after this, Russo was actually WCW champion. At this point you may as well have set fire to the company for the insurance money. Of course, he vacated it a week later when he decided that he wasn't actually a wrestler, so there had been no real purpose doing the switch in the first place. If you look at the WCW Championship history, 'Vacant' is an incredibly decorated multi-time champion.

Bischoff was gone from WCW again in July 2000, with Russo now involved in a feud with Goldberg that may well have been legit. It's genuinely headache-inducing to even try and think about the logic in the company at this point. Ratings were worse by the week, and the well of money had run dry. By the end of the year, Russo would be gone, his reputation in tatters. While he'd been responsible for some great things in the WWF and had, to an extent, his hands tied in WCW, knowing that one company tanked when he joined it while the other one rose to new heights was something that he'd never fully recover from. He remains around wrestling, although much of what he does now involves provoking arguments with other people in the business. If he ever reads this I'm sure he'll get into it with me, although for balance I will say that my business partner Glen Joseph absolutely adores everything that Russo's ever done.

The Time-Warner media juggernaut bought the Turner empire in 1996, including WCW. Remembering how wrestling helped his fledgling network back in the 1970s, Turner was always loyal to WCW and wanted to help them out. Time-Warner had no such loyalty, especially knowing that WCW lost $60 million in 2000. But Turner was still the largest shareholder in Time-Warner so could keep it running – that was until AOL merged with Time-Warner.

In early 2001, AOL Time Warner started looking into selling off WCW. Having been given a heads-up in late 2000 that this may happen, Bischoff headed up a group of investors called Fusient Media Ventures who *nearly* bought it. When the sale looked imminent, the Turner TV Networks cancelled the WCW timeslots due to atrocious ratings. With no network, the company had no value. It was an eerie parallel to Black Saturday back in 1984, with everything hinging on TV time. WCW was finished.

On 23 March 2001, just $3 million was enough to purchase the WCW video library, 24 wrestler contracts (the higher paid wrestlers were contracted to AOL Time Warner) and all company trademarks. Who was the savvy bargain-hunter who made the deal? Vince McMahon. The last ever *Nitro* was opened by Vince himself, and I would have lost my mind if he wore the same outfit as he did on Black Saturday. Again, the similarity to 1984 was immense. On that show, Booker T won the WCW Championship from Scott

Steiner, but the last-ever match was reserved for Ric Flair and Sting, two WCW stalwarts until the end, with Sting never leaving the company at all during his career up to that point. After a standing ovation for both men, Shane McMahon appeared, making the acquisition a storyline as *he* took over WCW.

WCW had pushed Vince hard for a good couple of years, but just like in the 1980s during the huge rock and wrestling explosion, he had won. And WCW wasn't the only rival that he acquired. ECW had enjoyed a great run, but talent was repeatedly lured away to WWF and WCW. In April 2000, Mike Awesome, the then-champion of ECW, turned up on *Nitro* unannounced in a protest over unpaid wages. Paul Heyman immediately filed an injunction so that Awesome couldn't appear with the belt, and also so he could get it from him to ensure that his company could continue without too much embarrassment. Heyman managed to pull something quite clever; he had Awesome lose the title to Tazz, who was on loan from the WWF as part of their ongoing cordial relationship. As I've mentioned previously, Vince would help ECW out financially from time to time; by having Tazz win the title it both surprised the ECW crowd and managed to somehow turn a small victory for WCW into a crushing, embarrassing defeat.

In October 2000, ECW lost its TV deal with TNN as the network took over the contract to broadcast *Raw*. For much of 2000, ECW had been pretty much the second most successful company in wrestling with WCW lagging as badly as it did. Its last ever pay per view, *Guilty as Charged 2001*, took place on 7 January. By 4 April the company was no more, and its assets were purchased by the WWF. Despite existing in various forms for only around a decade, the influence of ECW cannot be overstated. It changed the style of matches, helped push the Atttitude Era and even gave rise to smarter fans, those who know the inner workings of the business and applauded good wrestling. I reckon that every single fan at the ECW Arena knew that wrestling was a work, and the product was all the better for it. The company's influence has rightly pushed Paul Heyman as a creative genius, and he would go on to other employment within the WWF. As a fan, I'll never forget the first time I saw the opening credits to *ECW Hardcore TV* and how it changed how I viewed wrestling. Even though shows were only in front of a thousand or so fans, we will still be talking about the little company from Philly in 50 years' time. It was just that important.

Chapter Seventeen:
Attitude Peaks

WrestleMania X7, Austin retires, Brock debuts

Just as Vince had turned a two-, sometimes three-horse race into a solo canter, the WWF held what I (and many others) consider to be their finest-ever showcase: *WrestleMania X7*. Held in Houston at the Astrodome in front of 68,000 fans on 1 April 2001, it was, from top to bottom, a wonderful card with some fantastic matches that underlined WWF's untouchable supremacy at the time.

The show opened with William Regal against Chris Jericho, two mainstays of WCW who had never broken into the upper echelons despite their many talents. I know I'm biased as Regal is my friend, but it's still amazing to see two men who had been undervalued by their previous employer opening the biggest show of the year for the WWF. That opening match at 'Mania is tricky, where you have to get the crowd pumped and let them know exactly what the show has in store. Like the opening slot at a comedy night, it has to be entrusted to people who know what they're doing.

Later, Shane McMahon beat Vince McMahon in a street fight with Mick Foley as the special guest referee. This match came about because of the WCW 'takeover' angle at the end of the last ever *Nitro*. Shane took a bump from the top rope through the Spanish announce table after going for an elbow drop on his father only for his sister to pull Vince out of the way. He'd win the match by delivering a coast-to-coast dropkick on his dad; leaping from one turnbuckle into the opposite corner where Vince was sat with a steel garbage can in front of him. While neither man would claim to be a wrestler on the same level as the rest of the roster, they were certainly better at it than Bischoff and Russo could ever have hoped to be.

If that match wasn't stunt-filled enough, next came TLC II: The second tables, ladders and chairs match between Edge and Christian, The Dudley Boyz and The Hardy Boyz. All three teams had such unbelievable chemistry, and the first incarnation of the match occurred at *Summerslam 2000*, garnering rave reviews. Just like the ladder matches between Shawn Michaels and Razor Ramon in the mid 1990s revolutionised high spots in gimmick matches, the two TLC matches pushed the bar even further. TLC II was a masterpiece, making legends of all six men involved. Edge and Christian would be victorious just as they were in the first match, with Bubba Ray Dudley and Matt Hardy taking a huge final bump from a ladder through four stacked-up tables at ringside and Rhyno helping Christian unhook the WWF Tag Team belts.

In the semi-main event, The Undertaker continued his streak of winning matches at *WrestleMania* by defeating Triple H, taking his number of wins to nine with no defeats. As the decade wore on, this accidental statistic would become more and more important to storytelling. Triple H had a memorable entrance, with Motörhead playing him down to the ring. This was one of The Undertaker's best matches to this point, with the Texan crowd reacting massively to his victory.

The main event summed up exactly why the WWF had won the Monday Night War, the men involved almost at the head of the victory parade. Steve Austin took on The Rock in a no-disqualification match for the WWF Championship. The stipulation was only added moments before the match began, as two titanic babyfaces met. The Rock, the champion going into the match, was about to embark on a career in Hollywood that many thought was silly at the time. By 2018, he had become one of the highest paid actors in the world.

The match started and soon broke down into a brawl on the outside, with both men using the ring bell as a weapon and bleeding. Blood wasn't used anywhere near as much as it used to be, but it still had a place in matches of this magnitude. With Austin being from Texas, he had the slight edge in terms of crowd approval as the contest wore on, even using his old Ringmaster finishing move, the 'Million Dollar Dream' sleeper hold as an interesting nod to the past. The Rock then used Austin's Stunner finisher on him, before attempting a pin after his People's Elbow; that was broken up by Vince McMahon who had arrived at ringside to observe. As The Rock went after McMahon, he was rocked by his own finisher, the 'Rock Bottom', from Austin. The match continued with an epic number of finishers traded and near falls counted, before Vince handed Austin a chair at Stone Cold's insistence. This turned Austin heel, in theory, as he walloped The Rock over and over with the chair in order to finally get the pinfall. The turn didn't work in the arena as well as everyone would have liked, with Austin in his home state, but it works for me symbolically.

The show closed with Austin as WWF champion, sharing a beer with Vince McMahon, their enemies in both storyline and reality absolutely destroyed. Wrestling always goes on, it's a never-ending story that has no off season. But the war was over.

So then what?

By 2001, Vince McMahon found himself in the odd position of not having any rivals. From presumably being motivated by his war with Turner and Bischoff to finding himself as the winner, the wrestling business was going great. Like a sportsperson who has won everything and seeks a new challenge, he went after something else and it's fair to say it wasn't a success at the time. Having been in the works since 1999, on 3 February 2001 the XFL was launched, a rival to the incredibly successful NFL, running during the lengthy gridiron close-season. It didn't catch on, critics pointing to Vince's involvement with wrestling to try and taint the product. The whole thing was finished after one season, with WWF and NBC posting a $35 million loss *each*.

Vince seems keen to learn from his mistakes though, owning up to them when announcing a relaunch of the XFL in a different way at the start of 2018. The relaunch is due to begin in 2020 and this time is not a subsidiary of the wrestling business.

With the McMahon family now owning WCW (in reality: Vince; in the storyline: Shane), it made sense to try and make the most of the acquisition to push TV ratings and PPV buys. A storyline known as *The Invasion* took up much of 2001, with the WWF feuding with WCW. At *WrestleMania* X7, newly acquired WCW talent could be seen watching the show from Shane McMahon's skybox. By *King of the Ring 2001*, WCW's champion Booker T was interfering in WWF business, attacking Steve Austin during the main event. One mooted goal was to have WCW take over one of the weekly shows as a brand, in a similar way to Eric Bischoff suggesting that nWo could take over one of the WCW shows before the company went under. Just like back then, when it was tried out it didn't go to plan. Booker T was a solid talent and worked hard, but he had a WCW Championship defence against Buff Bagwell on an episode of *Raw* that was universally panned and made WWF management head in a different direction.

WCW was portrayed as the villainous group, and then a third group was added to the equation as ECW representatives Rob Van Dam, Tommy Dreamer and Paul Heyman formed their own side, pulling in many of their old alumni from the good old days at the bingo hall. Eventually, WCW and ECW would join sides, with WCW owned by Shane and ECW owned by Stephanie, calling themselves The Alliance and going after their father's WWF. Everything would come to a head at the *Invasion* pay per view in July 2001, with Steve Austin joining up with the WWF side on the episode of *Smackdown* right before the event.

The show was built around Alliance representatives doing battle with WWF talent, and going into the main event (dubbed 'The Inaugural Brawl') the scores were tied at five victories apiece. Representing the Alliance was Booker T, The Dudley Boyz, Diamond Dallas Page and Rhyno, facing off against the WWF team of Austin, Kane, Undertaker, Chris Jericho and Kurt Angle. The finish to the match came as Austin turned on his own team, claiming that he felt unappreciated by the WWF, thus joining the Alliance. The show remains the highest-grossing PPV outside of *WrestleMania* shows that the WWF has ever presented, with nearly 800,000 buys.

After *Invasion* though, the Alliance was gradually weakened. Truth be told, apart from the former ECW talents who had been in the WWF for a while and guys like Booker T, a lot of the former WCW talent didn't catch on with the fans and in the case of one team, KroniK (Brian Adams, formerly Crush, and Brian Clark, formerly Wrath) were so bad that they were let go after one pay-per-view performance. With wrestlers jumping sides fairly often, what could have been one of the most exciting storylines of all time was over before the end of the year. The reality of the war between the brands was always more exciting than the storyline anyway.

With no real competition in terms of televised wrestling to speak of, the WWF had busied itself signing up everyone talented from WCW and ECW and by March 2002 it had a roster that was bulging at the seams. As the Invasion storyline hadn't panned out well enough to give WCW a show of its own, it was decided to make wrestlers exclusive to either *Raw* or *Smackdown*. A draft lottery was held, which I remember being very excited by at the time. Each brand chose 30 superstars to populate their roster, with Vince controlling *Smackdown* and Ric Flair controlling *Raw*. In the storyline, Flair had bought the WWF stock of Shane and Stephanie in order for them to be able to buy WCW and ECW respectively. The first picks were The Rock (*Smackdown*) and The Undertaker (*Raw*). The draft also made some titles exclusive to certain brands once their holder was drafted – for example, the Intercontinental Championship which was moved to *Raw* when holder Rob Van Dam was drafted fourth. The brand extension lasted until 2011, before being rebooted and used again from 2016. As well as giving more talent the chance to be involved with storylines, it also meant that house-show business could pick up, with two separate crews doing a show each per night.

That wasn't the biggest change that fans and talent alike had to get used to though. The WWF had been arguing with the *other* WWF (the World-Wide Fund for Nature *aka* the World Wildlife Fund) since the mid 1990s about the use of the acronym. At the time, peace was achieved when the World Wrestling Federation agreed to try to not use the letters 'WWF' as much as possible. They didn't exactly stick to their end of the bargain, and in 2000 the other WWF sued, leading to the rebranding of the company as 'World Wrestling Entertainment' in May 2002. It was incredibly confusing for a while, a little bit like at the turn of a new year when you keep writing the old one down. I'm just relieved that I can finally type WWE nearly every time I mention the company from now on – you have no idea how hard it's been.

Ironically, the last-ever *WWF* champion was some guy called Hulk Hogan, who enjoyed a one-month reign between April and May 2002, and was back in the fold for a few more years at least. You wouldn't have expected his career to last longer than the only man arguably bigger than him in terms of lasting impact on the industry, but it certainly did.

Steve Austin wasn't exactly giddy about the decision to turn him heel at *WrestleMania X7* and has spoken about it many times since the event. As a villain he rapidly became part of a team with Triple H: The Two Man Power Trip, with Austin holding the WWE title, HHH the Intercontinental belt and both men holding the tag titles. Before the gimmick really got going, Triple H tore his quad and was out for an extended period. After turning face for a while by joining Vince's side during the Invasion storyline, Austin was soon a heel again by joining the Alliance and started his tedious 'What?' catchphrase which still permeates through some wrestling crowds now. It was funny for about two weeks when it first started. That one word helped turn him back babyface – which shows you just how odd wrestling audiences can sometimes be – and helped push Austin back into the title picture as the WWF and WCW titles were combined to form the Undisputed title, first won by Chris Jericho at *Vengeance* in December 2001.

Austin had a decent feud with Booker T that was notable for their brawl inside a supermarket, before turning down the chance to wrestle Hulk Hogan at *WrestleMania X8*, allegedly because he was unhappy at the prospect of losing to an older Hogan, a man he remembered debuting in WCW when he was still there and wasn't exactly a fan of. Austin was rushed into a feud with the new nWo instead, meeting Scott Hall at *'Mania* while the show was stolen by the 'Icon v Icon' match between Hogan and The Rock, the crowd in Toronto choosing to cheer the heel Hogan. After The Rock won, Hogan was attacked by his own nWo stablemates Hall and Nash, with The Rock making the save and the two men posing together, making Hogan a babyface for the first time since 1996. This wasn't even the main event; in that contest, Triple H captured the Undisputed championship, continuing his rise to the very top of the card that had been interrupted by injury.

Away from the ring, Austin was embroiled in a well-publicised domestic dispute with his wife Debra that led to their divorce. By his own admission, he was also drinking heavily at the time and not exactly the most fun person to be around. He started openly criticising the writing and storylines that the WWE creative team was putting out at the time, and most notably vetoed losing to monster rookie Brock Lesnar. On 3 June 2002 he made his last appearance on *Raw* until early 2003, no-showing the next week as his position within the company became blighted by squabbles and ill-feeling. He was allegedly unhappy with the positions in the company of both The Rock and Triple H, although these issues were resolved upon his return. He was also fined $250,000 for walking out on the company.

WrestleMania XIX in 2003 would be Austin's final-ever match, and unlike many wrestlers he has firmly stuck to this, apart from hitting the odd Stunner here and there. Having chosen personally to wrestle on against doctors' orders after his neck injury in 1997, Austin could easily have been paralysed or even killed if he had taken a move slightly wrong during this time. It seemed most apt that he would face The Rock one last time, with Austin the babyface and The Rock the smug heel, revelling in his early status as an actor and going all Hollywood. Austin's leather waistcoat had the initials 'OMR' stitched into them, symbolising 'One More Round'. After the Rock won, Eric Bischoff (yes, everyone got a chance in WWE at some point) 'fired' Austin the next night on *Raw* for medical reasons, an echo of when he actually fired him in the mid Nineties for having the temerity to be legitimately hurt.

Austin went on to have sporadic appearances on *Raw* and *Smackdown* for the rest of the decade, always in a non-wrestling role; his impact on the industry from 1996–2003 was absolutely amazing for such a short space of time.

The main event of *WrestleMania XIX* nearly saw someone else's career end, albeit by accident. Brock Lesnar, the rookie that Austin didn't want to put over in 2002, was a standout amateur wrestler, a former NCAA Division 1 Heavyweight Champion, won while at the University of Minnesota. At six feet three inches tall and weighing 286lbs of solid muscle, he's arguably the most terrifying man in the history of wrestling and has managed to achieve this without having a gimmick other than him being a monster. Raised on a farm, from his very first day in professional wrestling he looked like he had been brought up tossing bales of hay around or juggling cattle, and if you learned that he'd killed a few people, you wouldn't be shocked. My wife remarked that he looks like a more frightening version of British murderer Raoul Moat.

Because of his freakish appearance – seriously, nobody before or after him has ever looked so intimidating – and his ability to learn everything in professional wrestling incredibly quickly (much like Kurt Angle before him), he was fast-tracked to stardom. He was on the main roster by March 2002, managed by Paul Heyman and he won the 2002 *King of the Ring* shortly after his debut, earning a title shot at *Summerslam*. There, he beat The Rock to win the Undisputed belt at the age of 25, just 126 days after his main roster debut. This win led to two belts, as Lesnar defended his on *Smackdown* (becoming the WWE title) and the big gold former WCW belt became the World Championship, defended exclusively on *Raw* and first awarded to Triple H by Eric Bischoff.

Lesnar's first pinfall loss came against the Big Show at *Survivor*

Series 2002, the defeat prompted by Heyman turning on him. This turned Lesnar face; in truth, people wanted to cheer for him in the same way that they wanted to cheer for Goldberg back in WCW: he was a monster who destroyed opponents. Going on to win the 2003 *Royal Rumble*, he met Kurt Angle in the main event of *WrestleMania XIX* for the WWE Championship, a contest borne out of both sports entertainment appeal and the legitimate backgrounds of both men. Angle had become a megastar and was having stellar matches with nearly anybody he was put up against, but the end of this match saw Lesnar try and overstretch himself. Taking to the top rope, the plan was for Lesnar to deliver a shooting star press, a forward-facing back somersault into a splash, impressive enough when a cruiserweight performed the move but something really special when done by a man of his size. He had been able to hit it in the past, during his days in OVW (Ohio Valley Wrestling), but he had never used it on the main roster. He tried it at 'Mania but didn't rotate enough, landing on the top of his head in a frightening manner and causing Angle to help improvise a finish where the right man – the shook-up Lesnar – still went over and won the title. After his first year in WWE, it looked like Lesnar was going to be a mainstay in the company for a long time to come. As it happened, by the next year he'd be on his way out.

JIM'S TOP TEN: MATCHES

There is every chance that this list will change within a few minutes of me writing it down, but here are my ten favourite matches of all time. I'm already questioning them. This could easily be a list of my top 100 matches, there's just so many great bouts to choose from.

10. Brian Danielson v KENTA, 16 September 2006, Ring of Honor *Glory by Honor V Day 2*

A crazy crowd in New York's Manhattan Centre at the peak of Ring of Honor's greatness made this really special, with RoH champion Danielson defending the title against Japanese standout KENTA (Kenta Kobayashi) in a brutal war which featured some of the loudest-ever singing of the Europe song *The Final Countdown*.

9. Eddie Guerrero v Rey Mysterio Jr, 26 October 1997, WCW *Halloween Havoc '97*

Eddie Guerrero, the ultimate dickhead heel (in this role, at least) took on the much smaller Mysterio in a title v mask contest; Guerrero's WCW Cruiserweight belt against Mysterio's mask. Even over 20 years on the match seems futuristic, with spots being performed by both men that were truly death-defying. Try to ignore the fact that Rey is dressed up like The Phantom though.

8. Samoa Joe v Kenta Kobashi, 1 October 2005, Ring of Honor *Joe v Kobashi*

You know a match has the potential to be special when the whole show is named after it. Ring of Honor standout Joe took on Japanese legend Kobashi in 23-plus minutes of unbelievably hard-hitting violence. Kobashi is one of the best ever; this match showed that Joe absolutely deserved his place at the top table of wrestling as well.

7. The Undertaker v Shawn Michaels, 28 March 2010, WWE *WrestleMania XXVI*

After a brilliant match the year before, this one was a no-disqualification encounter that put The Undertaker's legendary winning streak at *WrestleMania* up against Shawn Michaels' career. It was hard to try and top the previous match between the two, but they managed it and then some, plus Michaels left and *stayed* retired, a rarity in wrestling.

6. Triple H v Cactus Jack, 23 January 2000, WWE *Royal Rumble 2000*

The first huge show of the new millennium remains one of my favourites, and this match between arrogant, new-to-the-main-event WWE Champion Triple H and the craziest of Mick Foley's personas, Cactus Jack, is a street fight with no rules, a lot of weapons and a fair bit of blood. I was distraught at the time when Cactus didn't win, and also squealed at the TV when barbed wire was produced.

5. Johnny Gargano v Tommaso Ciampa, 7 April 2018, NXT *Takeover: New Orleans*

Former tag team partners collided in an emotional, brutal war between the beloved babyface Gargano, trying to win his job back, and the bitter Ciampa on his return from injury. An absolute work of art that recalls the brutality of matches from the 1980s like Tully Blanchard v Magnum TA; it's the best match I've ever seen live and is made even more special for me by being between two friends of mine.

4. Bret Hart v Steve Austin, 23 March 1997, WWE *WrestleMania 13*

Conducted under submission-only rules, this match managed to turn both wrestlers; Hart to becoming a hated, Canada-obsessed villain and Austin to the working-class, blue-collar hero that the world embraced. The end came when Austin was locked in Hart's Sharpshooter hold, refusing to give up, his face covered in blood. By passing out he never submitted but Hart was awarded the match, the fans now finally having an excuse to cheer for 'Stone Cold' thanks to his heroics.

3. Kazuchika Okada v Kenny Omega, 4 January 2017, NJPW *Wrestle Kingdom 11*

2017 was easily one of the best years in the history of wrestling, and this match was the best match on an amazing show right at the start of the year. Fans will argue forever which of the three encounters between Okada and Omega they preferred that year; I love this one, awarded six stars out of five by *The Wrestling Observer* newsletter. Omega, the Canadian gaijin up against the virtually unbeatable 'Rainmaker' Okada. Some of the bumps in this match are quite brutal, and Okada manages to make even simple moves like a dropkick look like it could kill a man.

2. Katsuyori Shibata v Tomohiro Ishii, 4 August 2013, NJPW *G1 Climax 23 Day 4*

I often show non-wrestling fans this match to illustrate exactly what I love about professional wrestling. This match between two long-term friends is one of the most brutal contests you'll ever see. Only lasting just over 12 minutes, it's so stiff that had it lasted any longer, it would have massively suspended everyone's disbelief. The two men go toe to toe from the start in what people *thought* would just be a regular round-robin tournament match. What the crowd got was a *war*. No gimmicks, no blood, nothing flashy. Just a fight. Shibata is now, sadly, retired, due to his physically punishing in-ring style.

1. John Cena v CM Punk, 17 July 2011, WWE *Money in the Bank 2011*

When I was a bit of a smark, if you'd have told me my favourite match of all time would include John Cena then I would have laughed. But as a promoter, I now see him differently. At the time, I wanted CM Punk to win this match so much but absolutely could not see it happening, with it being his last match before his contract ran out and the match being for Cena's WWE title. In front of Punk's hometown Chicago crowd, the match has a couple of slip-ups, but the atmosphere turns what could be just a very good match into the absolute best match. I rewatch this match once a month, on average. It's that good.

Chapter Eighteen:
New Stars and Career Peaks

Michaels returns; WWE creates new main-eventers; Guerrero and Benoit reach the top of the industry

While Lesnar was a bright new star and Austin was making his way out of the company, another man made his return in 2002: Shawn Michaels. Reintroduced as a member of the new version of the nWo in June, they were disbanded a month later and he took to trying to convince his friend Triple H to reform D-Generation X with him. After seemingly convincing Triple H to join the *Raw* roster on his return from injury at *Vengeance 2002*, the next night on TV Triple H turned on Michaels, setting up a no-disqualification street fight at *Summerslam*. Billed as 'unsanctioned' to give the match a sinister gravitas because Michaels was coming back off a severe, seemingly career-ending injury, I always had an issue with that. If it was unsanctioned, why was it on pay per view? The match was wonderful though:

a long, bloody, drawn-out contest that signalled just the start of a long feud between the two men.

Michaels had used his time away from the business to start his own wrestling school and become, for a short time at least, a sports commentator for a local TV news network. By the time he made his return he was a much easier person to be around than he had been in the past, having become a born-again Christian upon meeting his wife and getting sober.

Michaels won the World Championship at *Survivor Series 2002* in the first-ever Elimination Chamber match, a huge cage structure where six men fight under elimination rules, two starting off and then four more being released from glass pods after set time increments. Triple H would win the title back in a Three Stages of Hell match at *Armageddon*, and the two men would feud on and off until 2004, while a feud with Chris Jericho bubbled alongside, leading to a great match between Jericho and Michaels at *WrestleMania XIX*.

With his new, revamped attitude, Michaels was a huge asset to the company and stuck around for the rest of the decade. He wasn't averse to still having the occasional old-school HBK moment though: check out the main event at *Summerslam 2005* where Michaels, unhappy at having to lose to an inferior in-ring performer like Hulk Hogan, absurdly oversells every single move to the point of flat-out comedy. That match remains one of my favourite-ever guilty pleasures.

Meanwhile, Triple H was becoming a mainstay of the main-event scene within the company. He'd rebranded himself as 'The Game' and would go on to be a 14-time World Champion. At the time of writing (because he's still an occasional wrestler), he has headlined *WrestleMania* seven times, more than any other performer. His involvement in various stables always kept him at the forefront of storylines, from his time in DX to the McMahon-Helmsley Faction, that saw him 'married' on-screen to Stephanie McMahon, and eventually divorced on-screen too, despite the couple *actually* getting married in October 2003 and placing Triple H, behind the scenes, as an important part of the family business. Father of three children with Stephanie, in 2011 he was named executive vice president of talent and live events; his influence behind the scenes would be felt more over the following decade.

Often criticised by internet fans as a beneficiary of nepotism, people forget that Triple H regularly used himself to put over talent on their way to mega stardom, doing, to borrow his later catchphrase, 'what's best for business'. As we'll learn when we look at the current decade, like him or not, Triple H is now one of the most important people in wrestling history and you'll hear his name a fair bit more before this book is finished.[3]

In 2003, Triple H was a big part of a stable that could be seen as an updated version of the Four Horsemen: Evolution. Consisting of Ric Flair (Triple H's hero) and relative newcomers Randy Orton and Batista, the four suit-clad, high-living villains dominated stories for over a year. By *Armageddon 2003*, all four men would hold titles and be as dominant as Flair and his old buddies in mid 1980s NWA.

Randy Orton is the son of 'Cowboy' Bob Orton, part of the main event at *WrestleMania I*, and the grandson of Bob Orton

[3] Side note: I had a conversation with HHH about Killer Kowalski, his trainer, when researching this book; he also once tweeted a photo of him with me that caused me to get a mixture of congratulations from many and hate mail from a few. My personal experience of him is that he's a good guy.

Sr. Discouraged initially from joining the family trade, young Randy was a marine but struggled with it and was punished for going AWOL before leaving the military. After getting injured shortly after his debut, he gradually turned heel while recuperating through various segments and vignettes, displaying arrogance that fitted his overall demeanour much better. Upon healing, he joined Evolution and was soon Intercontinental Champion, adopting the nickname 'The Legend Killer' as he went after veterans of the industry. At *Backlash 2004* he took part in a bloody hardcore match with Mick Foley that featured barbed wire and thumbtacks; by *Summerslam 2004* he was the youngest-ever World Champion at 24 years old, breaking Brock Lesnar's record.

Batista is probably better known to non-wrestling fans as the actor Dave Bautista, who plays Drax in the *Guardians of the Galaxy* movies. A bit like Brock Lesnar and Randy Orton, he picked up wrestling fairly quickly although he didn't come into the business until he'd passed the age of 30. In the late 1990s he tried to become a wrestler through the WCW Power Plant school but was told that he didn't have what it took to be a star despite extensive bodybuilding experience. By 2000 he was in OVW, performing under the name Leviathan, then was called up to the main WWE roster and given the gimmick of 'Deacon Batista', enforcer for D-Von Dudley as he worked as a solo competitor with a heel, religious gimmick.

By *Armageddon 2002* he was just plain old Batista, aligned with Ric Flair before joining up with Evolution. He was injured for a long period, and upon his return was the first to show dissent with his Evolution stablemates, leading to Triple H telling him to keep out of the title picture and Batista winning the 2005

Royal Rumble to get a title shot of his choosing. In a great moment, the imposing Batista fooled his stablemates into thinking he would go after the *Smackdown* WWE Championship at *WrestleMania 21* by giving them the thumbs up, before turning it, Nero-like, into a thumbs down, and turning face, attacking Flair and Triple H. '*Mania* that year did fantastic numbers on pay per view as Batista won the title from Triple H, his ascent to the top of the company being great fun to watch at the time.

There was another muscular chap who started making his name within WWE at this time, and while his ascent to the top took slightly longer, he remains there to this day. Beloved by kids, despised by the smarkiest of smart fans, and supporter of the tea towel industry: John Cena.

Like seemingly everyone else at that time, Cena had his period in OVW in 2001, using the same gimmick he'd used in the Californian independent scene: The Prototype. With chiselled muscles and a buzz cut hairdo, he adopted robotic mannerisms and portrayed himself as something of a cyborg. In June 2002, during WWE's 'Ruthless Aggression' period, he answered Kurt Angle's open challenge on TV, narrowly losing but looking like a promising, if green, rookie in the process. Later that year he would become a heel during a feud with Billy Kidman (the last and only time he's been a villain in his career), and accidentally invented a gimmick during a Halloween special edition of *Smackdown*. Having dressed up as Vanilla Ice and delivered a freestyle rap, that became his character, delivering insulting (and often very funny and near the knuckle) lyrics to crowds around the USA as he started going after various titles. He was even given the ludicrous nickname of 'The Doctor of Thuganomics' which makes me giggle to this day.

Because he was so good at his new gimmick, Cena started getting over and fans started cheering for him. By the time he lost a title match to Kurt Angle at *No Mercy 2003*, he was a fully-fledged babyface. At *WrestleMania XX* he won his first title, the US Championship by delivering his finishing move, the 'FU' (since retitled, cleverly, as the 'Attitude Adjustment') to the massive Big Show. By the next *'Mania*, he would be WWE Champion for the first time. While he is a polarising character nowadays, with kids adoring him and grumpy smart fans chanting 'John Cena sucks', you can't deny that Cena's body of work (as well as his tireless contributions to the Make a Wish Foundation charity) makes him *the* franchise player for WWE over the last decade or so. He even learned Mandarin when WWE started expanding into China. The guy is a model employee.

Some stars got to the top after a slower burn. Edge and Christian, storyline brothers but really best friends from Canada, had a great run as a tag team, being part of the historic TLC matches and combining exciting in-ring work with a genuine sense of humour and commitment to character, their 'five-second pose' and use of kazoos entertaining fans. Like most tag teams, only one half ever seems to go on to enormous superstardom, even if both men did enjoy storied careers. Edge won the 2001 *King of the Ring*, splitting the team up. Winning the first 'Money in the Bank' match at *WrestleMania 21* by grabbing a briefcase hung above the ring, Edge was granted a title shot at any point within a year of his victory. It came nine months later at *New Year's Revolution 2006* when he would finally cash in to easily win the title from John Cena who had just won an Elimination Chamber match. From here, 'The Rated R Superstar' was born, celebrating the next night on *Raw* with what Edge promised to be a 'live sex celebration' with Lita. By this point, Christian had already left WWE, but he did make a name for himself elsewhere.

Edge's real-life relationship with Lita put a whole new spin on the long rivalry between two former tag teams, Edge and Christian and the Hardy Boyz. Starting as jobbers when they were under age, Matt and Jeff Hardy had risen up the card at WWE, their willingness to take high risks and their 'Team Extreme' with Lita making them incredibly popular. Matt and Lita were in a relationship for quite some time before Lita embarked on a real-life affair with Edge; the Hardyz tag team was split up in 2002 with Jeff seemingly destined to become a star but unreliable outside of the ring due to addiction issues. He was released in April 2003 but would sporadically return to WWE. Matt, meanwhile, became 'Matt Hardy Version 1', a fun gimmick that saw 'Matt Facts' appear on the screen during his entrance. In April 2005, real-life issues stemming from his relationship with Lita saw Matt released, only to be rehired and with the affair between Lita and Edge public knowledge, everything turned into a storyline.

While new stars were being built up all the time on both *Raw* and *Smackdown,* for long-term fans like myself, the biggest thing in 2004 was the rise to the top of the tree of two veterans; two men that I had watched on grainy tapes that I'd ordered from Japan or of their days in the early, pre-pay-per-view ECW. Little did I know that the joy I had watching them in 2004 would eventually be replaced by sadness.

Eddie Guerrero had been sent to rehab in May 2001, and then in November that same year was arrested for drunk driving. This led to him leaving the WWF and having a brief run on the growing independent scene while he got clean. In April 2002 he was back in the WWE fold, enjoying various runs as a tag team champion and US Champion, as well as a memorable feud with his nephew Chavo Guerrero. Eddie's best friend Chris Benoit had missed a year out of his career after getting hurt in 2001, returning to form a tag team with Kurt Angle on *Smackdown* and having a WWE title match with his partner at the 2003 *Royal Rumble* that is one of the finest matches of the decade, if not ever. Guerrero and Benoit then had a brief feud over Eddie's US Championship, with both men starting to get massive reactions from crowds.

The thing was, Eddie had a character. He would 'lie, cheat and steal' during backstage skits, and could deliver promos nearly as well as he could deliver his 'Frog Splash' finisher, adopted from his late tag team partner Art Barr. Benoit was different; he couldn't really speak but had an intensity to him that made you pay attention to the screen, a stiff in-ring style that made him look like a legitimate badass and a likeness to the legendary Dynamite Kid. Benoit would win the 2004 *Royal Rumble* after entering the match first, deciding to jump to *Raw* and challenge Triple H for the World Championship at *WrestleMania XX*. This led to Guerrero winning a 15-man *Royal Rumble* match on *Smackdown* at the end of January to determine the number one contender to the WWE Championship. At *No Way Out* in February, Guerrero, a massive underdog, beat Brock Lesnar for the title to an overwhelmingly emotional response. Bill Goldberg was involved in some interference in that match, having been around WWE since March 2003, feuding with Chris Jericho and Triple H before entering into a rivalry with Lesnar.

There was a reason that Lesnar had to drop the title before 'Mania. Despite being at the very top of the business, he wanted to go and do something else. With hundreds of pro football players moving from gridiron to wrestling, he wanted to be the first to try and go the other way. Despite having not played football since high school, Lesnar wanted to try out for the NFL and so gave his notice to WWE. Goldberg was also leaving, his one-year contract up.

At *WrestleMania XX*, the two faced off in a match during which the fans constantly gave them grief for leaving, the news having broken on the internet. Only special guest referee Steve Austin got any form of positive reaction in what remains one of the weirdest *WrestleMania* matches of all time. A few weeks after 'Mania, Lesnar was in an accident on his motorcycle that hampered his ability to operate at 100 per cent. In June he was signed by the Minnesota Vikings but only played in pre-season games before being released. A short run in NJPW would be next for him, then the world of MMA. He'd be reunited with Goldberg in a WWE ring over a decade later.

Eddie Guerrero defended his WWE Championship against Kurt Angle in a fine match at *WrestleMania XX*, before Benoit entered the main event against Triple H and Shawn Michaels for the World Heavyweight Championship. Benoit would eventually get the victory, leading to an emotional end to the show with Guerrero joining him in the ring, two best friends with their titles aloft, finally at the top of the industry after years in Mexico, Japan, bingo halls and being ignored in WCW. Unfortunately, such a happy moment was not the end of the story for either man.

John Bradshaw Layfield, formerly Bradshaw of the Acolytes

tag team, was a bullish, stuck-up, rich cowboy who entered into a great feud with Guerrero, featuring a full 1.0 Muta scale blade job by Eddie in their match at *Judgement Day 2004*, with a bloody Eddie retaining his title after losing the match by disqualification. JBL (as he was abbreviated to) would win the title from Eddie at *The Great American Bash*. It was rumoured that Eddie spent much of his reign worrying about the pressure of being champion, so he had no issue when storyline dictated that he dropped the title.

On 13 November 2005, Eddie was found in a hotel room in Minneapolis, dead from heart failure at the young age of 38. He had apparently been feeling unwell for some time, and after spending so long getting himself clean and sober it was a devastating blow to the entire industry, especially as he was such a popular figure both in front of the camera and behind the scenes. There was a massive outpouring of sadness from his colleagues, a feeling that still resonates today when you realise just how influential he was on the current generation of wrestlers.

After Eddie's death, WWE implemented something called the Talent Wellness Program, started in February 2006 to screen talent for drug, alcohol and health issues (primarily cardiac problems, which were causing most early deaths for wrestlers). There had been a steroid screening programme in place in the early 1990s, around the time of the Dr Zahorian issue, but this was the first step to ensuring that talent was not abusing drugs, be they recreational or steroids. There was a three-strike system set in place, with the first violation leading to a 30-day suspension, the second 60 days, and the third termination of the wrestler's contract. WWE has been keen to reach out to past performers with substance abuse issues and pay for their rehabilitation, with stars like Scott Hall taking them up on their offer.

Unfortunately, in June 2007, wrestling would witness something even more heartbreaking.

Chris Benoit hadn't quite hit the heights that he did in 2004 again, but he remained one of the best in-ring performers of all time. A grizzled veteran with a missing front tooth (that he actually lost not in a match, but by clashing heads with his dog), he built a reputation in Mexico and Japan as Wild Pegasus and the Pegasus Kid, before his runs in ECW and WCW introduced him to American audiences. In the late 1990s and early 2000s, Benoit was my favourite wrestler. Because of his actions over one weekend in mid 2007, I can never see him in that same light again. I know he did amazing things inside the ring, but something inside his brain went awfully wrong and triggered arguably the saddest story in the history of wrestling.

On Monday 25 June 2007, police entered the Benoit family home in Fayetteville, Georgia, after being contacted by WWE representatives who were worried about Chris Benoit missing shows over that weekend. They found the bodies of Benoit, his wife Nancy and their seven-year-old son, Daniel. Nancy had been murdered the previous Friday, strangled by Benoit after putting up what the coroner believed was a struggle. Her limbs were bound, and her body was wrapped in a towel, a Bible placed next to her body.

On Saturday, Chavo Guerrero had received a voicemail from Benoit saying that he'd overslept and would be late for the house show that night in Beaumont, Texas. Benoit didn't show up at all, but spoke to Chavo that afternoon and stated that Nancy and Daniel were both sick. In reality, Daniel was now also dead, having been smothered after being sedated with Xanax. He was likely already unconscious before he was murdered. He also had a Bible placed next to his body.

In the early hours of Sunday, texts were sent from both Benoit and Nancy's phones to co-workers, giving their home address and cryptically saying that the dogs were in the pool area and that a side door to the garage had been left open. Benoit then no-showed *Vengeance: Night of the Champions* that night. At some point after the texts had been sent out, Benoit used a weight machine to hang himself.

On Monday, the discovery of the bodies and the talk of a major police investigation initially made people think it was a triple murder, so *Raw* that night was dedicated to Benoit, showing his old matches and the like. The next night on *ECW on Sci Fi*, Vince started the broadcast himself, saying that the true nature of the situation had come to be known and that Benoit would no longer be mentioned. He has since been gradually erased from WWE history as the company, quite rightly, distanced itself. Many wrestler autobiographies have had to deal with the complex nature of having a friend commit murder; I'm just a fan and I find writing about this very difficult. I can't imagine how his friends must have felt. He wasn't mentioned by name again on WWE television until 2015.

There has been much speculation as to why Benoit did what he did. Concussion expert and former wrestler Chris Nowinski has hypothesised that Benoit had repeated, untreated concussions. Tests on his brain showed severe Chronic Traumatic Encephalopathy (CTE) and brain damage consistent with a sufferer of Alzheimer's Disease. Others blamed alcohol (none was found in his system) or steroids, but it's hard to argue that this was 'roid rage' when everything was so planned and meticulous. The truth is that we'll never know exactly why he did it, but we do know that the attention to the case has gradually led to less chair shots to wrestler's heads (there are now none at all in WWE; Benoit would happily take them at his own suggestion, unprotected, even to the back of his head).

This hastened, around the time of the *WrestleMania* match that this book is named after between Ric Flair and Shawn Michaels, a change behind the scenes that saw shows gradually getting less violent. Blading would, pretty much, become a thing of the past in a few short years. Extreme matches would seem tame compared to those of the late 1990s and early 2000s. In the summer of 2008, WWE TV programming was quietly changed to be PG-rated, after years of Attitude had taken the company to stratospheric heights. By 2009 *Raw* would become more showbiz, with guest hosts appearing weekly on the programme in the same way that they would a chat show. The grittiness of Austin's rise to fame and crash TV was long in the past.

Wrestling wasn't done with innovating yet though. Not by a long shot.

Chapter Nineteen:
New Challengers

TNA, Ring of Honor, events in Japan and even WWE launches new brands

In 2002, two new challengers entered the wrestling scene. TNA was started up at the same time as another new company, Ring of Honor, as smaller alternatives to WWE programming.

Ring of Honor was started first, by Rob Feinstein of RF Video. His company needed something to stay afloat after ECW went bust in 2001, as ECW had provided most of his bestselling tapes. He decided to start his own company, with the first show in Philadelphia on 23 February 2002. It quickly became known for tremendous in-ring competition, with shows usually staged in the North East of the USA, the former ECW heartland.

Feinstein would be gone from his own company by 2004, after he became the victim of an internet sting that embroiled him in a sex scandal. This in turn led to the company being seen in a bad light by other promotions like TNA, putting an end to talent-sharing. Once RoH was in the hands of new owner Cary Silkin, the gradual expansion began. I can't overstate how important RoH was for a fan like me in the mid 2000s; their shows felt out of this world and while I still loved WWE, it felt very much like I was on board with something new and underground. It also helped that so much of the company was designed to feel different, from the 'code of honor' that meant wrestlers shaking hands and eschewing cheating (so when somebody *did* cheat, it really meant something), to the way that title challengers were decided based on the more sports-like win/loss records rather than storyline feuds.

The rise of RoH led to a legion of wonderful talents who have nearly all gone on to bigger things, but three names in particular stand out as standard-bearers for the company and among my favourite wrestlers of all time.

Touring in a Polynesian dance troupe as a kid is one of the more unusual groundings for a professional wrestler, but Samoa Joe did that before starting to train in his native California. What was meant to be a one-shot deal as a burly enforcer in RoH became a long stint thanks to his impressive in-ring work; stiff strikes, great submission moves and wonderful agility for a bigger guy. Less than a year after his RoH debut, Joe was their world champion, holding the belt for 645 days and helping the promotion expand, built around him and his growing reputation. In 2005 he would sign with TNA, going on a long undefeated streak and being part of the best match in that company's history, a brilliant three-way between himself, AJ Styles and Christopher Daniels. From there, he moved to a terrific feud with Kurt Angle who had moved from WWE after citing concerns over his health with such a busy schedule. It would be 2015 before Joe would make it to WWE, but his work on the NXT brand and on *Raw* shows that he hasn't lost a step since he was one of the most exciting wrestlers on the planet a decade earlier.

I once got a parking ticket because I took Joe to Nando's in London when he worked for PROGRESS. I've never been happier to get fined.

CM Punk is the man who eventually made it easy for me to explain what being Straight Edge is, with him arguably being the most prominent practitioner of the drink- and drug-free lifestyle that I also follow. It was a no-brainer for me to latch on to his character, but his in-ring work was also stellar. His first RoH feud was with former ECW standout Raven, comparing him to his own alcoholic father and somehow making sobriety a heel trait. A 2004 classic series of matches with Samoa Joe put Punk in the shop window. In May 2005, he had a tryout match for WWE, signing with the company in June. Brilliantly, Punk then won the RoH World title from Austin Aries, starting the 'Summer of Punk' and threatening to take the belt with him to WWE. In a moment of absolute genius, he even signed his contract on the actual title belt.

He eventually lost the title to James Gibson (known in WWE as Jamie Noble) in a four corners match, but would revive some aspects of the Summer of Punk in 2011 to fantastic effect. Punk remains the coolest person to ever have a soft drink logo (Pepsi) tattooed upon him. I am ranked about 100,000 (Coca-Cola).

Third in my trifecta of favourites is Brian Danielson, a founding father of RoH and a huge part of the company until leaving for WWE in 2009 and becoming Daniel Bryan. Trained at Shawn Michaels' school in Texas, he got a WWE developmental deal and formed a friendship with William Regal who was a key figure in his development (which is why Danielson always wore burgundy-coloured trunks and boots, as a tribute). Regal recommended that he spent time in the UK doing holiday camp shows for All Star using his 'American Dragon' gimmick. Blending technical skill with a hard-hitting style, he won the RoH title from Gibson in September 2005 and held it for 462 days. His title run was notable for him acting incredibly viciously but never really becoming a full heel; fans would sing along with his *Final Countdown* theme music (yes, that 'banger from the 1980s by Europe) and then shout along with what became his catchphrase, leaving on holds to the very last second with an assured yell of 'I have till five, referee'.

TNA was started by Jeff and Jerry Jarrett, father and son coming up with the idea on a fishing trip after WCW had folded. Their idea was to start a company reliant on pay per view, not a television deal. In July 2002 they were joined by Vince Russo, and the company was allied with the NWA organisation. Initially called NWA-TNA, the 'TNA' stood for 'Total Non-stop Action'; it also helped that it wasn't a million miles away from 'T and A', suggesting that the content would be nearer the knuckle with it not being governed by TV regulations.

In 2004, the company changed tack from the unusual concept of weekly pay-per-view shows, launching *Impact!*, a new weekly television show and moving to monthly pay per views. *Impact!* would be taped at Universal Studios in Orlando, and for a little while it seemed that WWE might have some actual competition. Fox TV ended their deal with the company in May 2005 though, and the show resurfaced on Spike TV in October of that same year after broadcasting on the internet during the dark months.

A highlight of TNA's programming was their X Division, showcasing high-risk, high-impact matches rather than weight-based bouts. It was mainly the domain of the lighter, nimbler wrestlers but both Samoa Joe and Abyss managed to have X Division title runs. TNA also had some big stars involved; Jeff Jarrett and Sting were arguably the biggest ex-WCW stars to not get picked up by WWE (although both are now in the Hall of Fame there) and they forged solid careers within the company. Up until 2007, the TNA champion also had the distinction of being the NWA champion, so they had that lineage to begin with, before breaking away eventually. The first breakout star that they really made themselves had also been a success in RoH until the Feinstein controversy: AJ Styles.

Styles actually had a WCW contract in 2001, right before the company went under. He wasn't picked up by WWE so worked for as many independents as he could, before making TNA his main home. In 2003 he was rapidly switched between face and heel (and of course, this had nothing to do with the influence of Vince Russo, oh no . . .) and would go on to win the NWA title three times, becoming the solid, exciting talent that the company could be built upon. I remember attending a TNA show in the UK when I knew precious little about the company and was blown away at the reception that Styles got. Just like Samoa Joe, it would take a while – and even more detours – for him to end up with WWE, but he got there in the end after a long time in the main event with TNA.

The final NWA champion associated with TNA was Christian, formerly of WWE and now with Cage as his surname. As the NWA relationship ended, the first-ever TNA Champion in May 2007 was Kurt Angle. Both men would have some excellent matches in TNA, and Christian would be back in WWE before the end of the decade. It would take Angle a while longer, and in a non-wrestling role, but he's currently the general manager of *Raw*.

Other independent companies started making names for themselves too. Chikara had a goofy take on wrestling that blended lucha libre with sports entertainment via almost comic book characters, and CZW (Combat Zone Wrestling) and IWA Mid-South kept the hardcore wrestling element of ECW alive and pushed it to the next ultra-violent level. Then there's the independent company that is the reason that I'm involved in wrestling in the capacity that I currently am: Pro Wrestling Guerrilla (PWG), based in Southern California.

Formed in 2003 by six wrestlers including Super Dragon, Excalibur and Joey Ryan, they started as a small, local independent then grew to become a super indy, now at a level where their shows in Reseda sell out in minutes and fans travel from around the world to see them. On my bucket list is eventually getting to a *Battle of Los Angeles* show, the three-day tournament that they started in 2005 and is responsible for some of the finest wrestling on the planet every year.

I met Excalibur in March 2017 when he commentated on the PROGRESS show in Orlando; I probably annoyed him by being a tedious fanboy and constantly thanking him for giving the world PWG.

Back to Japan. Companies there were fracturing at a rapid rate. In January 1999, Giant Baba died, leaving ownership of the company to his wife Motoko and having standout star Mitsuharu Misawa as company president. But Misawa didn't care for the direction that Baba's widow wanted to take the company in, so he left and set up his own company in May 2000: Pro Wrestling Noah. Nearly everybody defected with him. This huge split immediately impacted on AJPW business and pushed Noah to be the number two company in the country behind NJPW. Misawa was keen not just to push established heavyweight stars like himself, Kenta Kobashi and Jun Akiyama, but also new stars over the course of the decade. In 2004 and 2005, Noah was named as best promotion by the *Wrestling Observer*.

Misawa, one of the all-time in-ring greats, died on 13 June 2009. During a tag team match he took a routine belly-to-back suplex as he had done thousands of times before. This time when he landed, his already worn-out neck and spine had enough; he received severe spinal damage and died in the ring. Akira Taue took over the reins of the company, but Noah then lost its TV deal the same year, before getting a new one, only to be embroiled in a Yakuza scandal in 2012 that affected business further.

A huge deal in the 1990s, Atsushi Onita's FMW (Frontier Martial Arts Wrestling) had popularised 'garbage wrestling', the Japanese – often more extreme – version of hardcore wrestling. By 1998, most of the hardcore matches the company had been built upon had been stopped as it tried to be seen more as sports entertainment. They still had one ace though, the high-flying, masked marvel Hayabusa. In October 2001, he attempted his signature springboard moonsault, leaping on to the ropes before flipping back into the ring. This time something went wrong though; he slipped, landing on top of his head and breaking his neck. He was paralysed instantly. With Hayabusa now retired, the company had no bankable star and owed money to various different organisations, some of them significantly dodgier than others. The last FMW show was in February 2002. Three months later, company president Shoichi Arai committed suicide, so his life insurance could be used to pay off his massive debts.

Another company filled the garbage wrestling void: Big Japan. Taking the death matches that FMW had put on in its prime and turning the nuttiness up to 11, it was a company with wrestlers willing to do some of the more extreme matches that have ever been dreamed up, including use of light tubes, razor boards, barbed wire trampolines and even scorpions, cactus, crocodiles and piranhas. At the other end of the spectrum was Toryumon, formed by Ultimo Dragon, a company based around lucha libre. This morphed into Dragon Gate in 2003, a company which is still active today and doing great things, often with younger audiences than companies like NJPW.

Wrestling in Japan is absolutely on fire at present, with All Japan, Noah and Dragon Gate all competing to be the second biggest company and more niche promotions like DDT and Big Japan also drawing great crowds. But it's New Japan that are at the head of the pack, by some distance, thanks to the rise of stars like Hiroshi Tanahashi and Shinsuke Nakamura in the mid 2000s. The annual 4 January show at the magnificent Tokyo Dome baseball stadium was rebranded as *Wrestle Kingdom* in 2007 and NJPW started to stretch out as national leaders; it's now the Japanese equivalent of *WrestleMania* and always an absolutely brilliant show. NJPW have also been helped by having very marketable stars on their roster in recent years, and if you attend any wrestling show in the world you'll see their T-shirts in the crowd.

The last time I was in the USA, my teenage daughter asked me to pick her up something from Hot Topic, the 'alternative' store that I needed in my life when I was a nerdy teenager. Browsing the T-shirts, I couldn't help noticing black ones emblazoned with the words 'Bullet Club'. This isn't pro-NRA stuff; this is pro wrestling. It's the biggest wrestling T-shirt trend since Austin 3:16 or nWo. If PROGRESS had sold that many T-shirts I'd be writing this from the Maldives on a solid-gold laptop.

Bullet Club was formed in May 2013 by fan favourite junior heavyweight Prince Devitt, an Irish wrestler who had risen through the ranks in Japan and massive Tongan Bad Luck Fale; they were soon joined by Tama Tonga, Karl Anderson, Luke Gallows and the Young Bucks Matt and Nick Jackson. Every Bullet Club match was riddled with interference, cheating and arrogance, the opposite of what Japanese wrestling had been built on. With Devitt as leader, he rose from the junior ranks to being able to challenge for the main title within NJPW, but it was the IWGP Junior Heavyweight Championship that remained closest to him – he held it for 14 months before losing it to Kota Ibushi in a wonderful match at *Wrestle Kingdom 8* in January 2014. Three months later, surprisingly, he left NJPW for WWE, where he would become Finn Balor.

Bullet Club needed a new leader, and they got one. Leaving TNA behind, AJ Styles took to Japanese wrestling incredibly well, making an immediate impact by winning the IWGP Heavyweight Championship after just one month in the company, thanks to the help of new Bullet Club member Yujiro Takahashi, the first Japanese member of the stable. Two years later and Anderson, Gallows and Styles would all be heading for WWE. Before he left, Styles had a tremendous match at *Wrestle Kingdom 10* with Shinsuke Nakamura who would also be heading Stateside.

At that point a 14-year veteran of both wrestling and some

MMA, Nakamura had been an IWGP Heavyweight Champion incredibly early in his career, winning the title just over a year after his debut by beating Hiroyoshi Tenzan for his first reign. For a company that often doesn't push wrestlers until they're in their thirties, this should tell you just how great he was even at the start. In 2009, he formed the then heel stable CHAOS and was soon in his third IWGP title reign. He has always had quite astonishing charisma without needing to speak and caught on quickly with audiences, moving around before a match like a cross between Freddie Mercury and Michael Jackson. When he went to the USA, initially to NXT where he was absolutely brilliant, it was a massive loss to NJPW. Luckily, they had a lot of talent still left behind.

'The Ace' of the company, Hiroshi Tanahashi has always been able to have at least a four-star match with absolutely anybody. Part of the 'new three musketeers' with Nakamura and Katsuyori Shibata, he's consistently been around the title picture, and success in the annual round-robin G1 Tournament. It's also worth talking about his hair, which is magnificent – like the plumped-up wings of a majestic, beautiful eagle. There are female hairdressers in Liverpool who would kill to have his hair. It is a thing of beauty.

He's had many five-star matches, including three absolute belters with arguably the biggest star in wrestling who isn't signed up to a WWE contract: Kazuchika Okada.

Okada is, as I write, somehow still only 30 years old. He trained in Toryumon between 2004 and 2007 before moving to the NJPW dojo and continuing to train despite being a well-appreciated wrestler at this point. His debut in the company was a loss to Tetsuya Naito, another superstar now and leader of

Los Ingobernables de Japon, another great stable and shifter of hefty amounts of merchandise.

Naito took a while to find a bankable gimmick, but he's morphed over the last couple of years into being an absolute nutcase and it's fun; he won the IWGP title and would just throw it over his shoulder to the canvas, uncaring, when he got into the ring. Now surrounded by characters like EVIL (yes, that is his name and his personality), his signature taunt is to hold one of his eyes open with his fingers. This comes from his time on an excursion in Mexico (where the LIJ idea comes from) where he would get racist abuse from fans for his narrow eyes.

After that debut loss, Okada was injured for about a year and then went on an excursion himself, to TNA. He was briefly called 'Okato' after Kato from *The Green Hornet*. It may not have seemed like a trip that set the wrestling world on fire, but Okada returned to Japan knowing that he needed a character to go along with his in-ring skills. He came up with one: Rainmaker. He would enter the ring to a shower of fake banknotes, have a special camera shot when he hit his finisher of the same name and join the CHAOS stable, so he could develop the arrogant, rich-boy persona he'd come up with. He won the G1 tournament in 2012 and entered into a brilliant feud with Tanahashi. His greatest opponent, though, is Kenny Omega.

Omega was, for many years, a brilliant wrestler from Canada who geekier fans really appreciated thanks to his work in PWG and the smaller Japanese promotion DDT. Fluent in Japanese, he got his chance in NJPW and became the leader of Bullet Club after Styles joined WWE. Initially seen just as a Junior Heavyweight, leadership of such an important stable boosted him up the card and into full-blown Heavyweight contention.

At *Wrestle Kingdom* in 2017, he had arguably the greatest match of all time with Okada, a match that required Dave Meltzer to change his star ratings system, awarding it *six* out of five. Amazingly, they would go on to have two more six-star matches that same year (one was actually six and a quarter stars), making them the Flair and Steamboat of their age.

Wrestling in Japan continues to thrive and develop. NJPW in particular are expanding as much as they can, with shows in Australia and in Los Angeles (that have sold out frighteningly quickly). The scene among the Junior Heavyweights is amazing, with wrestlers like Will Ospreay, Hiromu Takahashi and Marty Scurll tearing it up. Bullet Club rumbles on, now with added Cody Rhodes giving it intrigue. There's a fruitful relationship with Ring of Honor, bigger attendances for their shows than ever before with fans travelling across the world for *Wrestle Kingdom* just like fans do for *WrestleMania*, and even genuinely shocking storylines such as Chris Jericho appearing in order to attack Kenny Omega that featured the first bladejob in NJPW for a long time.

I thought Japanese wrestling was brilliant when I first started getting tapes of mid-Nineties AJPW; it's arguably even better right now.

In June 2006, WWE revived the ECW brand, putting out a weekly show on the Sci Fi network that ran for nearly four years. Having acquired the ECW tape library in 2003 and producing a well-received *Rise and Fall of ECW* documentary, in June 2005 WWE held the first *ECW One Night Stand* pay per view in the Hammerstein Ballroom in New York, once home to many ECW shows. This show harked back to the ECW of old, with the entire card looking like it could have come from any point between 1996 to 2000. The 2006 version of the show is one of my favourite ever pay per views and remains essential viewing for the raucous, often dickheaded crowd and a couple of great matches: Edge, Lita and a heel Mick Foley against Tommy Dreamer, Beulah McGillicutty and Terry Funk, and the main event of Rob Van Dam against WWE Champion John Cena.

When Cena made his entrance, the crowd absolutely went to town on him with offensive chants. When he threw his T-shirt to the crowd, as was his signature gesture, they threw it back at him. When Van Dam beat him for the title, the place became unglued; this was an early example of Cena doing a great job in front of fans who absolutely wanted to hate him. Van Dam would hold the title for just a month, also taking it as the new ECW title, meaning he technically held two belts at once just as the new ECW TV show, *ECW on Sci Fi,* was being launched. But as he was arrested on drug possession charges, he dropped the WWE title to Edge and the next day the ECW title to the Big Show.

ECW on Sci Fi did okay, ratings-wise, to begin with. But with the show eventually being filmed in the same way as *Raw* and *Smackdown*, it didn't have the gritty edge that the old *Hardcore TV* shows did in the late 1990s. Rules were observed more too, taking away the Wild West nature of the old ECW shows and only going 'Extreme' in matches that warranted it. The relaunched ECW would have its own pay-per-view shows too, but apart from a brief run by Kurt Angle as a killing machine on the brand and the first steps to megastardom within WWE for CM Punk, the relaunched brand is now largely forgotten while the original remains as lauded as ever. In 2010 the show would be replaced with something totally different: *NXT*.

NXT started out as a quasi-reality-based competition show in 2010, eventually morphing into a brand that is the perfect halfway house for fans like me; it's part sports entertainment in the most classical WWE sense, but it's also the best of independent wrestling for those who enjoy PWG, RoH or the stuff from Japan or the UK.

WWE has always had developmental territories: promotions that they have sent rookies to in order to get extra training and ring time before they're ready to be called up to television. OVW produced many of the biggest new stars of the 2000s; by 2010 the company was using Florida Championship Wrestling (FCW), based out of Tampa. The show concept for *NXT* was to pit rookies (often very experienced independent workers, they were only 'rookies' in the eyes of a WWE TV audience) against each other through a series of physical and creative tasks, with each rookie coached by their own pro, an experienced member of the main roster. Similar to *America's Got Talent*, it would be up to the pros to decide who remained on the show each week. The winner of the first series would get called up to the main roster and a title shot, thus blurring the reality and sports entertainment boundaries further. I remember at the time absolutely *hating* this concept. Having rewatched it for research since, it's actually pretty interesting, a potential gateway for new fans into wrestling without giving the entire business side of things away.

The original *NXT* ran for five seasons between 2010 and 2012. The most memorable was the first season, won by British wrestler Wade Barrett. As soon as the season was finished, all of the competitors from the show formed a stable called The Nexus with one of the most remarkable angles on an episode of *Raw* for years. Barrett walked down the entrance ramp while his stablemates leapt over the guardrails, attacking everyone in sight: John Cena and CM Punk who were in a match against each other; Luke Gallows, who had accompanied Punk to the ring, commentators Matt Striker and Jerry Lawler, ring announcer Justin Roberts and more. It was abject chaos and it was *brilliant*. In among the melee, Daniel Bryan – the former RoH standout Bryan Danielson, who was one of the first eliminated during the series – choked Roberts out with his own tie, and spat in the face of John Cena, showing the intensity and aggression that saw him being so feted on the indies. He was subsequently let go by WWE for going too far. Luckily, he'd soon be rehired and emphatically bounce back from that setback.

In 2010, desperate to reignite the Monday Night Wars, TNA made a couple of quite astonishing decisions: not only would they choose to hire Hulk Hogan for his second stint within the company, but they would also take on Eric Bischoff – what could possibly go wrong? As well as both men being given roles in front of the camera, they were entrusted with decision-making behind the scenes. They hired a cabal of ex-WWE stars such as Rob Van Dam, Jeff Hardy and Ric Flair who'd already returned from retirement. They abandoned their six-sided ring in favour of a traditional squared circle and decided to put their TV show *Impact* on opposite *Raw*, starting on 8 March. I must stress that the show was already far from a rating success. I'm not entirely sure what putting it up against the most successful wrestling show on TV was meant to achieve.

Fair play to them, in the first week ratings were actually pretty decent as fans tuned in to see if the hype over a new war was real. But viewer numbers quickly slid off the edge of a cliff, plummeting so rapidly that the show was rescheduled to

Thursdays. The entire experiment lasted less than two months and only added to the perception of TNA as very much minor league compared to WWE.

I've been to some live TNA shows and they were fantastic, and the company has enjoyed some awesome matches and feuds. That two months trying to compete with *Raw* exposed the promotion badly though. However, it would briefly bounce back a few years later thanks to some incredibly bizarre tactics.

Suffering with declining ratings and attendances and with some ownership issues, TNA did something oddly revolutionary. With Matt Hardy and Jeremy Borash (recently hired by WWE, he is one of the most underrated people in wrestling who did nearly every job at TNA for a long time), they were willing to do something quite different and crazy. Matt feuded with his brother, Jeff. Nothing special there; they'd done it before in WWE. But this time Matt adopted an overblown, melodramatic, mad genius persona, dying a blond streak in his hair and back-combing it to make it massive, calling himself 'Broken' and only referring to Jeff as 'Brother Nero'. They would use drones to film unusual segments at the Hardy Compound in North Carolina, something that may have influenced WWE having an 'off campus' match called 'The House of Horrors' between Bray Wyatt and Randy Orton, that felt to the viewer like you were playing a *Resident Evil* video game.

One special episode of *Impact* that came from the compound was called *Total Nonstop Deletion* and dependent on your view-point, is the greatest or worst thing in wrestling history. It's got wrestlers in it. But it's not really wrestling. I'm still not sure what it is. It's part wrestling, part film, part video game, part insanity. There's a ring, but there's a drone and a boat and side characters and . . . look, it's probably best to just watch it. I am not qualified to do it justice. The finish to the 40-odd minute long main event 'Tag Team Apocalypto' match had Crazzy Steve fall into a volcano and get fired into the ring to be pinned. It might have been daft, but it was *different*; somebody has to try and push things, just like the Gold Dust Trio did back in the day.

JIM'S TOP TEN: SOON-TO-BE-HUGE STARS

Now hopefully people are still reading this book in 2030, so this list may well make for interesting debate at that point. But as I write this in 2018, here's ten wrestling stars who will, in the space of the next few years, go on to dominate the wrestling industry and headline *WrestleMania* or *Wrestle Kingdom*:

10. Flamita
One of my favourite luchadors in the world, Flamita has mastered both the Mexican style and put a Japanese twist on it by spending time in Dragon Gate. Capable of doing some of the most insane things I've ever seen in a wrestling ring, he's also got enough strength to throw his opponent around too. And you can sing his name to the tune of *Maneater* by Hall and Oates.

9. Joey Janela
Dubbed 'The Bad Boy', Janela is based in the North East of the USA and is rightly getting a great name for himself as more and more companies around the world realise that he's not only a special talent inside the ring, but he's a brilliant, insane genius of a character outside of it.

8. David Starr
The man with a thousand nicknames (I wish I could memorise them, I'm honoured that I'm allowed to add one to it on our shows), Starr is a world traveller who has caught on massively in Europe thanks to his work in Germany and the UK. It's only a matter of time until one of the big boys come calling for him.

7. Hiromu Takahashi

Having worked overseas under the name Kamaitachi, Takahashi returned to NJPW under his real name in 2016 and was quickly recognised as one of the very best junior heavyweights in the world, with a creepy charisma that sets him apart from everyone else and makes him ideal for the LIJ stable. He'll certainly move into the heavyweight division at some point in the future.

6. Travis Banks

Leaving his native New Zealand behind to follow his dream of becoming a professional wrestler, Banks worked in Japan and the USA before settling in the UK, winning plenty of titles here as a singles wrestler or in tag team competition. Having now appeared for Evolve and PWG, his style is reminiscent of Brian Danielson in his Ring of Honor prime.

5. Tyler Bate

I watched Tyler make his debut for PROGRESS when he was 17 years old, meaning that technically he was too young to actually get into the venue that day. In January 2017 he became the first-ever WWE United Kingdom Champion, a few months later he was in the NXT match of the year. Still technically an independent wrestler, by the time he's 25 he'll be so good that it's genuinely scary.

4. WALTER

Yes, just like PROGRESS it's meant to be typed that way. The massive Austrian has been getting rave reviews around the world for his hard-hitting style; his match with Timothy Thatcher at PROGRESS in January 2018 may be one of my favourite ever. A chop from this man would cave an average man's chest in.

3. Matt Riddle

Formerly of the UFC, where he had a professional MMA record of 8 wins, 3 losses and 2 no-contests (he won those two fights but tested positive for marijuana afterwards; if you ask me, if you can win a fight when stoned then you can have *two* wins on your record), Riddle hasn't been wrestling for long, but has arguably picked it up quicker and better than anyone else ever has. Once marijuana is legal he'll no doubt be in the WWE; he's great in ring and looks like a Greek god.

2. Will Ospreay

Technically *already* a megastar in Japan where he spends a lot of time for NJPW, Will was the first British – and youngest-ever – winner of the Battle of Super Juniors tournament, the first-ever British-born winner of the IWGP Junior Heavyweight Championship, and the first (and only) person to moonsault off a balcony at a PROGRESS show. The sky is – pun intended – the limit for the 'Aerial Assassin'.

1. Pete Dunne

At the age of 24, Dunne is, for my money, already one of the finest wrestlers in the world. He's already been in the business for over a decade and has evolved from a fine Indy wrestler into the second coming of William Regal. His match with Tyler Bate at *NXT Takeover Chicago* in 2017 was the best match on American soil that year and propelled him into the stratosphere. I was at the Manchester Arena the day he made his debut on *Raw* with his WWE United Kingdom title and the pop was enormous. Won't be long till he's there all the time.

Chapter Twenty:
The Best in the World Around the World.

CM Punk and Daniel Bryan.
The Network. The streak ends. Hogan.

There are hundreds, maybe thousands of wrestling matches that fans will point out as being one of the best ever. It's all subjective of course, I could easily list a hundred matches that I think are of exceptional quality and then someone else could come up with their hundred and maybe only half on each list would cross over. Promos are *very* different. You can normally reel off a list of all-time greats and a lot of the same segments come up: Dusty Rhodes' 'Hard Times'; Mick Foley's 'Cane Dewey'; Steve Austin's '3.16'; Ric Flair's *Nitro* reformation of the Four Horsemen after falling out with Eric Bischoff; and the promo and aftermath I'm about to discuss: CM Punk's infamous 'Pipebomb'.

This promo led to one of my favourite-ever matches, a contest that I watch every few months to be reminded of how utterly brilliant it is. For me, it's the greatest match in WWE history, although subsequent years have seen a *lot* of great wrestling so it's only a matter of time until something at least runs it close. At the start of 2011, Punk was the leader of the New Nexus, a rejigged version of the stable that had originally made such an impact in 2010 after the conclusion of season one of *NXT*. By June of that same year, Punk's star was shining brightly with a series of big wins, climbing back to the top of the card. It then emerged that after the upcoming *Money in the Bank* pay per view in July his contract would be expiring. Always outspoken, he seemed to have no desire to re-sign.

The promo that is called the 'Pipebomb' actually doesn't include the phrase; it was used in the next promo that Punk did, going back and forth between him and his nemesis John Cena. The original segment remains absolutely unbelievable even now, especially for how much the whole thing even worked the smartest of fans at the time.

Coming out on *Raw* and sitting cross-legged in the entrance aisle, Punk just cut loose. He spoke of Cena mistakenly claiming to be the best, because Punk believed that he was, as his nickname and merchandise suggested, 'the best in the world'. He mentioned Hulk Hogan and The Rock – as 'Dwayne' – describing them both as 'ass-kissers'. He even mentioned breaking the fourth wall, turning to the camera and waving as he did so. The motivation behind what was intended to be a heel promo was his annoyance at not being the face of the company despite having a stellar record since making his debut. He wanted to be on souvenir cups and on TV chat shows and showed bitterness at

The Rock being announced already for the main event at *WrestleMania* the next year. As fans cheered, he even rounded upon them for hassling him at airports.

He then made the statement that worked me: On 17 July, he said he would win the WWE Heavyweight Championship from John Cena at *Money in the Bank* and he would be leaving with it. Well, I remembered the 'Summer of Punk' and I knew how that turned out. I was a smart fan. I knew his contract was up. Vince was too smart to let him leave with a title. It would be a good match, but Cena would win, and normal service would be resumed. Then the promo got even *more* bizarre, with Punk saying that he would maybe head to New Japan or back to Ring of Honor, taking time to turn to the camera to say hello to his best friend Colt Cabana, who he spent a long time there with and who had been let go by WWE in 2009. From there, he described Vince as the 'millionaire who should be a billionaire'. As Punk went to talk about the WWE anti-bullying policy, the mic was cut.

I remember being stunned at this promo, as was the entire wrestling community. I *thought* it was a work, but some points were so raw (no pun intended). It turned out, as subsequent weeks taught us, that it was the finest ever worked shoot in wrestling history, the kind of thing that Vince Russo would have killed to have been behind when he was doing three on every episode of *Nitro*.

As *Money in the Bank* was in Punk's home town of Chicago, the atmosphere was destined to be absolutely unbelievable. I think it's the best atmosphere for a wrestling show in an arena of all time, only rivalled by some WWE shows in Canada in 1997 when Bret Hart was still a babyface there.

The match itself was mammoth, with the added stipulation placed on Cena that if he didn't beat Punk, he would be fired, making it seem even more likely that Punk would lose on his way out. The match had nearly 35 minutes of action with so many false falls that after I watched it live, the adrenaline was such that I couldn't sleep properly when I took myself off to bed at 4 a.m. Technically, it is not the best match ever because there were a few slips from both men, but that was understandable in such a pulsating atmosphere and sometimes, a great match is as much down to the audience as the moves performed.

At the time I was a Punk fan and I knew he really was one of the best in the world; this is the match that changed my opinion of John Cena. Sure, some fans despise him, but he's been in dozens of utterly tremendous contests, and this match wouldn't have been as special if it was just down to the work of Punk. It took two, and they blew everyone away.

After half an hour, Punk's enemies Vince McMahon and John Laurinaitis (WWE's head of talent relations who had transitioned into a corporate villain role on TV; he is the brother of Animal of the Road Warriors and worked himself in Japan for many years as Johnny Ace) headed to the ring to distract Punk. Cena locked on his step over toehold facelock (STF) submission and McMahon, in another nod to Montreal, asked for the bell to be rung. Cena refused to take a tainted victory. He left the ring to go after Laurinaitis and as he returned, Punk grabbed him, hit his 'Go 2 Sleep' finisher and pinned him for the title. The building came unglued.

But it wasn't over yet. McMahon summoned *Raw* Money in the Bank winner Alberto Del Rio to the ring, and you could hear the crowd sigh as they expected the title to switch again, instantly, allowing Punk to leave. Before Del Rio could cash in his Money in the Bank contract though, Punk kicked him in the face, left the ring and hopped a guardrail, leaving through the crowd with the title belt. He blew an exasperated McMahon a kiss as he went, the crowd almost weeping with joy at their home-town hero doing what pretty much everybody thought was impossible.

Watching at home, I was absolutely stunned. I was certain Punk wouldn't win the title. I didn't know that he'd actually, secretly, signed a new contract. Over the next week he would be seen outside of WWE, celebrating his big win and flashing the title belt around.

A new champion was crowned in Rey Mysterio, who quickly lost the new title to John Cena, prompting Punk – after only two weeks – to make his return, using his old RoH music ('Cult of Personality' by Living Colour) on *Raw* to make a match between Cena and himself at *Summerslam 2011* to decide the one true champion. Punk won that, but after the match Kevin Nash attacked him and this time Del Rio did successfully cash in his opportunity to leave with the title. By *Survivor Series* though, Punk was champion again and would go on to hold it for a record breaking 434 days as champion, eventually losing to The Rock at the 2013 *Royal Rumble*. Not bad at all for someone who wanted to leave.

After a *huge* shock at *WrestleMania XXX*, (we'll get to that in a while) the WWE needed something to lift the crowd back up. Luckily, they had something up their sleeve. Daniel Bryan, at this point, was wonderfully popular but didn't have the best *WrestleMania* record. In 2011 he was in a pre-show match against Sheamus for the US title. The next year he lost to the same man in just 18 seconds while the World Heavyweight Champion and a heel. I was at that show in Miami and despite really liking Sheamus, I remember being incredibly annoyed and spending quite some time explaining to a ten-year-old kid why I wasn't happy. In 2013 he was in a tag team title match as champion, defending the belts that he held with veteran Kane in a short match against Big E Langston and Dolph Ziggler. By 2014 he was a main-event-level star and audiences around the world clamoured for him to be given a chance on the biggest stage. Small for a WWE superstar, Bryan was a bearded, quiet, unassuming vegan who had made a connection with the crowd thanks to his pluckiness and technical skill. He'd also developed a personality that showed he could resonate as well with kids as he could smart fans, a result of spending time on the camp shows in the UK over a decade earlier.

Bryan won the WWE Championship at *Summerslam 2013*, beating John Cena (that man again) in a great match where Triple H was the special guest referee. As soon as the bell had rung, Triple H attacked Bryan, allowing Money in the Bank contract holder Randy Orton to come out and win the title, giving birth to 'The Authority' stable. They would repeatedly describe Bryan as a 'B+ player', insisting he wasn't of the calibre to carry the company. Every wrestling fan has experienced one moment in their life when they've been told that they weren't good enough at something, so this very simple dynamic resonated with everybody. Bryan would be thwarted at every turn as he tried to win the title back. At *TLC*, Orton unified the WWE and World Championships (it was now the WWE World Heavyweight title), beating Cena and meaning that only one title would be up for grabs at *WrestleMania XXX*. On that same show, Bryan was beaten in a three-on-one handicap match by the Wyatt Family, making it look very much like he was being de-pushed, the deck constantly stacked against him.

At the 2014 *Royal Rumble* Bryan lost again, this time in a singles match to Bray Wyatt. The Rumble match itself was notable for two things: the return of Batista, and how much the fans hated the fact that he won it. Everyone was expecting Bryan to make an appearance and win the match, but he didn't. When entrant number 30 was revealed to be perennial fan favourite Rey Mysterio, the crowd even booed him. Batista was positioned as a babyface and they hated him winning to get the *WrestleMania* title shot.

At the next show, *Elimination Chamber*, Orton retained his title ensuring he'd be at 'Mania, eliminating Bryan after Kane interfered. The main event at the biggest show of the year would be Orton against Batista, which was now a heel-on-heel contest as fans had rallied so much against Batista's reappearance in WWE.

A challenge was issued by Bryan to Triple H, which by now was the equivalent of asking your boss for a quick punch-up in the office car park. The match was agreed, and then it was also decided that the winner would go on to be part of the main event at 'Mania, making that contest a three-way match. Bryan and Triple H kicked off the show, with the two personalities portrayed by their entrances; Triple H's elaborate, over-the-top, powerful entrance was like something out of *Game of Thrones*, while Bryan, the man of the people, just came out to his 'Ride of the Valkyries' music, looking intense and ready for a fight. After 26 minutes, Bryan won the match with his running knee finisher, ensuring he would be in the main event, but Triple H attacked him after the bell, injuring him.

As for the main event, it was another epic, with Triple H and Stephanie McMahon interfering to try and keep the title away from Bryan. In the end, he resisted all of that and made Batista submit to his 'Yes Lock', sparking off wild celebrations. It was a great way to structure a show and Bryan was made to look like a superstar in victory, showing the WWE were listening to the fans. The cynic in me says that maybe they always had it planned exactly how it panned out, and every fan was worked into a frenzy by Bryan's road to *WrestleMania*, but whatever the truth, the final result was wonderful, and fans went away incredibly happy.

Sadly, Bryan would only hold the title for two months before vacating it because he needed urgent neck surgery. He returned to the ring in January 2015, and when he was eliminated from the *Royal Rumble* match the fans booed nearly as much as they did the previous year when he didn't appear. He did win something at *WrestleMania 31* though, picking up the Intercontinental title in a ladder match; but again, he would have to hand this back due to concussion-related injuries in May 2015. He had been keeping them hidden, but he had been having seizures. Having suffered ten concussions in his career (and a detached retina in his RoH days), a lesion was found on his brain and in February 2016, he retired.

His fellow RoH standout CM Punk also left wrestling behind, but his exit was slightly more ill-tempered. The day after the 2014 *Royal Rumble*, where he lasted an hour in the showcase match, Punk walked out of *Raw*. In July, he was quietly removed from the list of active competitors on the WWE website, having been fired after six months absence.

A few months later, Punk sat down with his friend Colt Cabana on his *Art of Wrestling* podcast to talk about what happened. This led to what is still an ongoing legal case, so I won't go into specifics, but towards the end of his tenure he was incredibly unhappy at his workload, injuries and creative direction, a little like the feelings he had that were behind the 'pipebomb' the last time he came close to leaving. Most tellingly to me, as a fan of his, he stated that never headlining a *WrestleMania* made him feel like a failure, which seems very harsh; I'll always remember his WWE career as being brilliant.

Punk went into UFC, but unlike Lesnar, he wasn't successful, losing his first contest. Credit to him for trying though, especially without a legitimate background. Punk returning to wrestling would be the most shocking thing that could happen at this point; let's see how well this book ages over the next few years, shall we?

I've just been to New Orleans for the 2018 version of *WrestleMania* where Daniel Bryan, after years of doctors' tests, made his in-ring return. When it was announced, I celebrated like my football team had just won the cup final. It's brilliant to know that a man who just wanted to carry on wrestling finally gets to continue his dream, and proof that when it comes to retirements in professional wrestling, worked or otherwise, you should never say never about a comeback.

In August 2011, the WWE brand split ended. Stars from *Raw* started appearing on *Smackdown* and vice versa, and show-specific pay-per-view events were phased out. That meant things were easier for the fans to follow, for sure. It also meant that opportunities at the top of the card would become more limited. Some stars would remain around the company, albeit part-time like The Rock, by then a massive Hollywood star. Another name came back in a similar way, picking and choosing his dates and certainly not doing the house show circuit. He'd tried football, he'd done MMA, he'd even had a stint in NJPW: Brock Lesnar.

Lesnar didn't need to rely on nostalgia when he came back. He'd left WWE as a very good but still relatively new wrestler, but through the success of UFC he'd grown his own brand massively. In only his fourth competitive MMA contest he won the UFC Heavyweight Championship from Randy Couture in November 2008. He held it for nearly two years before losing it to Cain Valasquez thanks to a first round TKO. He retired (for the first time) from MMA just over a year later after losing to Alistair Overeem and a battle with diverticulitis that saw him having twelve inches of his colon removed in a lengthy operation. On 30 December 2013 he returned to *Raw*, reunited with Paul Heyman, and went on a killing spree. The only man to stand up to him was The Undertaker, who attacked Lesnar in February to set up their match at *WrestleMania XXX* in New Orleans. That match would be historic for a couple of reasons. People tend to remember the show for that match and forget that it was the first *WrestleMania* to be shown on the new WWE Network.

First planned in 2011, the Network was initially expected to be quite a different form of pay TV channel. When the launch hit the USA in 2014, it became Netflix for Wrestling, a huge archive of shows for fans to enjoy, as well as live events that you could stream instead of buying via pay per view. All of this for $9.99 per month. It wouldn't launch in the UK for another year, so I was one of many people scrambling around for a USA zip code so that I could sign up – I ended up using one I found for a WalMart in Arizona.

I had to have it; every big show from the history of WWE, WCW, ECW and more; and eventually every *Raw* and *Smackdown* alongside episodes of Mid-South, World Class, AWA. It changed the industry overnight and has now expanded to most of the globe with 1.6 million paid subscribers at the time of writing. It pretty much ended the lucrative pay-per-view business in wrestling though, and showed how viewing habits had changed with more people taking to the internet for their entertainment.

The success of the Network had a knock-on effect to independent wrestling, with it being cheaper and more convenient to have all of your shows on an on-demand site with paid subscribers rather than making DVDs and selling them at shows or online. Easily accessible on-demand online services brought the whole world closer, and helped to trigger a resurgence in British wrestling from 2012 onwards. I'm biased towards my own company, of course; PROGRESS started in March 2012 and after a year or so the whole landscape in the UK had organically changed. Not because of us, I hasten to add; we were part of a scene that included ICW (Insane Championship Wrestling) in Scotland, Rev Pro in the South, Attack in South Wales and the Midlands, Fight Club Pro in Wolverhampton, Southside in Nottingham, Futureshock in Manchester and many more, plus new companies would spring up all the time. After a few years in the shade, all of a sudden, we had a wealth of tremendous British talent, with the UK now seen as a territory as fertile as the North East of the USA was in the mid 2000s, companies all intertwining and doing great things.

Back to *WrestleMania XXX* in New Orleans. With The

Undertaker meeting Brock Lesnar, most fans – myself included – presumed that The Undertaker's streak of *WrestleMania* wins would go on forever. Lesnar was obviously fodder, especially as Lesnar wasn't even full time, even if he had been on a path of destruction. The match came from the briefest of confrontations at *UFC121* after Lesnar had lost his UFC Heavyweight Championship, and three years later the two men finally met in a match for the first time since Lesnar's first WWE stint.

During the 25-minute-long match, 'Taker was legitimately hurt early on, receiving a concussion as both men traded heavy blows. He soldiered on, everyone expecting the usual Undertaker *WrestleMania* result, the streak continuing. To start with, winning every year at 'Mania didn't mean anything, it was just a coincidence. The longer it went on, the more it mattered and also, the better the matches got. The first great Undertaker streak match for me was in 2002 against Ric Flair at *WrestleMania X8*, giving him his tenth win. The streak was actually named and referenced for the first time at *WrestleMania 21* in 2005, when 'Taker moved to 13–0 against Randy Orton. Going into the Lesnar match, he had two bouts with Shawn Michaels (*WrestleMania XXV* and *XXVI*), including retiring him; two contests with Triple H (*WrestleMania XXVII* and *XXVIII*) and a match with CM Punk (*WrestleMania 29*). All five of these matches were absolutely stellar.

Except this time, the usual ending didn't happen. Lesnar hit The Undertaker with three of his F5 finishing moves and pinned him to stunned, bewildered silence. After the bell rang, they didn't even play Lesnar's music. They just let the crowd react to the result, many people in absolute disbelief. One man's reaction became a meme within about 30 seconds, such was the shock etched on his face. The streak was over. Undertaker was 21–1. The crowd chanted 'Thank you 'Taker' as he slowly left the ring.

The feud wasn't done, with the two men hooking up again after Lesnar's dominant march to the WWE World Championship, with a push built off being the 'one in 21 and one'. He beat John Cena at *Summerslam 2014* by pretty much murdering him, hitting him with 16 suplexes. The title would switch to Seth Rollins at *WrestleMania 31*, with Lesnar defending against Roman Reigns, and Rollins, now a heel after turning on his Shield teammates, cashing in his Money in the Bank contract to get the title off Lesnar. The Undertaker feud continued, with 'the Dead Man' getting a win back at *Summerslam 2015*, before Lesnar ended the feud at *Hell in a Cell* two months later, not only using the cage structure to beat his opponent but also destroying the ring canvas so he could pummel Undertaker on the exposed wood of the ring.

Hulk Hogan was a man who had spent most of the last decade and a bit skipping between WWE, TNA and a couple of other places like Memphis and Australia. After the aborted attempt to start a new Monday Night War in 2010, he returned to WWE in 2014. He handled the *WrestleMania XXX* intro with Steve Austin and The Rock, three of the biggest icons in the history of the business and certainly the three biggest money draws. He did slightly ruin it by calling the venue the Silverdome, which was incorrect. He was in the New Orleans Superdome. He thought he was at *WrestleMania III*.

In July 2015 his contract was terminated, and he was instantly edited out of a lot of WWE content, making previous fall-outs with Vince and the WWE seem tame. The termination happened at the same time as an exposé on Hogan was making the rounds in the *National Enquirer*, talking about a leaked sex tape that Hogan was part of. The sex part of the tape didn't seem to be the issue, it was more that Hogan appeared to hold some very racist views, liberally used the n-word, insisted he never wanted his daughter to be with a black man and even said that, 'to a point', he was a racist. He apologised in August in a TV interview, but hasn't been near WWE since, any toys or merchandise bearing his likeness dropped. Hulkamania didn't end in the ring, it ended on a video tape.

JIM'S TOP TEN: FEUDS

If you want to sell tickets to wrestling shows, you have to build good feuds. Here's ten of my favourites (and I apologise for choosing one of them that I'm massively biased towards):

10. Magnum TA v Tully Blanchard

A feud so heated that it could only be settled in the 'I Quit' cage match, that final match in the rivalry was preceded by several gory matches and a NWA United States title switch that was caused by Blanchard's manager Baby Doll handing him a weapon while dressed as a security guard. Despite being over the secondary title in the company, the feud was a big-money programme.

9. Toshiaki Kawada v Mitsuharu Misawa

In Japan, wrestling doesn't have the same amount of pageantry that it does in the USA, so the feud between these two men was based around them constantly having brilliant, brutal matches with each other. Former tag team partners, they had some tremendously stiff contests in the mid 1990s, including the infamous 'Ganso Bomb' incident. If Misawa hadn't had left and formed Pro Wrestling Noah, they would have been fighting till the day he died.

8. Shawn Michaels v Chris Jericho

In 2008, Chris Jericho reinvented himself as a heel with none of the traits that made fans cheer for him at all and embarked upon a feud with Shawn Michaels that absolutely blew everything else in wrestling away. Based around morality, with Jericho irked that Michaels was still being cheered despite using underhanded tactics in a match. The feud's biggest point involved Jericho accidentally punching Michaels' wife during a promo, leading to an unsanctioned match between the two men to settle things.

7. Dusty Rhodes v The Four Horsemen

It was mainly Ric Flair and Tully Blanchard that Rhodes had issues with, but the fairly new stable was firmly established for their attacks on Rhodes, their high-flying lifestyles the opposite of Dusty's working class 'common man' gimmick.

6. CM Punk v WWE

In 2011, CM Punk dropped his 'pipebomb' promo and put everyone on notice that he was leaving the company and hopefully taking the title with him. In Chicago at *Money in the Bank* he did just that, after weeks of shoot-style promos that turned him into a massive babyface and had Vince McMahon and his lackey John Laurinitis trying to foil him at every turn. Would be higher, but Punk returned after only a couple of weeks away, holding the company to ransom.

5. Mick Foley v Triple H

Triple H's ascent to the top of the card in WWE was because of this feud in late 1999/early 2000, and it also reminded fans that Mick Foley, someone who made them smile as Mankind, could also be one of the most vicious wrestlers in the world under the guise of Cactus Jack. Their two matches – at *Royal Rumble 2000* and *No Way Out 2000* – were brutal, bloody masterpieces. The second one, a Hell in a Cell match, was meant to signal the retirement of Foley, but you know how wrestling is . . .

4. Jimmy Havoc v Will Ospreay

Sometimes two wrestlers will seem destined to fight forever. Jimmy Havoc, during his 600-plus day run as PROGRESS Champion, beat Ospreay repeatedly and at one point, even nearly cut his ear off. When Ospreay finally beat him to win the title (a certain person writing this may have counted the pinfall) that wasn't even the end of the story; over a year later the two men would have changed alignments and would try to kill each other all over again.

3. Raven v Tommy Dreamer

ECW did a lot of things very well in the late 1990s, and the feud between Raven and Dreamer was one of the very best. Portrayed as childhood friends who had fallen out over a girl (Beulah McGillicutty, who is now Dreamer's real-life wife), this brutal feud lasted over the course of several years, even being reignited when Raven returned to ECW after a couple of years with WCW.

2. Kevin Steen v El Generico

A feud that spanned two of my favourite companies (RoH and PWG), this is proof that long-term friends often have great matches and killer chemistry. When both men (sorry, one man and another man who certainly *looked* like an unmasked version of Generico) signed with WWE, the turn from Steen (now Owens) on Generico (now Sami Zayn) was masterful, even taking place after the show-ending copyright logo had been flashed on screen.

1. Steve Austin v Mr McMahon

The best wrestling storylines work if the audience has empathy for one of the characters involved. In this case, who wouldn't want to be able to punch their boss in the face? This is the feud that reinvented wrestling, the standard face/heel dynamic, and is the reason the WWE is still such a global sensation. Those episodes of *Raw* in 1998 that built this feud remain some of the best television in wrestling history.

Chapter Twenty-One:
Changing Times

NXT takes over. New Stars.
Full Stadiums. The Women's Revolution.

The rise of the WWE Network aided the rise of NXT as a brand as it transitioned from reality show to actual wrestling promotion within a larger wrestling promotion, like an impressively muscular Russian doll. In June 2012, all FCW events became NXT shows, and the TV show began in the form that we now know it, going from talent show to *actual* wrestling show. Helmed by Triple H in his behind-the-scenes role, it combined the best of independent wrestling with WWE Sports Entertainment elements, making it a hybrid product for smart fans who would be able to find something that they enjoyed on each show. The list of NXT Champions is a who's who of brilliant wrestlers and talent that have usually made the step up to *Raw* or *Smackdown*. By February 2014 and *NXT Arrival*, the first-ever live show on the

Network, the brand was putting on excellent regular specials that were often among the best shows of each year.

The growth of NXT as a brand goes hand in hand with the establishment of the WWE Performance Centre in 2013. Inside an unassuming facility on an industrial estate in Orlando, there is a state-of-the-art gym, several wrestling rings, studios to record, practise and break down matches, a medical facility for performers who are rehabbing injuries and room for up to 70 wrestlers to learn the finer points of the business before they are ready for the next level. At any one time, there can be a mixture of independent talent who are being shown the WWE way before making their debut at NXT, to talent who have no wrestling background at all and have arrived from other sports, to talent from overseas who have to learn all about their new home as well as wrestling.

The first NXT Champion was Seth Rollins, formerly known as Tyler Black in RoH and previously part of one of my favourite stables of all time, The Age of the Fall with, among others, Jimmy Jacobs (who would go on to be a WWE writer) and Necro Butcher (who was in the film *The Wrestler*). That stable used blogs and fan message boards to set up their debut and work fans; at the time (2007) it all felt incredibly futuristic and cool. Jacobs as something of a cult leader – at one point hanging Mark Briscoe upside down and having his blood drip all over his white suit – was quite something.

By the time Rollins made his main roster WWE debut, he was part of The Shield, a heel trio who wore black combat gear and worked as hired guns for anyone who wanted their help, initially CM Punk. Their statement was to destroy opponents with a triple powerbomb, and Rollins was joined by two other NXT standouts.

Dean Ambrose began his career in the indies as Jon Moxley, even going as far as taking part in CZW's *Tournament of Death* in 2009. He had a fantastic feud towards the end of FCW with William Regal, which allowed him to both show off his wrestling ability and how brilliant a talker he could be, in some ways a blending of Mick Foley and Roddy Piper. The third member had the least experience but was identified early on as having the biggest potential by WWE. Part of the Anoa'i family, he wrestled as Leakee after making his debut in FCW in 2010. Once The Shield ended up on *Raw*, he had a new name: Roman Reigns.

The Shield would end up being a big part of The Authority I mentioned previously, which had started in mid 2013 and was run by Triple H and Stephanie McMahon, quickly growing into the most dominant heel group. It was part of the strange double life of Triple H; on one hand, hated heel wrestling character who was usually by far the biggest villain on television; on the other hand, Paul Levesque, the man behind NXT who would be cheered whenever he started off their events or made a point of lauding his talent on that roster.

In 2016, WWE managed to beat the attendance record they set at *WrestleMania III* with *WrestleMania 32* in Arlington, Texas. The official attendance was 101,763, and although that number apparently includes some ushers and staff, it was still an absolutely enormous crowd. Nowadays WWE always uses a massive stadium for 'Mania, the attendance for the annual showcase usually exceeding 70,000. It's huge business, with front-row tickets costing thousands of dollars as part of exclusive travel packages that include hotels, tickets to *Raw* and *Smackdown* after 'Mania and The Hall of Fame Ceremony, *NXT Takeover* and *WWE Axxess* before the big show.

In front of that enormous crowd in Texas, a few important things happened. Firstly, on the pre-show, the new Women's Championship was introduced by Lita, replacing the Divas Championship that had been in use for a few years. It was more than just a cosmetic belt change though; it signified the beginning of improved equality within the business for women – from this point on, they would be known as Superstars, the same as the men, rather than the 'Diva' tag that they'd started using in the late 1990s. The first holder of this belt was Charlotte, daughter of Ric Flair and one of the most important cogs in the women's wrestling revolution; more on that shortly.

There was also the in-ring return of Shane McMahon, who had been away from the WWE since 2009, spending his time on media deals in the Chinese market and just flat out not being involved with wrestling. He'd now be a performer only, known as much for his crazy stunts that he'd been part of over the years as he was for being the son of Vince. He lost to The Undertaker in a Hell in a Cell match, and of course he took his standard ridiculous bump from the cage.

The main event saw Triple H defending the WWE World Heavyweight Championship against Roman Reigns, who had been built up as a monstrous babyface challenger. The problem is, when Reigns won, he got a negative reaction from a lot of fans. You certainly won't hear me criticise Reigns; I think he's great. Looking at him from the point of view of a promoter, he looks great, is a very good wrestler and doesn't tend to have bad matches. For some reason, probably as much down to the speed of his rise over anything else, fans just tend to boo him. I've been at shows where kids absolutely love him, but it's fans that look like me that tend to give him grief. Sometimes they'll chant

'You can't wrestle', which is absolutely ridiculous. You are only allowed to suggest that a wrestler is a worse wrestler than you if you can actually wrestle. When you're an untrained fan, it just seems insulting to address someone like that when they're risking their health to entertain you.

Cena has always garnered a similar response and as I said earlier, I never used to appreciate him like I do now. Look at both Cena and Reigns; they do what they're supposed to do inside and outside of the ring. At *WrestleMania 32* Reigns didn't react well to the boos and catcalls, but he's mellowed about it since. The next year in Orlando, at *Raw* the night after *'Mania* he delivered the best four-word promo that I've ever seen, waiting through boos for ten minutes before saying his thing ('It's my yard now') and leaving.

Is he a face or a heel? He acts like a face but has heel tendencies. You can't deny he's a star though; people do pay for tickets to see him, it's just unclear whether it's to see him win or lose. The days of clearly defined faces and heels died a long time ago. If he started acting properly evil now, chances are that fans would cheer him. It's weird.

With so many stars and the performance centre and NXT starting to bear fruit, brand extension was needed once again to make sure that half the roster wasn't just sat around clicking its heels. NXT was by 2016 a massive brand in its own right with the *Takeover* shows having some fine contests. Asuka v Ember Moon from *NXT: Takeover Brooklyn III*, Andrade Cien Almas v Johnny Gargano from *NXT: Takeover Philadelphia* and Aleister Black v Velveteen Dream from *NXT: Takeover Houston* are three fine examples of wonderful matches, but I could easily list a dozen more.

Smackdown moved to Tuesday nights and also went from being taped to live as of July 2016. Another draft was held, with Dean Ambrose being selected for the Tuesday show. As he held the WWE World Heavyweight Championship, this left *Raw* without a main singles title, so a new one was needed. I can only presume that the brainstorming meeting about it asked the question: what's bigger than the world? The new belt was christened the WWE Universal Heavyweight Championship. It has yet to be defended on Mars.

After earning his shot through episodes of *Raw*, the first-ever Universal Champion was Finn Balor, the creator of the Bullet Club. Coming just a month after he had been called up to the main roster after nearly two years on NXT, Balor won the title by beating Seth Rollins in his main roster pay-per-view debut, but unfortunately sustained a serious shoulder injury during the match and had to vacate the belt the following day. He wouldn't return until after *WrestleMania* the next year, although he did appear at a PROGRESS show while on hiatus in order to play musical chairs with me and the fans. (I'm really not making that up.)

Of the next three Universal Champions, the first was Kevin Owens. Called by his real name, Kevin Steen, on the independent circuit, Owens is one of my favourite wrestlers of the last decade. Acerbic on social media and the greatest practitioner of heel tactics that you'll ever see, he was another NXT graduate after doing brilliant things, usually feuding with El Generico (a masked wrestler who disappeared the second that the unmasked wrestler Sami Zayn showed up in NXT) in RoH and PWG. Not what you'd expect from a WWE star, he's not super-tall, not super-toned, but I guarantee that if you watch one of his matches, you'll want to watch more. At one point, wrestling Finn Balor in Japan, he threw the flowers he was given by the ring attendants before the match into the crowd, then when the fans started getting excited that he'd do some kind of exciting moves, he locked on a chin lock, telling them they didn't deserve it.

Great fact: raised in Quebec, he couldn't actually speak English until he was 15, French is his native language. He picked up English while watching wrestling, and you'd never know if you heard one of his excellent promos.

Ironically, Goldberg was next. Yes, him again. In 2016 he returned to WWE, his first appearance since the ill-fated encounter with Lesnar at *WrestleMania XX* that all the fans turned on. Challenged by Paul Heyman on behalf of Brock Lesnar, the two men went head to head again at *Survivor Series 2016* with Lesnar still in the midst of a killing spree. Goldberg, amazingly, beat him in a minute and a half, with such a rapid result showing that wrestling could be just like MMA if it needed to be: a match can end at anytime, anywhere. That one unexpected result managed to reset the expectations of every single wrestling fan by doing something so very different. He won the Universal title at *Fastlane* and after a confrontation during the *Royal Rumble* match between himself and Lesnar, set up the *WrestleMania 33* match between the two where Lesnar won the belt. That was Goldberg's first-*ever* clean loss. That's how you protect a gimmick. At the time of writing, Lesnar is still the champion. He remains the most terrifying part-time employee in the history of everything.

With the Network being such a success, it has meant an ever-bigger appetite for content. Sure, the archive of everything is amazing, but WWE also had to start making new programming to attract and retain subscribers. They became very keen on a tournament, which suits me as I love them. It also suited me because my little company ended up getting some welcome publicity out of them.

In Summer 2016, a tournament called the Cruiserweight Classic was held to crown the first WWE Cruiserweight Champion, taking 32 of the finest wrestlers under 205lbs from around the world. It showed the marrying of WWE to independent wrestling, with many of the participants not initially being signed to WWE deals and companies like Evolve, Rev Pro and PROGRESS holding qualifying matches. Our company held two and it really helped us get extra attention in a year when we were trying to do bigger shows than normal. Britain was well represented in the tournament with stars like Jack Gallagher, Zack Sabre Jr and Noam Dar; Gallagher would be in the *Royal Rumble* just a few months later. Japanese maverick Kota Ibushi was involved, having arguably the match of the tournament with Cedric Alexander. TJ Perkins was the eventual winner and first Cruiserweight Champion as a roster was signed and a new weekly show called *205 Live* was launched, following *Smackdown* on Tuesdays on the WWE Network. This show would eventually be bolstered by NXT talent and main roster standouts like Neville.

By January 2017, WWE had another idea which is obviously close to my heart: The WWE United Kingdom Championship tournament, held in Blackpool over two nights. I was there on the first night and, oddly, was shown on TV with my business partner Jon – one of the first times 'rival' wrestling promoters had ever been shown on screen and acknowledged by WWE.

Much of the PROGRESS roster was part of these two evenings, finished off with a wonderful final between Pete Dunne and

Tyler Bate, with Bate, who was 19 at the time, winning the rather beautiful UK Championship. At *NXT Takeover Chicago* Dunne would win the title in a fantastic rematch with Bate, a bout that NXT viewers voted the match of the year, in a year full of crazy matches. I remember watching that match and, as they're both friends of mine, feeling genuinely emotional when American fans started chanting 'UK! UK! UK!'.

Another tournament followed in Summer 2017, the Mae Young Classic that showcased female talent, wrestlers from all over the world putting on fantastic matches with some involved earning themselves WWE contracts. The winner was Japanese superstar Kairi Sane, and the popularity of the show in general was mainly down to the revolution within women's wrestling that had been taking place over the previous couple of years.

As I write this, we are a couple of months removed from the first-ever women's *Royal Rumble* match. Better still, it wasn't cut down and half size, or hidden away on the pre-show. It was the main event of the entire show. In the 1980s, the Women's Championship did have some prominence, being around the Rock and Wrestling movement with Cyndi Lauper. There were even Women's Tag Team titles for a brief while; 30 years ago, at *Royal Rumble 1988* they were defended in a classic two-out-of-three falls match between The Glamour Girls and the wonderful Japanese team, The Jumping Bomb Angels. In the 1990s the Women's Championship vanished for a while before being around the waist, most of the time, of Alundra Blayze, who became Madusa when she jumped to WCW and dropped the title in the trash.

Portrayals of women during the Attitude Era were reflective of the hyper-masculine environment that that show thrived within; crowds of men baying for more flesh and violence and bad language. Matches and competitors were often more about titillation than competition, with several of the Diva generation going on to pose in *Playboy*. It's not that there wasn't great talent in the division over that time, though; wrestlers like Trish Stratus, Lita, Ivory, Molly Holly and of course, Chyna, blazed a trail for those who followed such as Natalya, Mickie James, Beth Phoenix and more.

In 2008, the Divas title was introduced as a *Smackdown* only championship and may well have been the tipping point for female talent wanting to be considered as equals. While the quality of the matches could be good, the actual belt design was the ugliest ever seen, a pastel-coloured, diamond monstrosity that appeared to look like a tramp stamp tattoo. Not that the use of the word 'diva' was always super negative; the reality show *Total Divas* actually helped paint the wrestlers as more rounded individuals and gave them increased screen time, making them stars in line with the male talent through increased exposure. AJ Lee, Paige and the Bella Twins (Nikki and Brie) all benefited from this era.

On NXT, women were doing great things. Often on *Takeover* shows, the female talent would be putting on matches as good as, if not better, than the men. The 'Four Horsewomen' who came through the Performance Centre could be relied upon to have brilliant matches with each other every single week: Charlotte, Bayley, Sasha Banks and Becky Lynch. Now all on the main roster, we're at the point where the women can main event *Raw* or *Smackdown* (and have done so). With women headlining UFC shows, this was exactly the right step to take, as was removing the Diva term and having a title belt that looked the same as the men's title belt, rather than some flash art from the wall of a tattoo studio in Blackpool.

The latest crop of female superstars has only bolstered the roster: Nia Jax, Alexa Bliss, Naomi, Ember Moon and the winner of the first women's *Royal Rumble*, Asuka. After she won that match, her celebrations were interrupted by the one crossover athlete who can definitely help propel the division even higher: Former UFC Champion Ronda Rousey, who was always nicknamed 'Rowdy' because of her wrestling obsession and love of Roddy Piper when she was younger. Things are looking bright for the future of women's wrestling, even if it has taken far too long to get to this point in the USA.

Conclusion

So then. That's about 150 years' worth of history. Where are we now?

I write this in early 2018. The year has started with some great shows, but 2017 is going to be hard to top. Over the last few years we have had some of the best matches I've ever seen, and some of the most amazing developments in the industry. The British scene is fantastic, promotions in Japan and Mexico are doing wonderful things and the WWE goes from strength to strength, constantly innovating to try and grow its audience. This year's *WrestleMania* was back in New Orleans, with another full stadium. But the weekend has grown into something like the Edinburgh Fringe with so many different shows on for all the fans that gather, with even PROGRESS getting the chance to go to the USA, Australia, New Zealand and Germany this year because wrestling fans are starting to try and seek out every last thing that they can find.

The Undertaker, as I mentioned at the very start of this book, allegedly retired at *WrestleMania 33* in Orlando. He was beaten by Roman Reigns at the end of the show, and the whole event closed with fans in disbelief, 'Taker's hat and gloves left in the ring to signify the end of the career of an icon. Undertaker was the reason I stepped away from wrestling, directly involved in the reason I came back to it and participated in some of the finest matches in WWE from my time as a fan. As I write this, he is no longer retired, having appeared at *WrestleMania* once again. That's the nature of wrestling; by the time this book is published a few people may well have come back for one last match, like criminals in Hollywood movies are tempted back for one last score. It's why I haven't made a bigger deal out of such a landmark event; everyone else who has retired that we've discussed I remain *fairly* confident that they'll stay that way.

Everything is great in the wrestling business right now. History tells us that wrestling will always have ups and downs, however. If you're reading this in ten years, there could well have been a massive crash and *WrestleMania* could be back in front of regular arenas, Japanese wrestling could have fractured into a million smaller companies and I could well have had my thumbs repossessed for overspending while trying to keep a once-successful wrestling company afloat. I'll tell you what, though: If that happens, I'll still love wrestling.

You could well already be a massive wrestling fan. You might have read this book and got into it more, or just be someone totally new to this crazy business and now you've got a list of loads of things that you want to delve into. Whatever kind of fan you are, let me say this: it doesn't matter what happens in the future, whether the industry crashes or goes on to even crazier things. You might not like whoever holds a title belt right now, but rest assured that someone you love will have their chance one day soon. And there might be storylines, angles or feuds that you don't care for, but remember that there are no season finales. Wrestling has been going in its current state for over 100 years and it's not going to stop now. It is a never-ending story of twists and swerves, and there will be something that you like coming around soon. Don't overthink it. Just enjoy it. I'm 40 years old and I've loved this since I was four years old. Writing this book has been an absolute joy.

Professional wrestling is the greatest thing in the entire world.

JIM'S TOP TEN: FAVOURITE WRESTLERS OF ALL TIME

As we've reached the end, it seems only right that I tell you who my ten favourite wrestlers of all time are. I'll be honest, this changes on a weekly basis depending on my mood, so I'm bound to read the final, printed version of this book and get annoyed that I didn't include someone . . . .

10. Chris Hero/Kassius Ohno

The artist formerly known as Chris Hero, now competing in NXT as 'The Knockout Artist', Kassius Ohno has been one of my favourite wrestlers for over a decade. He first travelled the globe as an independent in both singles competition, and then as part of the Kings of Wrestling with Claudio Castaglioni (now known as Cesaro in WWE) before his first run in NXT. During a brief time back on the indies, he was in some absolutely stellar matches in PROGRESS. Throws the best elbows and punches in professional wrestling and is one of the nicest men on the planet.

9. Katsuyori Shibata

I once described Shibata on my podcast as looking like he works in a bank and then hurts people for money at the weekends. Part of the *new* Three Musketeers of NJPW in the 2000s with Hiroshi Tanahashi and Shinsuke Nakamura, Shibata dipped out of wrestling for a while to do MMA, returning to it and developing a hard-hitting, believable style that is exactly my cup of tea. Sadly, after a match with Kazuchika Okada in April 2017 he collapsed with a brain injury, forcing him to retire. Always a man of few words, he would return at the G1 Climax Finals that same year to tell fans: 'I am alive. That is all'.

8. Samoa Joe

I loved him in RoH, followed his journey in TNA and lost my mind when he ended up in WWE. As much of a gentleman outside of the ring as he is an absolute animal within it, I have fantasy-booked many scenarios where Joe becomes the biggest champion and heel in WWE.

7. Eddie Guerrero

I've already written at length about Eddie, but his career spanned so many wonderful chapters. Dickhead heel in Mexico and WCW, the masked Black Tiger in Japan, technical wrestler extraordinaire in ECW, World Champion at the peak of his redemption in WWE. As a reformed addict, I've always seen Eddie as a man to look up to after conquering his demons; it's just so sad he was taken from us so soon.

6. Brian Danielson/Daniel Bryan

As I write this, Daniel Bryan, one of the very best ever to lace a pair of boots, has just returned to in-ring competiton after what we all thought was a certain retirement due to injury. I greeted the news by punching the air with delight. His RoH title run was wild, his accidental rise to be the biggest face in WWE was one of the happiest memories I'll ever have as a wrestling fan.

5. CM Punk

The Summer of Punk in RoH was the prototype for the wonderful 'pipe-bomb' era in 2011 and the subsequent record-breaking run as champion for the straight-edge superstar. From mammoth matches with Samoa Joe in the mid 2000s to brilliant main events galore for WWE before he decided to walk away, Punk may be a controversial figure within the industry but as a fan, he'll always be one of my favourites.

4. Mick Foley

The only wrestler on this list whose image I have tattooed on me, so that's definitely enough to get him on the list. He's also, as I've repeatedly stated, the reason that I fell back in love with wrestling, as well as being the best brawler of all time and the best talker. He's been very kind to me in person too, having him support me on numerous tours and helping PROGRESS take off when it was just a very silly idea between friends.

3. William Regal

He spends most of his time on social media giving me grief, but I don't care. For my money, the finest British man to ever carve out a career in any industry in the USA; a gentleman, a fountain of knowledge, one of the funniest human beings in the world, and a man who could turn his hand to any style of wrestling and make it look realistic, hard-hitting and brilliant. An artist. He'll be reading this and trying to find a way to tell me I need a sandwich.

2. Johnny Saint

The reason I fell in love with wrestling as a kid. No Johnny Saint, no PROGRESS, no podcast, no book that you're holding right now. A man who showed me that wrestling wasn't all grunting and groaning, it could be graceful and hard-hitting and look better than any fight in the movies. Also, thanks to Mr Regal, the first time I ever met him he asked me if I wanted a sandwich before laughing his head off. I enjoy being mocked by two legends.

1. Kenta Kobashi

I've watched more Kobashi matches than I could possibly remember, spending my time devouring them as quickly as I could get them on tape as a student. Despite injuries, he was always the hardest-working, hardest-hitting individual in the Japanese wrestling that I have always held dear. I remain enormously saddened that I have never seen him wrestle in person or had the chance — like I have nearly everyone on this list — to tell him how much his hard work has meant to me.

Appendix

A Viewing and Reading Guide

As I've banged on about wrestling in its many forms for so long, it only seems right that I give you some tips on where to watch things and some further reading. Trying to cram everything that has ever happened in wrestling to approximately 100,000 words is a pretty tough task, so my recommendations below can give you some further, more detailed insight.

VIDEO

The rise of on-demand services means that it's possible to watch just about everything that has ever been filmed in the world of wrestling. You can access a lot of footage via *YouTube* but, please, only stuff that has been posted there with the copyright holder's permission. Don't steal wrestling through nefarious means; small companies (like my own) rely on internet money to survive. If you like and enjoy something, pay for it and help the industry.

WWE NETWORK – network.wwe.com

Pretty much everything that WWE have ever produced is available on this service for £9.99 a month, including live events like *WrestleMania*, every big show that they've ever held and, thanks to Vince McMahon winning the Monday Night War, all of the WCW and ECW libraries as well. Also includes a lot of original content like round-table discussions and documentaries, as well as some of the archives of other companies from the past like AWA and SMW (Smoky Mountain Wrestling), and WWE's developmental brand NXT.

NJPW WORLD – njpwworld.com

The best (and most easily accessible) on-demand service from Japan, and like the WWE Network presents a way to watch the latest live events as they happen too. Archive-wise, they don't have everything from the company's history up yet, and some of the smaller shows are filmed with a camera set-up that will feel a little alien to Western viewers. However, it's worth it just to watch all of the *Wrestle Kingdom* showcase events.

You'll see a little flag at the top of the page that makes it easier to sign up as English translation is available for most of the site. At the time of writing, AJPW was also setting up an online archive, and other Japanese companies like Dragon Gate and DDT are starting to embrace the on-demand medium.

PIVOTSHARE – pivotshare.com/wrestling

One of the on-demand services used by many independent companies (including PROGRESS: demand-progress.com), each company charges a small sign-up fee and then you can enjoy all of their events. Highlights (yes, as well as my company) include the Highspots Network (highspotswrestlingnetwork.com) that has a huge archive from many companies; ICW (icwondemand.com) and Revolution Pro Wrestling (rpwondemand.com).

DOCUMENTARIES

There have been some excellent documentaries made about the world of wrestling, these are all certainly worth a view. These don't include the dozens that WWE have made and are up on the Network now (including *The Rise and Fall of ECW*, the excellent *Monday Night Wars* series and *The Spectacular Legacy of the AWA* among many others). A swift Google search of all of the below will locate them either on DVD or available to download or stream.

Hitman Hart: Wrestling with Shadows (1998)
Louis Theroux's Weird Weekends: Wrestling (1999)
Beyond the Mat (1999)
The Backyard (2002)
Lipstick and Dynamite: The First Ladies of Wrestling (2004)
Forever Hardcore (2005)
The Wrestling Road Diaries (2009)
Bloodstained Memoirs (2009)
The British Wrestler (2012)

Dynamite Kid: A Matter of Pride (2013)
The Last of McGuinness (2013)
The Sheik (2014)
Nine Legends (2016)
This Is PROGRESS (2018)

BIOGRAPHIES

Before Mick Foley's first book was published, biographies were rarely put out by wrestlers, let alone written by them. Now it's the norm for a retired grappler to do a book. Here are some of the very best that I've enjoyed:

Have a Nice Day: A Tale of Blood and Sweatsocks – Mick Foley (1999)
The Rock Says – The Rock (2000)
It's Good to be King . . . Sometimes – Jerry Lawler (2001)
The Stone Cold Truth – Steve Austin (2001)
Foley is Good: And the Real World is Faker Than Wrestling – Mick Foley (2002)
To Be The Man – Ric Flair (2004)
Walking a Golden Mile – William Regal (2005)
Heartbreak and Triumph: The Shawn Michaels Story – Shawn Michaels (2005)
Cheating Death, Stealing Life: The Eddie Guerrero Story – Eddie Guerrero with Michael Krugman (2005)
Controversy Creates Cash – Eric Bischoff (2006)
Hitman: My Real Life in the Cartoon World of Wrestling – Bret Hart (2007)
A Lions Tale: Around the World in Spandex – Chris Jericho (2007)

Behind the Mask – Rey Mysterio (2009)

Adam Copeland on Edge – Adam Copeland (2010)

Hooker – Lou Thesz (2011)

Cross Rhodes – Goldust (2011)

The Road Warriors: Danger, Death and the Rush of Wrestling – Joe Laurinaitis with Andrew William Wright (2011)

Wrestling Reality – Chris Kanyon (2011)

Dusty: Reflections of Wrestling's American Dream – Dusty Rhodes (2012)

The Hardcore Truth: The Bob Holly Story – Bob Holly with Ross Williams (2013)

King of the Ring: The Harley Race Story – Harley Race with Gerry Tritz (2013)

Andre The Giant: Life and Legend – Box Brown (graphic novel; 2014)

Yes!: My Improbable Journey to the Main Event of WrestleMania – Daniel Bryan (2015)

Backlund: From All-American Boy to Professional Wrestling's World Champion – Bob Backlund (2015)

Accepted – Pat Patterson (2016)

Crazy Is My Superpower – A J Mendez Brooks (2017)

FURTHER READING

Much of my wrestling knowledge comes from reading the *Wrestling Observer Newsletter*. Dave Meltzer has been putting it out weekly since the 1980s; it's worth signing up for it online (www.f4wonline.com) and going back through its archives.

And here are some other books I'd recommend for in-depth knowledge on certain issues within wrestling:

The Wrestling – Simon Garfield (1996)

The Rise and Fall of ECW – Thom Loverro (2007)

Shooters – Jonathan Snowden (2012)

The Death of WCW – Bryan Alvarez and RD Reynolds

Lions Pride: The Turbulent History of New Japan Pro Wrestling – Chris Charlton (2015)

Sisterhood of the Squared Circle: The History and Rise of Women's Wrestling – Pat Laprade (2017)

The Raw Files are a series of books by James Dixon, Arnold Furious and Lee Maughan that look at every episode of *Raw* for a year. I've read every one from 1993 to 2001 and they're definitely worth checking out.

The same authors have also put out *The Complete WWF Video Guide*, Volumes 1 through 6 that look at every WWF/WWE video or DVD that was put out between 1985 and 2004.

Index